DELINQUENT
BEHAVIOR

principles

and practices

Prepared by

WILLIAM C. KVARACEUS

WILLIAM E. ULRICH

with the collaboration of

JOHN H. McCORMICK, JR.

HELEN J. KEILY

JUVENILE DELINQUENCY PROJECT, WILLIAM C. KVARACEUS, DIRECTOR
NATIONAL EDUCATION ASSOCIATION OF THE UNITED STATES
1201 SIXTEENTH STREET, N.W., WASHINGTON, D. C.

Copyright 1959
National Education Association of the United States

Library of Congress Catalogue Card Number: 59—12323

Reprinted January 1960

38982
Feb. 1960

contents

foreword

Delinquent Behavior: Principles and Practices, the second document published by the National Education Association's Juvenile Delinquency Project, has been prepared as a guide for those who administer and work in or with schools and who are concerned with ways and means by which their schools can help in the prevention and control of norm-violating behavior.

The aim of this document is to provide general principles and specific guidelines for school action based on research-oriented theory and to illustrate how many of these operational principles have been implemented in different school systems throughout the United States. At the same time, this report refrains from offering simple recipes, convenient package mixes, or easy do-it-yourself kits in answer to what is a many-sided and complex problem.

The material and suggested procedures in this report have been assembled and organized within limits prescribed by available time and financial resources; moreover, the very nature and functioning of the school agency itself set certain natural limits to the scope of this document. Within these limits, the Juvenile Delinquency Project has sought to present an integrated consideration of the school's role in and responsibility for helping the delinquent youngster; the basic principles and guidelines in this document view the problem from a particular perspective and hence are highly selective. To offer a potpourri of ideas, some of which may be questionable, conflicting, or even irrelevant, would do little to help either the delinquent or the school in its effort on his behalf; likewise, action programs consisting of "practical approaches" lacking any research or theoretical frame of reference may easily result in "impractical-practical" programs which often prove either ineffective or irrelevant to the problem of delinquency. With this in mind, the NEA Juvenile Delinquency Project attempted to formulate a valid set of school practices which would be consonant with a stated theoretical approach to the meaning and causes of delinquent behavior and with the unique or special functions of the school as an institution for learning and teaching.

It is, unfortunately, impossible to acknowledge the contributions of each of the persons who assisted in the preparation of this report. Prior to final publication more than 500 lay and professional workers representing schools as well as youth and family welfare agencies had contributed their knowledge, experience, and insight in a series of 11 preliminary workshops and in the National Invitational Conference on the Prevention and Control of Juvenile Delinquency, held under the auspices of the NEA Juvenile Delinquency Project, May 14-15, 1959. Their suggestions, their criticisms, and even their disagreements proved most helpful to the Project staff in preparing the final draft of this report.

The practices, which comprise the greater part of this document, were submitted voluntarily or at the direct invitation of the Juvenile Delinquency Project. In all, several hundred schools and other state and community institutions and agencies furnished descriptions of various aspects of their programs that deal directly or indirectly with the prevention and control of juvenile delinquency. Without the help of these cooperating schools and agencies, this document would not have been possible. Because of the large number of individuals participating in this phase of the document, the limitations of space prevent our giving credit to each respondent for his particular contribution; but his credit is reflected in the name of his community, which precedes each quotation.

Special acknowledgement is due William E. Ulrich, classroom teacher at Experimental Project, Boys Junior-Senior High School of the Public Schools of the District of Columbia, who played an important part in the planning and writing of this report. Mr. Ulrich, a teacher of norm-violating youngsters and a student of cross-cultural differences, was a particularly valuable addition to the NEA Juvenile Delinquency Staff. His services were made available through the cooperation of the Offices of the Superintendent of the Public Schools of the District of Columbia.

6

Helen J. Keily, professor, State Teachers College, Salem, Massachusetts, served as a consultant in planning and organizing the National Invitational Conference, which was designed as a workshop for review of a preliminary draft of this document. Additional help was rendered, through the Council for Exceptional Children, by John H. McCormick, Jr., editor of *Exceptional Children*, who assisted the Project in various stages of this endeavor. Elizabeth Nelson, NEA Publications Division, assisted in planning, revising, and preparing the document for the press.

Responsibility for organizing, collating, and writing this report in this form rests largely with the director of the Juvenile Delinquency Project.

In the organization, administration, and conduct of the Delinquency Project the director was fortunate to have the able assistance of Margaret B. Morgan. Her complete and untiring commitment to the Project helped insure the successful completion of this endeavor.

The Juvenile Delinquency Project owes much to the guidance and leadership of William G. Carr, executive secretary, and Lyle W. Ashby, deputy executive secretary of the National Education Association, at all stages and in all phases of the year's study.

Delinquent Behavior: Principles and Practices, like its predecessor, *Delinquent Behavior: Culture and the Individual,* constitutes a report to the National Education Association and does not necessarily reflect the official policy or thinking of the Association.

WILLIAM C. KVARACEUS, *Director*
NEA Juvenile Delinquency Project

chapter 1 **INTRODUCTION**

What can the school, as one community agency, do to prevent and control norm-violating behavior of children and youth? What kinds of action can be undertaken within the scope of the school's responsibility and which would be most relevant to causation and treatment? These questions represent the major concerns of the Juvenile Delinquency Project's second report to the National Education Association.

The aim of this publication is to provide basic principles and specific guidelines for school personnel—school board members, superintendents, principals, special service personnel, and teachers—who wish to maximize the school's contribution in a broad community approach to the prevention and control of juvenile delinquency. This report does not prescribe or provide simple school recipes; it does spell out and illustrate many action-principles which have been derived from several sources in the different phases of the NEA Juvenile Delinquency Project. Before presenting the results of this aspect of the delinquency study, it would be advisable first to set forth the over-all aims and objectives of the Project, which started September 15, 1958, and terminated June 15, 1959.

Aims and Objectives of the Project

The general aim of the NEA Juvenile Delinquency Project is to offer help to the school administrator and the classroom teacher in understanding, educating, and rehabilitating the predelinquent and delinquent student, an objective reflecting a reciprocal concern for pupil-teacher welfare.

Because of the complexity of the delinquency phenomenon, the necessity for community-wide cooperation in prevention and control of delinquency, and the limitations of funds and time available to the Project, it was of utmost importance that reasonable and practical objectives be set for the study. At the same time, in formulating these goals, care was taken to avoid both the inference that the school should assume responsibilities beyond its unique functions and the implication that delinquency is primarily the school's problem.

The specific purposes of the Project were:

1. To identify various roles and functions of the school in dealing effectively with the aggressively troublesome youngster and, in particular, with the extremely difficult case who can jeopardize both the education of the class as a whole and the welfare and morale of the teacher

2. To suggest some specific and desirable school practices and adaptations based on concepts distilled from research-anchored theory of the various disciplines and a survey of current school efforts that will help prevent and control delinquent tendencies

3. To enable the school to do a better job of early identification of the potential delinquent so that the school and community can take preventive measures

4. To indicate some ways the school may participate in an all-out community effort designed to reduce delinquency-producing factors and to replace these with positive forces

5. To indicate how some schools may be more successfully articulate in their efforts to inform the public and to obtain popular support for their programs of prevention and correction.

The Two Publications of the Project

The findings of the NEA Juvenile Delinquency Project are being presented in two separate publications. Document 1 of this series, *Delinquent Behavior: Culture and the Individual,* was published in the spring of 1959, and its approach was primarily theoretical. The present volume, Document 2, is directed toward action measures which schools may utilize in meeting the problem of juvenile delinquency. Because the theory presented in Document 1 is helpful in understanding the present document, it is necessary that a few of its salient points be briefly reviewed here. At the conclusion of this summary, the sources, plan, and organization of the present work will be discussed.

The Theoretical Statement

Delinquent Behavior: Culture and the Individual defined juvenile delinquency as *norm-violating behavior which brings the youngster to the attention of official authority or official agencies.* Seeking to provide a sound theoretical understanding that would be useful as a basis for preventive and corrective school action, Document 1 examined delinquency, including its causative aspects, in terms of the interaction of personality with cultural and subcultural forces.[1] The document accepted Walter B. Miller's convincingly supported hypothesis that the bulk of norm-violating youngsters stem from the lower-class milieu and reflect in their behavior a complex interplay of cultural forces tending to re-enforce or encourage such behavior.[2]

The term, "lower class," as used in both Documents 1 and 2, refers not to an isolated minority but to a way of life followed by a large segment of the present-day population of this country whose concerns, values, and characteristic patterns of behavior are the outcomes of a well-formed cultural system. Although social stratification has been clearly demonstrated by many reputable sociological surveys and although the layman readily acknowledges class differences by the frequent use of such terms as "lower class," "middle class," and "upper class," there is a tendency to overlook the cultural implications and the realities of class differences.[3] Unquestionably, all people in the United States share to a degree a "general" national culture, and there is significant and frequent overlapping among the different American classes and subgroups; nevertheless, meaningful differences do exist

11

among social classes, and these cannot be ignored if the phenomenon of juvenile delinquency is to be correctly understood.

The terms "lower class" and "middle class" here refer to systems of behavior and concerns—in other words, to *cultural systems*—and not to economic groups as conventionally defined. In the contemporary United States class status is no longer necessarily determined by salary, automobile "brand," and ethnic origin, as once it was; class differences now are often more evident in patterns of behavior and preferred values than in material symbols of financial status. Document 1 maintained that distinctive, though sometimes overlapping, lower-class and middle-class cultures exist within this country; that each has its own set of specifically emphasized values, concerns, and patterns of accepted behavior; and that what is important, acceptable, and even "right" in one culture is not necessarily so in the other. Moreover, within the larger cultural systems there are found subcultural systems; a youngster's "street corner gang" is an example of a subculture that is of particular significance in a study of norm-violating behavior. Generally, the "official" culture of this country may be characterized as predominantly middle class; middle-class norms and values enforce and are re-enforced by many institutional systems, including the school and the codified legal system.

Normative Systems and Their Rule Books

The definition of juvenile delinquency as norm-violating behavior immediately raises the complex question, "Whose norms and what norms are being violated?" Usually, the answer to this question is "the norms of middle-class culture as exemplified in the school and legal codes." However, this answer does not simplify the real problem, for, as Document 1 pointed out, a wide variety of normative systems exist in all communities in the United States. These different normative systems include those of street corner gang; lower-class adolescent; middle-class adolescent; lower-class adult; middle-class adult; Church A, B, C, and D; the school; and, of course, the legal system. Each of these normative systems has its own rule book; and although there is much overlapping among the rules and regulations of the different systems, there is also much variance among them and often variance between the explicitly stated code and an individual's implicit conduct. For example, a middle-class adolescent who is trying out various roles in an effort to discover his identity, who often "rebels" against adult authority to achieve independence, and who is preoccupied with the preliminaries of "mate finding" is not expected to have the same concerns as those of his parents, which are centered around the maintenance of a stable family unit; a street corner boy who swears frequently in communicating with his gang differs markedly in "acceptable" language patterns from a middle-class member of a local Boy Scout troop; or Church A might sanction card playing or beano, an activity that Church B would not countenance.

Most adults working with delinquent youngsters, including some school personnel, tend to observe and assess the delinquent through the perspective provided by the middle-class normative system. To these observers norm-violating behavior often appears as deviant and atypical behavior, although it may be close to "standard" or even "demanded" behavior in the youngster's primary reference group. For the boy in the street corner gang, shooting craps, drinking, truanting, swearing, and staying out all night may represent status- and prestige-achieving conduct within his gang—his primary reference group—although these activities may violate rules and regulations of the legal-societal system.

In understanding the delinquent's behavior and in assisting him to adapt and to live in such a way that he does not come into conflict with the legal-societal normative system, professional and lay workers need to be aware of the normative system of the youngster's primary reference group and the interplay of forces within his milieu. It is, therefore, necessary to examine briefly some of the factors contributing to norm-violating behavior, particularly in the large urban centers in the United States.

13

Focal Concerns

Behavior within a given cultural system appears to be motivated by the "focal concerns" emphasized in that system. Generally, the dominant concerns for an individual in the middle class include deferment of immediate pleasures and gain for future goals; accumulation of material goods and maintenance of property; achievement through directed work effort; education and intellectual improvement; ambition to "get ahead"; heavy stress on child rearing and maintenance of the stable two-parent household. The youngster raised in a middle-class environment, because of the emphasis these concerns receive in his home, will tend to reflect them in his behavior, which will accord, on the whole, with the established "rules" of official society. This should not imply, however, that there is no delinquent behavior among middle-class youngsters. On the contrary, middle-class youngsters frequently may rebel against the values and concerns of their surroundings, and the result can be delinquent behavior. Nevertheless, it may be said that, generally, the bulk of serious and frequent norm-violating behavior on the part of middle-class youngsters seems more often to stem from psychological factors than from cultural forces.

Lower-class culture, on the other hand, emphasizes a different set of "focal concerns," which may tend to produce behavior that violates the norms of school and society. These concerns include: trouble, toughness, smartness, excitement, fate, and autonomy. Getting in, staying out of, or making trouble are important aspects of life to lower-class youngsters; they hear the word constantly from their parents and peers, and their reputations, whether good or bad—depending on the circumstances—may be determined by their involvement with or avoidance of trouble. Smartness, or to "con" another person while never being duped oneself, is a concern of great importance in lower-class culture; to the youngster from this background the academic skill of his teacher may be much less impressive than the fast line and smart repartee of the con man and the bunco operator. Toughness—physical prowess, ability to take it, and athletic skill—is highly

14

prized in lower-class culture, and much prestige is accorded the individual who is really tough and can take it and dish it out. The desire for excitement, as an escape from boredom and monotony in the home or on the job, often leads to activities—rumbles, joy-riding, and a night on the town with its usual mixture of sex and drinking—that involve risk and court trouble; although the outsider might view the often-resulting violence as aggressive and antisocial, to the participant the action partakes of high adventure within a range of "acceptable" conduct. And over all these activities presides the goddess of fate, or Lady Luck, who is invoked to explain any benefit or mishap that befalls the individual— "I had bad luck" or "Someday I'll strike it lucky." Finally, the concern for autonomy is voiced in the frequent protestation that "No one is going to push me around—just try!"; yet, the insistence on autonomy is often a covert way of indicating a need for dependency, a plea for authority to exercise its control and show that it cares.

However, this discussion of focal concerns should not imply any typical or "standard" behavior for all members of the lower-class culture. The large number of law-abiding lower-class citizens, for one thing, discounts any such construction. Indeed, within the dimensions of these focal concerns there are many alternatives for an individual. Much depends upon the family's orientation towards the focal concerns, for the individual lower-class family may be oriented positively or negatively to trouble, toughness, and the other concerns.

The youngster born and bred in the lower-class milieu who engages in serious and prolonged norm-violating behavior may do so for a number of reasons. First, he may be a daily witness to norm violations on the part of adults or other prestige figures in his family or neighborhood. The presence of a successful bookie or numbers operator openly at work in a neighborhood can provide a model for the youngster to imitate. At the same time, the success and prestige which the adult law violator enjoys can engender disdain or disregard for law and order. In other instances the lower-class

15

youngster may engage in norm violations because they represent an "easy way out" or the achievement of some goal or object with the least expenditure of energy. But in most cases the delinquent in this milieu turns to norm-violating behavior because he feels this to be the surest route to prestige and status within his primary reference group, the street corner gang.

Aspiration and Achievement

There is among lower-class youngsters a clearly discernible subgrouping which is very significant in understanding much of the delinquency "fallout." When considered in terms of levels of "aspiration" and "achievement," youngsters in lower-class culture may be further classified according to the following three categories: (a) the successfully aspiring lower-class individual who has the will, capacity, and means to lift his status—a much less common "case" today than most people realize; (b) the aspiring, but conflicted, lower-class youngster whose levels of aspiration exceed his realistic potential or whose reasonable aspirations are thwarted by almost insurmountable obstacles; (c) the youngster who neither aspires nor has any realistic possibility of achieving his aspirations—a member of the "stable," or "staying," lower class. Of these three groups, the second—aspiring, but conflicted—tends to produce the largest number of norm violators, for in this "stalled" group, friction, conflict, and frustration are inevitable; such ferment may beget aggression that overtly manifests itself in norm-violating behavior. It is interesting to note that for the middle-class youngster trouble is likely to arise when his capacities or achievements are not up to the level of aspiration his parents have set for him. The lower-class youngster, in contrast, who does aspire to higher status and academic achievement must "buck" a milieu that is often essentially hostile or indifferent to his endeavors and goals.

Female-Based Household

Dr. Miller has identified a prevalent type of household unit in lower-class communities as the *female-based household*.[4]

In this household one frequently finds a grandmother (or other female relatives) and one or more daughters who are child bearing; the "father" is either absent from the home; only sporadically present; or, when present, only minimally or inconsistently involved in the support and raising of children. Frequently the child-bearing female lives with a succession of mates or temporary "husbands," and the children are the issues of different fathers. The female-based household, a fairly stabilized form of household in many societies, is much more common in large urban centers than the majority of people suspect; Dr. Miller has estimated that between 25 and 50 percent of all household units in lower-class urban neighborhoods, particularly in and around large housing projects, fall into this category. It has many implications for the psychosocial growth and development of youngsters who are reared in such a home setting.

The psychosocial implications of the female-based household point to a number of hazards to healthy growth and development of children and youth. Lacking a positive father figure, a boy living in such a family may experience more than the ordinary amount of difficulty in personality growth, especially when trying to resolve the Oedipal phase of the growth process. At the same time, the presence or the shadow of an inadequate, negative, or unsuccessful father figure and the reiteration of such messages as "Don't be a bum like your father" or "All men are no good" may lead the youngster to reject or disassociate himself from the male-parent figure as a model for identification. If there are no positive male figures around the youngster—older brothers or other male adults—the lower-class youngster may not be adequately sustained even by the traditional matriarchal family structure, in which the mother plays the male role as well as she can. The youngster may need, consequently, to turn to his street corner group and seek his male identification through this association. In testing and proving his masculinity, he may engage in feats and episodes involving norm-violating behavior which bring him to the attention of an official authority and agency. Inasmuch as personality formation is greatly affected by identification with the appropriate parental figure, the preponderance of the female-based household may have special significance in the higher delinquency rates of lower-class culture.

Incidence and Pathology

The first document presented a simple typology of the distribution of "delinquent" youngsters based on two variables: (a) the degree of pathology or emotional disturbance and (b) the severity of the norm-violating behavior in terms of these criteria: seriousness, form, frequency, prior behavior, and individual history. The first variable provided for a degree of pathology ranging from none to severe; the second allowed for a range of behavior from norm conforming to seriously norm violating. Four ideal, or basic, types emerged from this bivariate treatment: Group 1—the "normal" youngster who was not norm violating and not emotionally disturbed—the large bulk of the juvenile population; Group 2—the norm-violating youngster, or delinquent, with little or no emotional disturbance; Group 3—the "delinquent" and "disturbed" youngster; and Group 4—the "disturbed" but not norm-violating youngster. It was estimated in Document 1 that the norm-violating behavior of a majority of delinquents (about 75 percent) stemmed, in the main, from cultural factors, and all but a small number of youngsters in this group were of lower-class origin. The norm-violating behavior of the remaining group—about 25 percent—represented "psychologically relevant" delinquency, and it was in this group that the largest number of middle-class youngsters were to be found. Document 1 pointed out that "a nonlower-class youngster who becomes involved in delinquency is much more likely to be emotionally disturbed than not; that some lower-class delinquent youngsters may manifest emotional disturbance, but their proportion is small compared to those who do not. . . . *the preponderant portion of our 'delinquent' population consists of essentially 'normal' youngsters.*" [5]

These projected estimates suggest that the psychodynamics approach via the child-guidance clinic and the one-to-one

18

counseling relationship in treatment may often or in many respects be irrelevant to the generic aspects of much delinquent behavior. They suggest also that preventive and corrective action, to a great extent, must be focused on the cultural situations and the way of life in the lower-class neighborhood. The singular lack of success in prevention and control of juvenile delinquency in many communities may be traceable to the fact that the majority of lower-class youngsters who come to the attention of official agencies are either immune or allergic to psychological and psychiatric approaches. Although the youngster subjected to conflicting cultural forces—for example, the family's values vs. the school's values—may eventually become emotionally disturbed, the problem is initially cultural and not psychological. It is often the neighborhood and the community that must be viewed as the patient. The key questions to be faced by those planning action programs are: "Can we modify the way of life of the lower-class community?" and "What techniques can be used to orient norm-violating individuals in lower-class population toward a law-abiding lower-class way of life?"

This strong emphasis upon the culturally determined delinquent does not, by any means, minimize the need for more and better child-guidance clinics; it does suggest, however, that this approach, by itself, may not get to the bottom of the problem for a majority of lower-class norm-violating youngsters. If anything, the theses in the first and the second documents reaffirm the value of the child-guidance clinic's diagnosis in confirming the extent of pathology evident in the behavior of the norm violator as well as the strategic importance of this approach for those norm violators whose problems stem from, or are complicated by, factors in the psyche.

Factors in Community Attitudes

Delinquency statistics are very responsive to the irritability index of the local community and to the changing frustration-tolerance level of adults. Consequently, it is often difficult

19

to determine whether delinquency, as such, is actually increasing or whether the increase in officially recorded cases of delinquency reflects only an increase in police activity brought on by the demand for "action" by a suddenly aroused community. In the resulting crackdown, local officials sweep up every minor and major offender, thus augmenting the official roster of delinquents.

However, spurts of irritated concern are often preceded and followed by long periods of complacency, for few communities dare to look into and stand up to the realities of their delinquency problem. When hysteria subsides, officials and citizens tend to point to the nearest urban industrial center as the place "where the delinquents will be found" and to deny or minimize "any real problem in our town." The attitudes of adults toward delinquency are extremely complex and, in many respects, contradictory; in a town where the existence of a serious delinquency problem has been denied, adults do not hesitate to solicit funds as an antidote to the threat of delinquency whenever seeking financial support for local recreational programs and organizations.

The irritating young delinquent appears to syphon off much of the adult frustration and aggression that are natural in a society as complex as ours; he serves admirably as a handy hate target—a classic case of the institutional scapegoat. Moreover, of all the exceptional children in the long litany of youngsters needing special help, the delinquent is the one who is most likely to get the back of the hand rather than the helping hand from adults. Many youth workers when queried indicate that the overt-aggressive norm violator is the one youngster with whom they would least like to work—if they had a choice.

Writers for such extremely influential commercial media as stage, screen, television, radio, and the press have contributed more than their share of the stereotyped image of the delinquent as ruthless and brutal:

The delinquent is black-jacketed and long-haired. He runs around on a bright and noisy motorcycle or in a souped-up hot rod. He is brutal. He is cruel. He is restless. He is dangerously free and uninhibited sexually. He is aggressive. He travels with a pack. He is heartless. And he is neatly tied in with that archenemy—the standardized villain—the lower-class American who dwells deep in the tenement holes of the big, dirty, and deteriorating city, so recently abandoned by those who have escaped to suburbia.[6]

This is an image which not only affects the adults in a community and leads them to look upon the delinquent as a moral monster, but it may often be a self-fulfilling prophecy. Seeing himself depicted as such a person, the delinquent will often strive to fill the role which has been created for him.

The adults in a community are explicitly and implicitly involved in many ways in the community's delinquency problem. Frequently they are themselves quite unaware of the nature of their own involvement, for norm violations by youngsters can fulfill a number of psychological functions for the law-abiding adult. The self-righteous clucking of many adults often only half conceals a vicarious thrill in the escapades of youth. If delinquency is to be prevented and controlled, it will be necessary that adults not only understand the reality of the problem within their community but also that they understand their own emotional needs, their own problems, and even the gratifications they might receive from the delinquency phenomenon.

Guides for School Action

The second document of the NEA Juvenile Delinquency Project, *Delinquency Behavior: Principles and Practices,* presents basic operational principles, guidelines for action, and illustrative programs outlining the school's role and responsibility for prevention and control of norm-violating behavior.

The material for this volume was obtained from three major sources. First, a series of workshops was held in different sections of the country in which different professional groups participated, including school and child welfare personnel. These discussions centered around desirable school practices and adaptations that stemmed implicitly from the theoretical orientation presented in the first draft of *Delin-*

21

quent Behavior: Culture and the Individual, which had been made available to all participants before the date of each conference.[7]

Second, a systematic search for school-community programs for delinquency prevention and control was undertaken early in the project by contacting state school officers and the executive secretaries of state education associations. At the same time, a careful check of the delinquency literature was made in order to discover other school programs designed to help the delinquent youngster. Officials operating such programs were invited to submit descriptions of their activities with other pertinent data. This phase of the project sought to identify, to describe, and to analyze specific school programs which in recent years have succeeded in denting the delinquency problem.

Third, on the basis of the information which came out of the first two steps, recommended principles and practices were outlined in a preliminary working paper. In turn, this preliminary document was submitted for study and discussion to the National Invitational Conference on the Prevention and Control of Juvenile Delinquency, which convened in Washington, D. C., under the auspices of the National Education Association. More than 200 lay and professional youth and family workers representing local, state, and federal institutions and agencies studied the material and made suggestions involving additions, revision, and deletions of many principles and practices; at the same time lines of responsibility within the community were clarified. Most of these suggestions have been incorporated by the Project staff in this revision of the original outline.

Plan and Organization of Document 2

The following eight chapters of this report are built around eight *basic principles,* each of which summarizes an important aspect of the school's fundamental and implicit responsibility to insure equal educational opportunity to the potential or active norm-violating pupil. The basic principle is followed by a set of *guidelines for action* that indicate ways in which the particular basic principle may be implemented;

22

these spell out in some detail how the school, in accepting its unique role and opportunities, may act to help the pre-delinquent and delinquent youngster. Presented in the form of a checklist, these guidelines may be used by school personnel as a source list of recommended practices as well as a guide in appraising local school programs dealing with the norm-violating pupil.

The basic principles indicate the implicit and essential school responsibility, and the guidelines represent ways in which the school can carry out its responsibility. The practices, which comprise a large part of each chapter, are, for the most part, direct quotations and illustrations of what some schools and communities are actually doing to help the norm violator. Reports on these practices, it should again be emphasized, were contributed to the NEA projects by individuals representing local school systems and community agencies that are actually engaged in programming for delinquency control and prevention. Material submitted in mimeographed or printed form is cited in the list of References found at the end of each chapter in this document. The practices themselves not only offer a variety of suggestions which other schools may follow, but, as a totality, they provide an over-all view of a nation-wide school-community effort to meet the problem of delinquency on the local level.

The document has been organized into two major parts, "School and Norm-Violating Pupil" and "School-Community and Norm-Violating Pupil." Part 1 is concerned with the school as it gives direct help to the potential or active norm violator within the limits of its own functions and organization. Part 2 discusses how the school in its effort to aid the norm-violating pupil may work with all community forces outside the school's organization—home, law enforcement and court, and all other youth and family agencies.

Before proceeding to a brief resumé of the chapters which comprise this volume, it may be helpful to sketch the sequence of steps taken by the school to help the norm-violating youngster.

First, the teacher identifies as early as possible the young-ster who gives indications of exposure or vulnerability to the development of serious and persistent patterns of behavior that point in the direction of legal norm violation. Help is then extended to the pupil through the resourcefulness of a competent and likable teacher in the regular classroom. Using all the planned experiences through an individualized cur-riculum, the school makes every effort to enable the pupil to achieve a measure of success that is commensurate with his learning potential. If the school is unable to help him in the regular classroom and through the resources of the school curriculum, judicious use is made of the special school serv-ices that are available to both teacher and student. For those learners who cannot profit from the regular school program even with the help of integrated school services and support, special placement in school or community may be indicated.

In addition to helping the pupil through the integrated effort utilizing all resources within the school and classroom, the administrator and staff reach out into the community on behalf of the youngster in need of help. The school gets in touch with the home and works closely with the parents. In the event that the norm violator comes in contact with the police and the courts, the school works side by side with these official agencies for the benefit of the youngster. And always the school remains alert to the assistance that might be rendered through the cooperative effort of other youth or family service agencies of the various public and private organizations that may be found in most communities. To sum up: the early identification of vulnerable or delinquency-prone youngsters, their study and diagnosis, the treatment program, and the attempt to influence their value systems or ways of life cannot be done on a hit-or-miss or trial-and-error basis. The school makes its optimum contribution, as would any other agency, by basing its program on research-oriented theory in a systematic, scientific, and humane endeavor to help the norm violator.

Document 2, which follows the general sequence of "events" outlined above, delineates the specific roles of school personnel in helping the norm violator as well as the special opportunities offered by school facilities. Part 1, "School and Norm-Violating Pupil," opens with a discussion of the teacher's role in identifying the predelinquent and delinquent at the earliest possible date (Chapter 2, "Identifying the Youngster Needing Help in the Classroom"). Helping the youngster within the classroom is explored in the next chapter; included in the discussion are instructional methods, the personal attributes and professional competencies of the teaching staff, as these relate to the norm violator; and the responsibility of the administrator in hiring and placing staff members and insuring their adequate inservice training (Chapter 3, "Providing Help Within the Classroom"). Curriculum planning and adaptations for meeting the special needs of those pupils whose emotional and cultural problems often handicap them in their schoolwork are next discussed (Chapter 4, "Providing Help Through Curriculum Adjustments"). The need for an integrated program of special services with an adequately manned and professionally trained staff—a necessary concomitant to the school's efforts to help the norm violator within the classroom—is the next topic considered (Chapter 5, "Providing Help Through Integrated Special Services"). The last chapter in Part 1 deals with organization, administration, and functioning of special classrooms and special centers established to help predelinquent and delinquent youngsters (Chapter 6, "Providing Help Through the Special Class").

In Part 2, "School-Community and Norm-Violating Pupil," a sequence of three chapters rounds out the report. The means by which school personnel can cooperate and work closely with the youngster's home and family is first considered (Chapter 7, "Working with the Family"). How the school may proceed to establish an effective working relationship with law-enforcement and court personnel in helping youngsters who have been brought to the attention of these agencies is next discussed (Chapter 8, "Working with Law-Enforcement and Court Personnel"). The concluding chapter in this document outlines ways and means for utilizing all available community agencies and institutions in an effective community-wide effort to reduce and contain delinquency (Chapter 9, "Working with Community Agencies").

The document views the problem of providing help for the norm violator primarily through planned programs within the school or by the school in cooperation with other community agencies. Because these place very real limits on the area of the school's responsibility, there are, inevitably, limits to the scope of this document.

Strategy of the School Agency

The school can occupy a most strategic role in the prevention of delinquency and in the rehabilitation of legal norm violators who already have a police or court contact. A school system exists in every community. It works with the children of all the people. It receives the youngsters early and maintains intimate and daily contact with them for 10 to 12 years. Hence, this considerable span of time is to great advantage in helping the norm-violating youngster. The school has professional personnel trained to deal with children and youth. In its major objectives the school aims to develop well-integrated and socially effective citizens in the tradition of the law-abiding citizen regardless of his class status. For the youngster entering the kindergarten or the first grade, these new experiences represent a first step away from the protective climate of the home and family—a step into a social experience that tests a large number of varied interpersonal relationships. At the same time the school—unlike many other agencies such as the police, courts, and welfare offices —has a natural relationship with parents; it is thus in a position to capitalize on this relationship for the benefit of the child or parent in need of help. In addition to teaching the fundamental language and arithmetic skills, the modern school has accepted a responsibility, which is shared with parents, for the personal and social growth of children as well as for their academic training and acquisition of knowledge. And, last, the school is in a unique position to identify at an early age the serious and even slight problems of the emotionally disturbed and/or norm-violating youngster. But the

26

school is only one agency in the community, and it has its limitations.

The school's approach to prevention and control requires a two-pronged attack. First, via the planned experiences in the curriculum the school tries to develop new and effective modes of behavior and adjustment and/or tries to modify and improve established but less effective modes of living of all youth. By changing the behavior of large numbers of children, the school can realistically hope to change or re-enforce the culture and the way of life. Via the second approach, the school attempts to render help on an individual basis and depends primarily, as many guidelines in Chapter 3 indicate, on the quality of the relationship that is established between teacher and pupil. Administrative and organizational provisions and adaptations, in and of themselves, are relatively ineffective except as they provide the settings in which positive teacher-pupil relationships are more likely to develop and in which a curriculum including all the planned learning experiences is more surely evolved.

Limitations of the School Agency

Norm-violating behavior is seldom of the school's manufacture alone, nor can norm-violating behavior be diminished solely by any "school cure." This statement should not be taken as discounting the school's tendency to precipitate norm-violating behavior. The school is only one agency in the community, but it is potentially a powerful and pervasive force for modifying and changing behavior.

Most norm-violating behavior has its origins in the home, the peer group, the neighborhood, and even the school, although sometimes its roots can be traced to factors in the youngster's psyche. The school works with the youngster as an individual and as a member of a group or class. As an agency, the school does not possess the means and the opportunity to work with the whole family, with the peer group, or with all the cultural forces in the neighborhood. Frequently other community organizations and agencies (church, settlement house, family casework agency, hospital, juvenile court, child-guidance clinic, group-work agency) can best provide guidance, diagnosis, help, or treatment. But always, as this report points out in Part 2, both school and community agencies can and must supplement one another. Each provides and receives help from the other in assisting the predelinquent or delinquent youngster, his family, or his peers.

The school is primarily concerned with prevention rather than treatment of emotional and social disturbances. When it plays a treatment role, it does so generally under supervision of another agency such as a child-guidance clinic, or incidentally through the utilization of milieu therapy, or through some special functionary such as a school psychologist, psychiatrist, or counselor. The school's primary function is not that of a hospital, institution, or warehouse to store children—good, bad, or indifferent. As a school, its major concern remains that of instruction and learning.

The school cannot become all things to all pupils. When it deflects from its original and unique function and/or when it lacks adequate financial support, it is apt to misfire on all fronts. But the school must always proceed with due regard to both the existence of other community resources and the willingness of the community to support an expanding program of special services in the school.

Basically, the school's responsibility to the delinquent is not different from its responsibility to all children or to other handicapped children—the blind, the deaf, the crippled, and the mentally retarded—or even to the gifted. The point may be made that the psycho-bio-social factors that impel norm-violating behavior may often be more susceptible to preventive and remedial measures than are many of those handicaps which receive a larger share of sustained community effort and financial support. The principle of universal education in the United States promises an equality of educational opportunity to all children, handicapped as well as "normal." In practice, this demands a diversified educational program. The central theme in this document turns on the conviction that the norm-violating youngster should be no exception to this rule.

The recommended and selected practices embodied in the principles and illustrative programs that have been gathered together in this report ultimately contribute to a definition of the "good school." The most direct and positive contribution that schools can make to delinquency prevention and control is for good schools to become better schools. It is believed that steps may be taken in this direction by following many of the guidelines and examples listed in this report.

The Lag Between Theory and Practice

There are many reasons why a serious lag exists between theory and practices in the behavioral sciences. Some of the reasons are to be found within the organization or agency such as the school; other reasons can be found in the community's inertia or ignorance. The New Jersey State Youth Study Commission, commenting on this problem in its third annual report, pointed out in straightforward language why schools sometimes fail to assist the youngster who needs help.

The basic reason for the inability of most schools to reach more students through special services and dynamic new programs lies in the attitude of the community. The spotty and in some cases grudging support given to schools only adds to the old inadequacies—low teacher status and poor morale, skimpy special services, traditional programs, and insufficient facilities.

If more communities will face up to their own educational crisis, then more educators may be encouraged to devise dynamic new programs and techniques to reach more students.

To succeed, these programs must overcome the following limitations of conventional schools: (a) the rigid middle-class measuring rod generally applied to children of all backgrounds; (b) the "custodial" approach assumed by many teachers and administrators in lieu of a "reaching-out" philosophy towards hard-to-reach youth; (c) the failure to meet with the real leaders of disruptive student groups to harness the power of group pressures behind mutually agreeable policies; (d) the paucity of adequate psychological and social work services for the guidance and treatment of disturbed children and their families; (e) the absence of imaginative school-work programs to hold

29

the interest of nonacademically oriented youths; (f) the failure to involve hard-to-reach parents in neighborhood-school projects and in adult discussion groups.[8]

Documents 1 and 2 of the NEA Juvenile Delinquency Project and the National Invitational Conference representing all community workers, including lay citizens, serve to re-emphasize that juvenile delinquency is everybody's business. At the same time such projects and meetings tend to bring out the difficulties that youth and family workers face in coordinating and focusing their efforts on prevention and control of norm-violating behavior. Differences in operational theory and in specialized vocabulary always present a potential hazard for disrupting community coordination and teamwork. There is a great urgency for continuing this type of interdisciplinary discussion and planning at the local level; and it is hoped that both NEA documents, *Delinquent Behavior: Culture and the Individual* and *Delinquent Behavior: Principles and Practices*, may be used as a working base to stimulate integrated thinking and, ultimately, coordinated community action. The professional youth and family worker must continually ask the question, "What are the facts?" He must view the hard facts—whether at the level of theory, community study, or individual case study—objectively and impersonally. And always he must be careful to act in behalf of the predelinquent or delinquent youngster, regardless of his own personal or emotional needs or even the entrenched interests of his own institution or agency.

To sum up, the value of such publications will always stem from the disagreements that must be reconciled as well as from the consensus that may be visible. In the combination of these two documents, which involve theory-based action, rests a promising approach to delinquency prevention and control for any school and community.

References

[1] A carefully selected six-man team of experts who embody broad, interdisciplinary experience with the delinquent engaged in a cooperative endeavor to provide the base for a comprehensive and integrated theoretical statement. The members of the interdisciplinary team included Milton L.

Barron, sociologist; Edward M. Daniels, M.D., psychiatrist; Preston A. McLendon, M.D., pediatrician; Benjamin A. Thompson, criminologist; William C. Kvaraceus, psychologist; and Walter B. Miller, cultural anthropologist. Dr. Kvaraceus and Dr. Miller prepared the report for publication.

[2] Miller, Walter B. "Lower Class Culture as a Generating Milieu of Gang Delinquency." *Journal of Social Issues* 14: 5-19; No. 3, 1958. April 1959.

[3] Vance Packard's recent book, *The Status Seekers*, is an attempt to interpret for the lay reader some aspects of the meaning and implications of class structuring in the United States. (New York: David McKay Company, Inc., 1959, 379 p.)

[4] Miller, Walter B. "Implications of Lower Class Culture for Social Work." *The Social Service Review* XXXIII: No. 3, September 1959.

[5] Kvaraceus, William C.; Miller, Walter B.; and others. *Delinquent Behavior: Culture and the Individual.* Washington, D. C.: National Education Association Juvenile Delinquency Project, 1959. p. 55.

[6] *Ibid.*, p. 27-28.

[7] In all, 11 workshops were held at meetings of the National Association of Secondary-School Principals (Philadelphia); Association for Supervision and Curriculum Development (Cincinnati); Department of Classroom Teachers (Salt Lake City); School, Youth and Family Workers Institute, University of Delaware (Newark); Department of Classroom Teachers (Hartford, Connecticut); Council for Exceptional Children (Atlantic City); American Association for Health, Physical Education, and Recreation (Indianapolis); Michigan Delinquency Conference for Elementary Teachers (Lansing); Special Service Personnel of Pinellas County (Florida); Special Service Staff, Los Angeles County Public Schools (Los Angeles); 28th Annual Governor's Conference on Youth and Community Services (Chicago).

[8] New Jersey Youth Study Commission. *New Ways to Reach Unreached Youth: A Challenge to New Jersey,* Third Annual Report and Recommendations of the State of New Jersey Youth Study Commission. Trenton: the Commission, June 1958. p. 9.

31

IDENTIFYING THE YOUNGSTER
chapter 2 NEEDING HELP IN THE CLASSROOM

basic principle: THE CLASSROOM TEACHER AS-
SUMES THE MAJOR RESPONSIBILITY FOR EARLY
IDENTIFICATION OF THE POTENTIAL NORM-VIO-
LATING YOUNGSTER. HE MAINTAINS RECORDS
AND ANECDOTAL REPORTS OF EVERY PUPIL HE
TEACHES, THUS INSURING THAT ACCURATE AND
UP-TO-DATE INFORMATION ABOUT INDIVIDUAL
STUDENTS AND THEIR BACKGROUNDS WILL BE
READILY AVAILABLE TO HIMSELF AND OTHER
PROFESSIONAL PERSONNEL.

Delinquent behavior should not be regarded as a 24-hour
malady. It rarely happens overnight. Habitual and serious
norm-violating behavior requires a fairly long period of time
for its development; this means that many youngsters give
some hints or signs well before a pattern of norm-violating
behavior is thoroughly established.

The classroom teacher who, as a trained observer, sees the
pupil for an extended period of time and who comes to know
him intimately is in an advantageous position to identify
those pupils who evidence need for emotional, psychological,
or cultural support. Through early referral of the delinquency-prone youngster to the appropriate agency, followed
by special help and treatment, the school can achieve preventive action in the literal sense of the word.

All youngsters, at one time or other, violate some minor, or
even major, rule or regulation. In a sense, every pupil may
be looked upon as a potential norm violator. But some
youngsters, because of their social-class status and milieu,
the interpersonal relationships within their family or peer
group, or other inner and outer forces, may be considered as

especially prone, vulnerable, or susceptible to norm-violating behavior as a mode of adjustment or as a solution to some personal-social problem.

In order to recognize the potential norm violator, the teacher will need to be aware of the tell-tale signs, the indicators, or the hints of the appearance of an adjustment that involves norm-violating behavior. These indicators will vary according to the youngster's social status or the cultural milieu in which he lives, works, and plays. For example, failure in several school subjects may be one indication of behavioral difficulty for the middle-class delinquent, but it may not have the same import for the lower-class youngster whose regard for school may be low and who expects to leave school as soon as it is legally possible. Research studies, such as Document 1 of the NEA Juvenile Delinquency Project, are beginning to point up some of the factors which are often associated with norm-violating behavior and which, if recognized, may alert the teacher to those boys and girls who have a high potential for, or who are vulnerable or susceptible to, the development of delinquent behavior.[1]

However, the day-to-day process of identifying the predelinquent still remains a subjective or clinical operation. There are no simple rule-of-thumb methods or measures that can be employed to sort out the predelinquent from those who are not likely to follow this patterning of behavior. The teacher will need to weigh the known factors in a youngster's personal make-up, in his peer-group relationships, and in his family. These factors must then be viewed against the background of his milieu or social status.

In identifying potential norm violators, the teacher must remember that there are stages or levels of readiness and that it is necessary to distinguish among them. Since all youngsters break a rule or regulation at one time or another, the teacher should not confuse the occasional norm-violating pupil with the more persistent and serious offender. He must remain alert to those youngsters who show a steady patterning of minor rule violations or who are involved in less frequent but more serious incidents. And always the teacher will need to watch for those pupils who give signs of persisting and serious norm violations, although these youngsters may be "predelinquent" only in the sense that they have not yet been designated as "official" delinquents by a juvenile court.

The school and the community should not wait until a youngster is on his way to court; it is possible through the processes of early identification and referral to forestall the development and habituation of many—even most—of the more serious norm violations.

The following guidelines spell out some actions that the classroom teacher may take in his efforts to identify the potential norm violator at the earliest possible time.

Guidelines

* In forecasting, the teacher is alert to the problem of labelling a youngster "predelinquent," for there is a constant hazard of a self-fulfilling prophecy, with the youngster acting out the role he has been given.

* The teacher, in validating his initial judgment of a youngster, intelligently utilizes all available sources of information, clarification, and guidance, including reliable individuals either personally or professionally knowledgeable. This supports his careful study of case records and cumulative folders and his own systematic observations of the child in the school and classroom.

* The teacher uses all the effective subindicators that are pertinent to the child's subculture and milieu. He notes such indicators as the student who shows conflicts in achievement-aspiration, who gains status via norm-violating behavior, who lives in a female-based household, who takes it out on people and property.

* The teacher evidences objectivity and balance in observing and assessing the different modes of behavior which are characteristic of varying culture patterns and is on guard

34

lest he misjudge every cultural pattern variant as a sign of potential norm-violating behavior.

* The teacher distinguishes between those symptoms in norm-violating behavior which reflect economic deprivation and cultural influences and those which are the result of inadequate personal relationships and psychological maladjustment.

* In those students who come from lower-class homes, the teacher recognizes the signs of friction and frustration that arise when the pupil's levels of aspiration exceed his realistic potential or when he is seriously thwarted in achieving his realistic level of aspiration.

* The teacher is aware of the special values inherent in contemporary child and adolescent culture—rebellion, independence, self-identity, group identification, sex roles—as they relate to the development of and the violation of different normative systems.

* The teacher not only identifies the vulnerable pupil but refers him to an appropriate source of help. The teacher exercises judgment in the making of referrals lest he err in too hasty referral or go to the other extreme of holding on to the youngster beyond the time when he may profit from available help.

* The teacher designates in his referral whether the norm violation appears to be culturally or emotionally based.

* The teacher recognizes that any prediction may be reenforced or invalidated by deterioration or improvement in the youngster's background and personal development.

Practices

Identification of the predelinquent is a continuing process. However, the earlier the identification, the more propitious the preventive effort. If the job can be done in the early grades, the school and community can bring their total effort to bear on the youngster and his culture with more hopeful results.   The following illustrations indicate how different communities are trying to spot the youngster needing help at various steps of the educational ladder.

In one New England town a concerted effort is made to identify these youngsters through a counseling process which involves the administration of psychological tests as a part of a preschool diagnostic evaluation.

WESTPORT, CONNECTICUT: We have . . . a full-time counselor-psychologist in each of our five elementary schools, and while their primary purpose is not that of identifying potential delinquents, we do feel that one of our major responsibilities is in that area.   Each incoming kindergarten child is tested during the month of July with the Stanford-Binet, and a conference held with his parents.   At that time, the counselor, who has seen hundreds of these children, attempts to make judgments about the differential capacities of the child and his probable adjustment to school.   In some instances it has been possible to identify a child who later showed fairly marked predelinquent characteristics.

Three large-city school systems, situated in widely separated sections of the country, have indicated their concern and their procedures for identifying the norm violator.   The statement from New York points up the strategy and responsibility of the classroom teacher; that from Los Angeles County indicates a general process; and that from Detroit lists specific hints and techniques.

NEW YORK CITY: Teachers of the lower grades are in an ideal position to observe the relative success or failure in social adjustment made by children who, for the most part, are experiencing their first major separation experience from home and family. The alert teacher, after several months of observation, can assess the child's ability to handle himself in the school and class setting.   Her experience further enables her to measure the individual child against her estimate of the normal pattern of adjustment of children who successfully manage the separation from the home.   Teachers are becoming increasingly alert in recognizing withdrawal symptoms of young children.   While such children tend to be quiet, unassuming and conforming, their adjustment patterns are often indicative of maladjustment.[2]

36

Los Angeles County, California: Teachers perceive these normal differences among children more precisely as they consider what is already known about the children and observe their daily behavior in the classroom. Health records and conferences with the school nurse often help teachers to discover quickly those children whose physical development will need special attention. Classroom activities should, of course, be adapted to the physical needs characteristic of the age group. There are, however, generally several children whose health and physical development necessitate such special arrangements as additional rest and favorable placement for better seeing or hearing. Sometimes the teacher's observation discovers physical problems which had not been noted previously.

The school records also may suggest differences in children's knowledge and understanding and their probable aptitude for successful school learnings. Previous teachers' notations of accomplishments in the arts, activities in social studies, or use of books and printed materials are helpful as the teacher plans ways of stimulating new learnings. Notations of children's performance on standardized tests indicate the range of differences within each group. As the teacher selects materials and plans a sequence of learning experiences, provisions must be made for these differences.

In most groups, there are a few children who, for many reasons, learn rather easily and experience repeated success. These children will need activities which enrich their learning and challenge their abilities. There are also generally several children who have more than usual difficulty in learning. This may be due to their particular aptitudes or because of limited background or because of unfavorable attitudes. Teachers attempt to discover the reasons for each child's difficulties in learning. Experiences are planned to draw upon each child's abilities and to insure many successes.

Through consulting school records, conferring with parents, and studying the community, the teacher gains insight into the differences in children's out-of-school lives. Social traditions and customs, the values and attitudes of the family, have a strong impact upon children. Sometimes these influences reinforce school learnings and sometimes they are in opposition. As teachers encourage children to reflect upon their experiences and to discuss their ideas, meanings are clarified and deepened.

Children constantly are helped to apply new learnings in their everyday lives.[3]

DETROIT, MICHIGAN: In studying the unadjusted child, co-operation between the school nurse, parents, and teacher is absolutely essential. First, make a careful inventory of the child's physical, mental, emotional, community, and family status. On the physical side, check his size, weight, and height in comparison with the normal; note physical defects, such as vision, hearing, respiratory, etc. Evaluate his mentality—is it good, average, retarded, extremely retarded, or is there mental imbalance? Visit the home several times; note the parent-child relationships, the feelings between brothers and sisters, the economic status, the feeding arrangements, and the type of physical care. Is the child happy and wanted in the home? Does he have home duties? Find out how he adjusts in the neighborhood, what are his play interests, whether he belongs to clubs or gangs, what cultural opportunities there are, what recreational outlets. Above all, try to appraise his emotional life: Has he a feeling of inferiority or of being unwanted? Has he many fears? Is he constantly feeling frustrated? Does he cry easily?

Make a chart showing his weaknesses and his strengths. Talk over his problems with him. Lead him, if he is old enough, to think through the reasons why he follows his impulses or withdraws from group activities.[4]

In a study of the unadjusted youngster, the making of charts, the examination records, and the observation and consultation with other school personnel, all play a part in helping the classroom teacher understand and aid the norm-violating youngster. However, unless the information is recorded and systematically organized, it will be of limited value to the teacher himself or to workers who in the future will deal with the same child. Therefore, keeping anecdotal reports and building a cumulative record and other case-study information becomes essential.

LOS ANGELES COUNTY, CALIFORNIA: A research study was completed regarding what school factors are found to be related to delinquency.

From out of the questionnaire data and from the fifty individual case studies used in the validation of the research data and illustrating and emphasizing the results therefrom, there

38

appeared a patterned list of techniques and procedures that, when utilized effectively by the secondary school, produced much improvement in the delinquency situation, and which further prevented many school predelinquent tendencies from developing into actual delinquency.

Overwhelming evidence was disclosed in favor of the necessity for adequate cumulative records in order to make correct diagnoses of delinquent or predelinquent cases. . . .

The results of the study showed that adequate cumulative records included fairly recent facts concerning identifying data, health information, standardized test data, school records and attendance, information regarding social situation, psychological and emotional data, educational history of student, identification of special interests, and follow-up and progress reports.

The effective interpretation of cumulative records to teachers was shown to have brought about teachers' knowledge and understanding of the whole student in his total environment, rather than just a knowledge of a segment of a student's life. Such an understanding generally was found to result in improved teacher attitudes and classroom methods. . . .

The techniques of questionnaire and autobiography . . . proved to be effective in many cases in making correct diagnoses, but some schools had not yet taken advantage of these methods of gaining information about their students. The facts disclosed by these methods often have thrown much light on the true picture of certain students having problems. In fact, even actual gaps or omissions in the autobiography have proved to be as meaningful as what was written. When these autobiographies have been placed in the cumulative record folders, a rich reservoir of pertinent fact has been provided the counselor and teacher that may hold the clue to solution of a serious but obscure student problem.[5]

To assist the classroom teacher in the process of observation and recording, which is essential to accurate and pertinent anecdotal reporting, the following guides have been set up for the school personnel in one Michigan school system.

PONTIAC, MICHIGAN:

Guides in Writing Anecdotes

1. The anecdote must be based upon a significant item of conduct.

2. The incident reported upon must be personally observed by the recorder.
3. The incident must be related as clearly, concisely, and accurately as possible and should be written immediately after the incident happened.
4. If conversations are included, they must be quoted exactly, if possible.
5. Do not inject statements into the anecdote which are not pertinent.
6. Observations should not be colored or influenced by personal feelings of the recorder.
7. Any interpretation and recommendation, if included in write-up, should come after the written observation and should be identified as such.
8. Do not record more than one incident in an anecdote.
9. Significant conduct which is favorable should be reported as well as that which is unfavorable. This is too often overlooked.

Other Factors

1. An anecdote should be a word picture of a student in action.
2. Anecdotes relating actions of students may be better than those reporting conversations.
3. Either recommendations, interpretations, or both are sometimes so obvious that they are not included in the written anecdote. If they are to be included, let them be short and to the point.
4. Any interpretation necessary for thorough understanding should be given.
5. Care should be exercised in making interpretations. It might be better to allow the reader to form his own conclusions.
6. Even if an interpretation cannot be given at the time, record anecdote if it seems significant. It may tie up with other anecdotes which have been accumulated in the pupil's folder.
7. The interpretation of an anecdote, if any, should be logically sound and fitting. . . .
8. Report only such data as helps us to understand the child better.
9. An anecdote should always be dated and bear the signature of the person reporting it.

10. Anecdotes should be turned over to the counselor for filing in pupil's cumulative folder.[6]

In addition, the same school system provides an elaborate information outline, "The Case Study Information Outline," to be used in gathering significant material relating to an individual pupil.

PONTIAC, MICHIGAN:

The Case Study Information Outline /

Introduction: The case study record is a written record of all significant information related to an individual. It is selective in that relevant details from other records are included. It is an evaluation and interpretation of the individual in that it seeks to present a cumulative picture of his total personality.

The Case Study May Be Used:
1. To study the growth and development of an individual
   a. For this purpose the material should be arranged in chronological order.
2. To study a special problem or the problems of the individual
   a. The information should center around problems and difficulties that have arisen in the development of the individual.
   b. The information should include enough of the normal development to secure a good perspective of the whole personality.

A. *Use of the Case Study Technique.* The exact classification and subdivisions of information used in a specific case study are not of great significance. The important thing is to give as clear and understanding a picture of the individual as is possible.

Unless the counselor has had training or experience in the making of case studies, it might be better for him to refer an individual whose problem indicates the need for *exhaustive study* to someone skilled in the technique. It should be remembered at all times that the case study must result in benefit to the individual concerned and that the material of the case study is *confidential.* Good judgment and discrimination will indicate the amount and kind of information necessary to give a clear and accurate picture. In those instances where personal and intimate details of family life and relationships are not relevant, they should be omitted.

41

When this information is necessary for the understanding and solution of the problem, the counselor must be sure that good rapport has been established between himself and the family and that the information requested will be given with confidence in the counselor's integrity and his ability to use the information toward the desired end.

B. *A Case Study Outline.* The following outline is one that may be used in the making of a case study; inclusion or omission of information will depend on circumstances.

   I. *The Introductory Statement.*

     A. The case study should open with a clear and concise statement giving the reason or the need for the making of the case study.

  II. *The Family Background.*

     A. *Father:* Age. Interest and presence in the home. Social relations of each member of the family with variation at different ages. Education. Work: type and different kinds, success, business relations. Civic interests. Religious attitudes and relations. Interests, hobbies. Orderliness. Temperament. Physical health and illnesses. Racial and national characteristics.

     B. *Mother:* (same as father).

     C. *Siblings:* (same as father) Also significant material under developmental history.

     D. *Other Individuals:* Having considerable contact with the individual studied, such as servants, collateral relatives, or boarders.

     E. *Economic Status:* Physical make-up of the home.

     F. *Neighborhood:* Economic and social environment, etc.

 III. *Developmental History.*

     A. *Infantile:* Mother's pregnancy: planned or not. Birth: normal or not. Weight. Age of smiling, sitting, crawling, walking, talking, etc.

     B. *Habits:*

       1. Eating: Whether breast fed, formula difficulties, weaning, good or poor eater—how handled. Food allergies. Special likes and dislikes. Regularity. Self-feeding.

       2. Training: When, bowel and urinary, day and night control. Methods used and when begun. Enuresis, soiling.

3. Personal care and appearance: Emphasis used by parents and methods.
4. Sleep: Time to bed and getting up, naps, wakefulness, night terrors, sleepwalking, and talking.
5. Nervousness: Fingernail biting, tics, restlessness, repeated mannerism. Attention span. Speech difficulties.

C. *Health:* Illnesses and their severity, injuries, operations, allergies, defects.

D. *School and Work Activities:* Responsibilities around home, voluntary and pay jobs outside home, academic record and accomplishment, academic difficulties. Group cooperation. Leadership. Dominating qualities. Following ability. Money and allowance.

E. *Social:* Outgoing, responsive to others; withdrawn. Ease of making friends, selfishness. Interest in others. Attention seeking.

F. *Sexual Development:* Curiosity about self, others, birth of babies, part father plays. When this curiosity developed, how it was handled. Sexual experiences; masturbation, and with others of same and of opposite sex. Attitude of parents and individuals to these.

G. *Dreams:* Pleasant, unpleasant. Examples.

H. *Other Personality Trends:* Temper reaction, self-control, sense of humor, seriousness, excitability, depression, evenness, suspiciousness, caution. Need to be superior. Complaining tendencies. Having phantasies.

I. *Intellectual Development as Revealed by:* Tests—general, verbal, performance in special subjects. Rate of development.

J. *Physical Status:* Size, strength, endurance, sensory acuteness, coordination, appearance. Nutrition. Teeth. Respiratory system. Cardiovascular, gastrointestinal system.

IV. *The Summary.*
A. The case study summary should be presentation of the situation or problem that has been under consideration as it is seen at the conclusion of the case study.
B. The summary should indicate how the knowledge gained through the case study is to be used for the

benefit of the individual concerned. It should state the steps that are to be taken and the facilities used to bring about desirable adjustments.

V. *Interpretation of Case Study Data.*

   A. The good interpreter of case study data has a repertory of sound [techniques in] reconstructing the total background of the case and in seeing probable cause and effect relationships. Systematically, he first examines the data for accuracy, completeness, and relevancy; then formulates the most plausible interpretations; and finally evaluates these tentative interpretations with the purpose of arriving at a best judgment. It is frequently necessary to verify these conclusions by interviewing the client or subject.

   B. It is helpful for the novitiate in the interpretation of the case study to examine the data with questions such as the following in mind:

What other information is needed?

What emotional trends are indicated in the whole situation and in the personalities involved?

Who are the persons most closely involved in the case? What are their attitudes? What effect do their attitudes seem to be producing in the individual? What are the factors in the parents' attitude that seem to wreck the child most seriously—to cause the most damage? What elements in the parents' backgrounds might account for their attitudes?

Which member of the family seems to be the most serious problem?

What elements does this person inject into the situation that make things more difficult for the case?

What are the recurring factors, if any?

What cause and effect relationships are apparent?

What mental status is indicated by achievement records, observation and the results of the tests?

Is there evidence of unalterable physical defects?

Where is the individual getting his satisfactions?

What normal satisfaction is not being obtained? What does he get out of his truancy or other misbehavior?

44

Does the difficulty seem to lie primarily within the individual or in the environment?
What avenues for further education are suggested?
What social activities seem to be called for?
What vocational paths are indicated?
What other problems may develop? [7]

Any school authority can provide leadership in developing programs for early identification and ways of helping children. The Michigan State Department of Public Instruction recently held its third annual workshop on a related theme, "The Elementary Teacher and Problems of Children." All state agencies and professions working with children and youth were involved in the planning and contributed to the conference; participants included guidance personnel, visiting teachers, probate court personnel, parents, juvenile officers.

On the West Coast a state department of education draws attention to one of the problems that may arise with youngsters from various types of homes and neighborhoods that reflect varying value systems.

THE STATE OF CALIFORNIA: In any one school class a . . . child who comes from a home which is to some degree different from the homes of the other children may be more likely to develop problems in school. . . .

Perhaps basic to any teacher's understanding of the adjustment of the children in her class is her understanding and analysis of the socio-economic status of the class group and the relationship of each child to the group values.[8]

The classroom teacher may work effectively with the school social worker in a cooperative effort to understand and support the youngster in need of help, providing both teacher and social worker understand the nature and limitations of their roles. The next statement discusses how this relationship may be achieved and also specifies some of the behavioral situations which call for mutual efforts of teacher, social worker, and psychologist.

HARTFORD, CONNECTICUT: The purpose of the program is to help the school identify children who present social and emotional difficulties which hinder school adjustment, and to provide

45

individual help for those children who cannot constructively use the group situation of the classroom. Thus, the school social worker serves as an auxiliary person to aid the classroom teacher with individual children whose problems lie outside the teacher's realm, since she is responsible for meeting teaching requirements and must have equal concern for all children in the classroom group. The school social worker does not take the child away from the teacher, nor does the teacher hand the child over to the school social worker for solution of the problem. Since the child's primary relationship in school is to the teacher, the social worker tries in every way possible to strengthen and reinforce the child's relationship to his teacher and his group. . . .

Individual psychological studies are made on children who are presenting some problem of educational, social, or emotional adjustment. More specifically, some of the situations in which these studies might be requested are as follows:

1. A child who is academically retarded for the group in which he is placed
2. The child who, on the basis of past intelligence tests, is known to be capable but is not able to achieve in the classroom
3. The child who shows indications of superior intelligence but does not achieve any better than the others in the group
4. When there are questions about the child's readiness (intellectual, social, or emotional) for placement at the next higher grade level
5. Pupils for whom group tests do not give an adequate estimate of ability
6. Children who give evidence of social and emotional adjustment problems
7. A case where there are wide discrepancies in past test results.

These studies are made at the request of school personnel and, in most cases, are made at the school which the child attends. Professionally trained psychologists, certified by the State Department of Education, are assigned to each school on a definite schedule.[9]

Another example of the use of a team approach by a school system is found in the next quotation, which is concerned with identification and study of youngsters with emotional problems.

San Luis Obispo, California: Our guidance and instruction personnel work with administrators and teachers, and conduct scheduled interviews with class teachers to identify children with emotional needs as early in their school career as possible. By using a team approach some of these troubled children are referred to an agency, a teacher, a nurse, the County Schools' psychologist, or the County Welfare Office for treatment. We work closely with the Judge and the Probation Office. We hold parent meetings, parent-teacher conferences, and meetings of coordinative groups. We work with the Mental Hygiene Society, which has a volunteer clinic for families or individuals who seek aid.

The wide variety of techniques, skills, and procedures that a school system may employ as a part of the study, diagnosis, and treatment involved in early identification have been listed by one county system.

Los Angeles County, California:

Diagnostic Techniques

a. cumulative records
b. testing program
c. individual case studies
d. classroom observation
e. home visits and parent conferences
f. individual counseling
g. expectancy studies
h. study to distinguish between limited ability and poor achievement of students
i. study to determine most effective media of learning
j. comparison of specific cases
k. clinical and psychological services
l. establishing rapport with the student
m. determining the physical condition and the physiological growth and development of the student
n. using the techniques of questionnaire and autobiography
o. selection of specific tests to meet particular purposes and needs
p. understanding and utilizing psychological assets and liabilities
q. analysis and interpretation of test data and cumulative records to classroom teachers.[10]

The two research reports which follow confirm the practicability of the teacher's role in identification of the norm violator at an early age.

NEW YORK CITY: In a research done on 90 case studies of boys . . . in every case, . . . asocial behavior was recorded early in the school career—usually beginning with the second grade—yet identification and referral had been delayed until these boys were in the sixth, seventh, eighth, or ninth year. Eighty-seven percent had been on probation or parole when admitted. The implication is that the regular schools must be equipped to discover and recognize the potential delinquent early in the school career, on a cooperative agency basis with a team approach.

There was a general pattern of retardation in reading and arithmetic, which also indicates the dire need for earlier identification of children in need of remedial instruction.

The early manifestations of patterns of truancy suggest a possible nonacceptance of the traditional school situation and teaching techniques or methods. This area should be given major emphasis by the schools.

The need for a carefully organized work-study program for boys identified as potential delinquents or drop-outs was another area recognized for emphasis.[11]

SACRAMENTO, CALIFORNIA: A brief summary of the aspects of the information collected by each teacher which differentiate the emotionally disturbed children (those selected by the clinicians) from others in the classes follows. . . .

1. The emotionally disturbed children scored significantly lower on group IQ tests. On psychological tests given individually, they approached the mean of all children included in the study.

2. The emotionally disturbed children scored significantly lower on reading and arithmetic achievement tests. The differences were greater and more significant on arithmetic achievement. The higher the school grade, the greater the difference between the emotionally disturbed child and others in the classes.

3. The emotionally disturbed children differed significantly from the other children in the classes in their self-perception as revealed in some of the items in the Personality Inventory. Emotionally disturbed boys exhibited greater dissatisfaction with self and their school behavior than the

other boys. Emotionally disturbed girls showed less dissatisfaction with self than the rest of the girls in the classes.

4. On the sociogram, "A Class Play," the other children in the class tended to select emotionally disturbed children for hostile, inadequate, or negative roles and failed to select them for the positive, good roles. Hostile children particularly were selected for roles consistent with their behavior.

5. The emotionally disturbed children came from homes which were not significantly different in socio-economic level from those of other children generally. . . .

6. Altogether 87 percent of the clinically known emotionally disturbed children were rated by their classroom teachers as among the most poorly adjusted children in the class. . . .

Some of the implications of the study were expected. Others are surprising. A few of these implications follow:

1. Children's judgments of other children's personality are surprisingly accurate and predictive.

2. Teachers' judgments of emotional disturbance are very much like the judgment of clinicians.

3. Teachers selected a greater number of children as being overly withdrawn or timid most of the time than as overly aggressive or defiant most of the time.

4. At least three children in each average classroom can be regarded as having emotional problems of sufficient strength to warrant the appellation "emotionally disturbed children."

5. The differences between emotionally disturbed children and the others seem to increase with each grade level.[12]

Once the teacher has identified a student as delinquent or potentially delinquent, what does he do? The next chapter presents reports on what teachers are doing in schools throughout the United States and discusses the norm-violating youngster in the regular classroom and the shared responsibilities of teacher and administrator in helping each youngster gain satisfaction and self-respect through optimum achievement.

References

[1] For full discussion, see *Delinquent Behavior: Culture and the Individual*, p. 132-38.

[2] Board of Education of the City of New York, Bureau of Education and Vocational Guidance. "Annual Report—Play Group Project, September 1957-June 1958." New York City: the Bureau, 1958. p. 3.

[3] Office of the Los Angeles County Superintendent of Schools, Division of Research and Guidance. "Preliminary Materials: Guidance Handbook for Elementary Schools." Los Angeles: the Division, 1956. p. 3-5.

[4] Detroit Public Schools, Department of Special Education. *Ungraded Classes for the Socially Maladjusted.* Detroit: the Department, 1953. p. 21.

[5] Office of the Los Angeles County Superintendent of Schools, Division of Research and Guidance. *School Factors Related to Delinquency.* Los Angeles: the Division, 1951. p. 1, 3, 13, 15.

[6] Pontiac Public Schools, Pupil Personnel Services. "Guides in Writing Anecdotes." Pontiac, Michigan: the Services, 1958.

[7] Pontiac Public Schools, Pupil Personnel Services. "The Case Study—Information Outline." Pontiac, Michigan: the Services, 1959.

[8] California State Department of Education. *A Process of Early Identification of Emotionally Disturbed Children.* Bulletin of the California State Department of Education XXVII: No. 6, August 1958. p. 48-50.

[9] Hartford Public Schools, Bureau of Guidance and Pupil Adjustment. "Handbook of the Bureau of Guidance and Pupil Adjustment." Hartford: the Bureau, 1957. p. 10-18.

[10] Office of the Los Angeles County Superintendent of Schools, Division of Research and Guidance. *School Factors Related to Delinquency.* Los Angeles: the Division, 1951. p. 3.

[11] Submitted at National Invitational Conference by Carol Cordes Smith, reporting on New York City "600" Program.

[12] California State Department of Education, *op. cit.*, p. 67.

chapter 3 PROVIDING HELP WITHIN THE CLASSROOM

basic principle: THE TEACHER MAINTAINS AN ATTITUDE TOWARDS ALL HIS STUDENTS WHICH RECOGNIZES AND UPHOLDS THE DIGNITY AND WORTH OF EVERY INDIVIDUAL, INCLUDING THAT OF THE NORM VIOLATOR. AS AN INSTRUCTIONAL MOTIVATOR AND GUIDE IN THE LEARNING EXPERIENCE, HE MAKES EVERY EFFORT TO ENABLE EACH PUPIL TO ACHIEVE A LEVEL COMMENSURATE WITH HIS ABILITY, DESPITE NORM-VIOLATING BEHAVIOR ARISING FROM EMOTIONAL OR CULTURAL PROBLEMS. THE ADMINISTRATOR IS RESPONSIBLE FOR ESTABLISHING CRITERIA FOR QUALITY TEACHER SELECTION, FOR APPLYING THESE CRITERIA, FOR STRATEGICALLY PLACING THE TEACHER, AND FOR PROVIDING OPPORTUNITIES FOR CONTINUED PROFESSIONAL GROWTH. THE ADMINISTRATOR HELPS TO CREATE AND MAINTAIN AN EFFICIENT NETWORK OF WORKING RELATIONSHIPS BETWEEN THE MEMBERS OF HIS STAFF AND HIMSELF.

The classroom teacher has a crucial and complex role to play in directly helping the norm-violating youngsters. Professionally trained to work with youngsters and brought into close contact with them for extended periods of time, the classroom teacher often represents the main line of defense for the norm violator in the big city or the small town, in the regular classroom or the special center. Frequently in smaller communities the teacher is the only agent, outside the home and church, who is equipped and ready to help the norm-violating boy or girl. The thousands of classroom teachers in the United States, individually and en masse, represent an ever-present and powerful force for modifying and improving the behavior of youth.

The teacher's effectiveness in the classroom will depend essentially upon the nature of the interpersonal relationships existing among the individuals in the group, including his own relation to his students. Needless to say, both learning and therapy presuppose effective personal interaction. The predelinquent or delinquent youngster who is disliked or rejected by his teacher or who does not like his teacher probably can not be helped through his classroom.

Every teacher plays many roles in his school day. He is a person "who knows"; he is a motivator and a "botherer"; he is a guide in the selection of learning activities; he is a mediator of middle-class culture; he is adult authority; he is a counselor; and, last, he is judge and evaluator. Obviously, some of these are conflicting roles. They may also affect the norm violator as confusing roles. For example, to befriend a delinquent who is entangled with serious and prolonged problems arising from a depressed and inimical home or neighborhood and, then, to hand out a report card which fails him completely and irrevocably because of the poor quality of his work and effort is to play the contradictory roles of benefactor and executioner. The teacher's part in helping the delinquent is always crucial and potentially beneficial, but it is never simple and easy.

In helping the norm violator, much depends upon the nature and quality of the teacher's personal and social traits and his conscious and subconscious job motivations. Unless the teacher enters and stays in the profession because he has a strong desire to live and work with children and young people—even difficult and dirty youngsters—his effectiveness with both the "normals" and the "delinquents" will be curtailed. Self-knowledge and personal-emotional adjustment are prerequisites to any job in which one must be the leader who tries to change and improve the behavior of individuals; these are absolutely essential for the teacher, who must work with large groups on a required daily schedule. And always the teacher must be ready to act to help each of his pupils, with all his professional knowledge and insight. Even when, or especially when, confronted by public apathy, ignorance, and hostility, the teacher acts in the best interests of children and youth. His role is to defend and to help, never to attack or to reject.

Even the most effective teacher will not be able to make full use of his talents and proficiencies without the cooperation of and support of the school administrator. One of the most important functions of the administrator is the procurement of the best teaching talent available. But he must also make good use of the talent he has hired. This will call for establishing a healthy work climate with sufficient freedom for teacher initiative in meeting the needs of the norm-violating pupil. And always the administrator will need to plan for the continued education of his staff through a wide variety of inservice training experiences.

In view of the heavy involvement of lower-class youngsters in the problem of juvenile delinquency, as emphasized in the Project's first document, the school through every teacher must try to build for the lower-class pupil pride in his past, confidence in his present, and to instill hope for the future. A constant and conscious effort must be made by the school to assist the vertically mobile and aspiring youngster in his individual growth and development. However, unless the teacher understands lower-class values and makes an effort to orient those pupils who do not or who cannot achieve middle-class status toward a law-abiding lower-class way of life, his contribution to the prevention and control of juvenile delinquency will tend to be limited and diffused.

There are many implications to be drawn from the basic principles and the guidelines in this chapter for those institutions that prepare teachers and for those school administrators responsible for inservice or continuing education of the teaching staff. The factors in the teaching personality, the substantive knowledge, and the professional competencies that are delineated or implied in the following pages will call for some reshifting of emphasis in the selective process when young people seek to enter teacher education, in the kinds of courses and practicum that must be provided in teacher training, in the recruitment and hiring practices of school administrators, and in the continuing education of the professional teacher.

Guidelines

Teacher

∗ The teacher can serve as an attractive and acceptable model of identification for lower-class youngsters and thereby can strongly influence them in the direction of positive change. However, in enabling the lower-class boy raised in a female-based home to achieve positive masculine identification, the woman teacher should see that the boy associates with male teachers and guidance counselors.

∗ The predelinquent, delinquent, or socially maladjusted youngster needs an adult with whom he feels free and to whom he may talk confidentially. Ideally, the classroom teacher can meet this need through his counseling role.

∗ The teacher maintains the respect of the pupils in his class as a person who knows the subject he teaches and understands the way of life in the youngster's milieu.

∗ The teacher develops a high degree of self-understanding so that he does not work out his own problems through his pupils, nor does he interpret the youngsters' problems solely in terms of his own social class values.

∗ The teacher's knowledge, interest, and concern for the pupils in his class goes beyond the classroom; he is cognizant of the home and family backgrounds of his pupils and of the conflicting value systems reflected in their cultural milieu. Because much of the information his pupils tell him and much of what he learns about their homes and family backgrounds is extremely confidential, he must maintain a constant sensitivity to professional ethics.

∗ The teacher plays his role as a group leader deliberately and effectively in the classroom.

∗ The teacher sets the standards of behavior in the classroom—including dress, coiffure, speech, and manners—

with due recognition of a realistic and positive teen-age image that will extend beyond the classroom.

* The teacher seeks to understand underlying motives beneath the manifest behavior and refrains from merely judging norm-violating behavior.

* The teacher makes an extra effort to understand, accept, and help the norm-violating youngster who is on probation or on parole from a state or county training school.

* The teacher provides encouragement and assistance to the lower-class youngster who is potentially mobile; the lower-class youth who by reason of his level of aspirations and abilities is not potentially mobile; the middle- and upper-class youth whose basic abilities are not consistent with the demands placed upon him by his primary reference group.

* The teacher makes every effort to retain and hold the youngsters in school, particularly the lower-class pupil who shows ability to carry school work at the high-school and college level.

* The teacher makes provision for individual differences by using a wide variety of methods which may enable every youngster to achieve a measure of success.

* The teacher's techniques for motivating students are based, in part, upon his awareness of the focal concerns of the youngster's subculture.

* The teacher is quick to recognize signs in a student of any developing reluctance and boredom and employs a wide variety of learning experiences beyond the usual reading, recitation, lecture, and writing to prevent or overcome this problem.

* The teacher uses remedial techniques in the basic skills inasmuch as these make an important contribution toward the prevention of norm-violating behavior as well as to the rehabilitation process.

* The teacher evaluates the pupil's growth in terms of both the competitive system and his abilities and goals. The teacher interprets the evaluation to the pupil in such a way as to minimize possible damage to their interpersonal relationship.

* The teacher, by means of discipline, provides a stable and predictable environment in which the norm-violating youngster has less difficulty in adjusting than in an unstable and unpredictable one.

* The teacher aims to involve youngsters in the solution of problems relevant to their age group. In order to insure development of self-discipline, which should be regarded as an ultimate goal for all members of the school society, opportunity is provided for young people in school to make moral decisions with a minimum of school supervision and direction.

* The teacher confers with the parent regularly and on special occasions concerning growth and achievement as well as norm-violating behavior.

* Teachers frequently must seek the help of other staff members when confronted with severe and special behavior problems. When the teacher reaches out for help and assistance, he does so without a feeling of guilt or failure, nor does he do so with the intent of ridding himself of the youngster with a problem.

* The teacher utilizes his working knowledge of the youngster's physical, mental, and emotional growth and development to enable him to collaborate with medical, psychiatric, psychological, and social-work professions.

* The teacher regularly participates in case conferences with other professional personnel in school and community.

* The teacher attempts to handle the problem of the norm-violating behavior within the classroom until it is so gross or extreme that it directly or indirectly upsets the classroom activities or negatively affects the other members of the group.

56

Administrator

∗ The administrator, when hiring a teacher, is as concerned with factors of personality and basic motivations as he is with intellectual qualifications.

∗ The administrator recruits teachers with a working knowledge of the mores and modes of living of different cultural and subcultural groups in the United States.

∗ The administrator seeks teachers who have had a carefully supervised internship—supplemented by workshops and seminars in which they have had first-hand experience in working with youngsters from various cultural and subcultural groups.

∗ The school administrator utilizes the probation period for orientation and training, thus insuring the classroom adjustment and maximum growth of the beginning teacher.

∗ Teachers with certain strengths and competencies are strategically placed in particular schools and neighborhoods. Those teachers less suited for these positions are not placed in such classroom situations where they may become a hazard to themselves and to some students.

∗ The administrator develops a healthy working climate based upon an effective two-way relationship with his staff.

∗ School administration encourages and assists individual staff members to recognize their own strengths and weaknesses in working with norm-violating pupils, particularly those from lower-class milieu.

∗ The administrator remains alert to the possibility that a teacher's personality can be a threat to the student; in such cases, he takes appropriate action to help the teacher and to protect the student.

∗ The administrator stimulates the continuous professional growth of his staff through staff seminars, inservice workshops, sabbatical leaves, cross-cultural travel experiences, and affiliated university programs.

57

* The administrator assists the teacher in defining and maintaining his role as a teacher through individual counseling and group processes.

* The administrator utilizes action-research programs in the area of discipline and delinquency for both the prevention and control of norm-violating behavior and the inservice training of the staff.

* The school administrator works out with his teaching staff a lucid and definite statement of the school's policies and practices regarding discipline. Such policies, which should be formulated to accord with basic mental hygiene concepts, are adapted to the local school community and neighborhood.

* In considering rules to be followed or regulations which have been transgressed, the school administrator and staff act with knowledge of the significant variations in the normative systems to be found in the various subcultures.

* The administrator makes available the necessary equipment and materials in the regular and special classes to insure an effective learning opportunity for the youngster with problems.

* The administrator organizes the school with classes of reasonable size to enable the teacher to establish effective personal relationships with each student.

* The administrator recognizes that a small fraction—usually less than 1 percent—of norm-violating pupils cannot be contained in the regular classroom. For these extreme cases, he either sets up special centers within the school organization or utilizes a separate and special facility which may exist in the community.

* The administrator is careful that the school does not hold on to the disturbed and maladjusted youngster too long, thus depriving him of help and treatment which he might obtain from some other community resource. The well-being of the teacher or other members of the class must also be taken into consideration. In the event that a

58

youngster is separated from the school, the administrator and teacher cooperate in studying the out-of-school adjustment and the conditions under which the youngster may return.

Practices

What the effective teacher "is" and what he "does" is a popular topic of the day in professional and lay circles. The nature of the teaching personality, the professional skills, and knowledge of a teacher are all a part of what he "is" and determine much of what he "does." In the next four statements, these desirable traits and competencies are described in considerable detail; and, as will be evident, for the teacher working with youngsters who evidence emotional or social maladjustment, they are of vital importance. A welfare council drafted the following list of qualifications for all youth workers; since teachers are youth workers par excellence, these prerequisites are particularly pertinent to the classroom teacher.

CHICAGO, ILLINOIS: Prerequisite Qualifications for all Youth Workers

A person who can differentiate between the act that is disapproved and the person committing the act.

A person who is secure in his identification with his own social group or groups.

A person with sufficient perspective and resiliency to cope with:
  a. having affection for people, but remaining firm when this is calculated to be helpful to those he serves;
  b. being the worker in a group, rather than a group member or a group leader;
  c. having those with whom he works become increasingly independent of his help;
  d. the disappointments represented in regressive behavior, the inability to get resources and human crises synchronized, and the length of time consumed in re-education for social competence;
  e. persistent and recurring temptation to compromise on values in the interest of expediencies;

59

f.　the discomfort of continuing exposure to values that are in conflict with those he holds.

A person who has a fundamental respect and an abiding affection for people.

A person who has the ability to recognize, understand, and work with the social systems developed by people in close proximity to each other. He also should have sufficient social background to permit his helping the neighborhood people to relate cooperatively to other social systems of the larger community.[1]

The above "prerequisites" defined the strengths and characteristics of the potential teacher, or other youth worker, through what he "is." The second statement emphasizes what a teacher "does." A comparison may be drawn between the statement of the Chicago Welfare Council and the following statement, which was prepared by a board of education.

NEW YORK CITY: Here is what the composite ideal teacher does to promote the development of "decency" and discourage tendencies toward delinquency:

　　a.　He helps children to become understanding persons by treating them with understanding. Stated conversely, he realizes that socially acceptable behavior is never taught to children by severe punishment.

　　b.　He knows that children are merciless with teachers who appear weak. He has mastered the art of being firm and kind, of being friendly without being chummy. He issues orders with a smile; he exerts authority without being punitive or requiring submission. Thus he helps develop wholesome attitudes toward authority.

　　c.　He inspires confidence by a businesslike competence. His dress is neat, his room orderly, his voice well modulated; and he is sparing with words.

　　d.　He see each child as an individual and makes provision for the child's growth at a rate commensurate with his capacities. He reduces tension by avoiding undue competition and emphasis on marks; he adopts realistic standards for slow children so that these young people are freed from fear of failure and the concomitant desire to retreat from learning.

　　e.　He treats all pupils with equal consideration. He encourages friendly relationships among children. He shows his respect for the dignity of the individual by providing opportunity for every child to secure satisfaction through achievement and success through sustained effort.

f. He has ideals which he transmits to the children he meets.

g. He gives support to children facing conflicts and obstacles. He tries to provide a healthful emotional climate in which children are given a sense of belonging and recognition.

If emotional disturbance is at the root of delinquency, such a teacher helps to give young people the feelings of acceptance and satisfaction all people need. When classes are small, teachers more readily can find opportunities for establishing such feelings in their students.[2]

A recorder's report from one discussion group at the Juvenile Delinquency Project's Invitational Conference provides another point of view. This discussion group consisted of four participants from public youth agencies, three from private community agencies, two school administrators, one teaching-principal, one school psychologist, one participant from the National Education Association, and a member of a college staff.

NATIONAL INVITATIONAL CONFERENCE: Qualities of "Good Teachers":

1. Objectivity—teacher's right to have access to basic information, not to serve as a therapeutic agent—"We want a therapeutic environment, not a therapist."
2. Self-accepting—ability to feel secure
3. Positive feeling toward others—understanding culture
4. Fairness
5. Consistency
6. Sympathetic
7. Breadth of interest in world
8. Imagination
9. Flexibility as a person and in control area
10. Dependableness
11. Ability to combine understanding of pupil and excellence in subject matter—recognize individual differences—sensitivity to recognizing problems
12. Values "inservice" activities, keeps contact with research findings, knows community agencies (cited: Massachusetts Department of Education Civic Behavior Seminars),

61

and studies own methods of working as partner with faculty groups and others

13. Intelligence—nothing so discourages the pupil as a teacher who is patently stupid

14. Well motivated—this is affected by salaries, supervision, the community's respect for (or not) of the teacher, spiritual elements in the teacher's own value system, e.g., satisfaction in *service*.

The last of these four summaries of what the teacher "is" and "does" was furnished by a large urban center, which has been active over the years in programming in the prevention and control of delinquency.

SAINT PAUL, MINNESOTA: Actions reveal attitude even more than words. Sometimes it is our own feelings which make it impossible to accept deviant behavior. Studies have shown that we do have different standards for different children.

Someone has said that in teacher-pupil relationships six persons are present:

"The teacher as he is

The teacher as he thinks he is

The teacher as the child thinks he is

The child as he is

The child as he thinks he is

The child as the teacher thinks he is."

Children react as others react toward them. Teachers sometimes say, "Think of the whole group. This child is too disrupting to the whole group." Studies show that generally it is the teacher who is more disturbed about the maladjusted child than the children are. Children tend to understand and accept that this child is different.

It is important for the teacher to understand that:

Behavior is caused.

We must search for the cause; then search for ways to bring about a change.

Certain conditions bring about deviant behavior.

Visiting moral judgment is unproductive.

Everyone is maladjusted in one way or another. Some people work out their maladjustments in ways acceptable to society; some use means not acceptable.[3]

The individuality of the child and his needs and the personal characteristics of the teacher were points specifically stressed in all four of the preceding discussions. These factors, then, become clues for the classroom teacher or the administrator in formulating discipline policy, teaching techniques, and procedures within the schools. These factors alert administrators to consider the importance of the teacher-pupil relationship, the assignment of norm violators to certain classrooms and certain teachers. For example, in the next comment the necessity of recognizing individual dignity is seen as an obligation requiring the school to undertake specific action on the individual's behalf.

LOS ANGELES COUNTY, CALIFORNIA: Every child, regardless of his differences and imperfections, should be accepted as a worthwhile person, possessed of dignity, and in these respects equal to all others. Whatever may be the individual's status with regard to physical, mental, and emotional health, he is still a person of infinite dignity and should be considered completely worthy of any efforts we make in his behalf. It is, therefore, a primary obligation for all school personnel, as individuals and also as a combined staff, to make a serious attempt to understand each pupil and the complex of characteristics, experiences, and situations that make him what he is. The mere acquisition of such understanding, however, is not an end in itself, for it is of little avail to understand the pupil unless that understanding leads to action in his behalf. Every effort should be directed toward the provision of appropriate school experiences, adapted to the individual abilities and needs of the pupil.[4]

"Adapt to the individual abilities and needs of the pupil" is the cry that can be heard in a great industrial city as well as in a small Southern town.

DETROIT, MICHIGAN: See that opportunities are given for success and approval in daily classroom contacts. Remember that most problem children are fundamentally immature, that they react on lower developmental levels. Help the child grow up by giving him some classroom responsibilities and by encouraging the home to do likewise. See that some recreational outlets are provided.

Provide children with a variety of experiences—crafts, art,

63

music, athletics, as well as verbal tasks and reading material— covering a wide range of difficulty and interests. Thus, it will be possible for every child to engage in some activity in which he can win outstanding success and to find some way in which he can be of service to the group.

Help him to gain skills and knowledge without unnecessary failure through effective practice and instruction; be on guard against occasions and incidents which might cause him to feel inadequate.[5]

GAFFNEY, SOUTH CAROLINA: The placing of pupils with certain teachers has proved to be an outstanding aid in curbing delinquency problems. During the early spring each year, sixth-grade teachers are required to fill out information forms on every pupil who is to be promoted to the junior high school. These forms give information concerning the pupil's ability as well as his personality traits. If this record indicates that the child has a tendency to become delinquent, his schedule is arranged so that he will have special teachers. These teachers are selected because of their patience, love, and understanding of children. Teachers of the same groups have regular meetings to discuss ways of helping the individual pupils in their classwork and in their adjustment to school and community life. This plan of teacher-pupil scheduling was not used during the first year that the junior high school was in operation, and we had more problems during that year than in all the other years combined. . . .

[After his arrival in the junior high school] our practice is to let each child choose the teacher with whom he would like to discuss his problems. Forms are filled out, and the information is passed on to that particular teacher. Appointments are made with the teachers for private conferences. We find that a child this age will confide in and take advice from a teacher that he has chosen far more quickly than from one selected by the administration.

Frequently in assisting the norm violator, the school can play its role most efficiently by offering the youngster a teacher who is, among other things, a good listener.

LOS ANGELES COUNTY, CALIFORNIA: The technique of proving to be a good listener was shown to have been effective in approximately [40 cases] and unsuccessful in only two cases. Interviews with the counselors disclosed descriptions of episodes where proving to be a good listener had accomplished almost the impossible with some students having serious problems. In fact, this was the first time these students had an opportunity to talk freely to someone interested in their problems. Always before, no one at home had ever listened to them; they had always been told they didn't amount to anything; they had repeatedly been made to feel rejected, unwanted, and inferior. The teacher-counselor who listened to their problems helped such students to build up a feeling of self-reliance, self-confidence, and a feeling of belonging.[6]

A citizens advisory committee in a Midwestern city made recommendations, with the attendant discussion comments, concerning the pupil, teacher, and personal relationships.

DETROIT, MICHIGAN: Recommendation: Assign pupils to a teacher to whom they can turn for assistance.

Discussion: This plan makes every teacher a counselor. In a large high school it is often difficult for students to receive guidance service appropriate to their needs. This arrangement makes it possible for a group of students to be assigned to a teacher for their entire high school career. They meet daily for a short conference period where their problems and concerns are discussed. Thus they have one faculty member to whom they can turn for help as problems arise from day to day. . . .

Recommendation: Utilize the best available resources for the improvement of the mental health of all pupils and staff.

Discussion: A broad program of mental health should be in evidence. Such a program involves selection of competent, well-adjusted teachers, availability of suitable instructional materials, opportunities for inservice training and a program in the class-room which is based upon sound mental health practice.

Teachers should help students to live with others with a maximum of happiness, usefulness and security. Psychological competence is as important to a child's achievement as are intellectual and physical competence.

Recommendation: Make a constant effort to build an over-all climate conducive to respect for learning and for those who learn.

Discussion: There should be renewed effort to encourage curiosity and industry. Recognition should be extended to those who have shown unusual scholastic achievement. Teachers encourage good scholarship during the hours of the day, and parents have the responsibility to give constant help during after-school hours. Such help includes providing a suitable place to study, supervising work habits, and giving the guidance which will result in competent and productive workmanship on the part of their children. All segments of the community should endeavor to restore a respect for the values of our culture and an interest in knowledge and learning.[7]

In a workshop session at Atlantic City centered on the Project's first document, Herbert C. Quay of Vanderbilt University drew the following implications for teachers:

Discipline, consistently and fairly applied, is a must for all children. Allowing the persistent or periodic rule violators to interfere consistently with the progress of the group as a whole is neither justifiable on the basis of maximum benefit for all, nor is it therapeutic for the violator himself. In regard to discipline, note that "toughness" is a quality admired by the delinquent group. It is not infrequent that the firm but fair individual has the most success with this group, both in terms of productivity and personal growth. The classroom teacher must have both the authority and the willingness to set limits and stand by them in the face of hostility and other behaviors designed to escape the limits being set. The limits set should be a function of the goals of the particular classroom situation.

Care should be taken, however, that discipline does not take the place of treatment. Discipline will not "cure" the delinquent, especially the emotionally disturbed group. It will, however, provide a stable and predictable environment, which, in the last analysis, will be easier to adjust to than a shifting and unpredictable environment.

A minority of the delinquent group, with and without pathology, cannot be dealt with successfully in the public schools. This group cannot be contained within the limits the school is able to set and maintain, nor can the school meet their particular needs. This small minority must be dealt with by other facilities, both for their own benefit and the welfare of the majority of children.

There is always the danger that a teacher may feel a deep sense of failure when confronted with a difficult discipline problem that cannot be resolved through his own efforts. As

66

the following statement indicates, every teacher may expect to encounter minor and major norm violations. At all times, the teacher should use those methods of discipline that prevent and ameliorate rather than intensify and accentuate the problem.

SAINT PAUL, MINNESOTA: It is not true that a good teacher has no disciplinary problems. Probably every teacher has encountered behavior problems, including some which she should have solved better than she did. It is true, however, that an excellent teacher is a good disciplinarian. . . .

1. Objectives of Good Discipline. Good discipline is more than the maintenance of school and classroom order. It has as its ultimate objective the development of socially approved self-control with due respect for democratically constituted authority. Policies and practices of discipline should be such as will help achieve this broad objective, while at the same time achieving the immediate objective of maintaining the desired degree of order in the classroom and in the school.

2. Sources of Good Discipline. Desirable discipline and its counterpart, good school morale, are the products of several forces, of which effective teaching and classroom management are the ones with which this bulletin is primarily concerned. It seems only fair, however, to point out some of the other forces: efficient administration of the schools; development of school ideals, traditions, and spirit; establishment of friendly relations between students and school staff, also among students in the classroom; the school curricula; recognition of the findings of educational psychology; and, above all, a sound philosophy of education.

3. The Teacher's Role in Discipline. The classroom teacher plays the most important part in the control of school discipline. Quoting Dr. Minard Stout, "To enable the school to succeed in its program of discipline, it is necessary that each teacher meet his responsibility in this area. This obligation may be said to be twofold. First, there will be specific assignments, such as classroom management, group sponsorships, and so forth, where the teacher is definitely charged with the responsibility for good order. Second, it is the duty of every member of the staff to be responsible for good order wherever he may be on the school grounds."

4. Basic Principles of Correction. Many behavior problems

67

can be settled with only a frown of disapproval or a reprimand. Others may demand the deprivation of privileges, or a conference between the teacher and the pupil, or the employment of differentiated-assignment techniques to substitute worthy activity in place of trouble-making activity. Occasionally there will arise situations in which correction demands assignment of penalties. Certainty of correction is a better deterrent than severity. Discipline should be just, but tempered by kindness, and should be adapted both to the offense and to the offender.

5. Corporal Punishment. It is the policy of the schools to discourage the use of any form of corporal punishment. A teacher should not have to threaten physical punishment, and should understand that, if he does administer such punishment, he does so at his own risk.

6. Sarcasm, Ridicule, Humiliation. More damaging to the child's mental health, and certainly as deplorable as physical punishment, is injury inflicted by humiliating a child in the presence of other children. A teacher should never belittle, ridicule, or humiliate a pupil, especially in the presence of another pupil. Correction or adjustment—not revenge—should be the aim of discipline. The teacher must always try to retain the respect and good will of every pupil with whom he comes in contact, even in difficult disciplinary situations.

7. After-School Detention. Some teachers find it effective to assign after-school detention as punishment for misconduct. The detention should be in the teacher's own room, should be under the supervision of the teacher who assigned the detention, and should be for the purpose of conferring with the pupil.

8. Apologies: Forced Versus Voluntary. Requiring pupils to make apologies, even in private (and certainly in public), to a teacher or pupil against whom the offender has transgressed seems clearly an unwise procedure. Being forced to make an apology is more than likely to lead to hypocrisy; to the feeding of fires of resentfulnes, antagonism, and vengeance; and to further complications growing out of the manner of the apology. It should be remembered that few pupils consider themselves entirely to blame and that frequently they are not. Some pupils will regard the apology as an easy way to escape any significant punishment, and the procedure becomes education in hypocrisy . . . . A sincere apology, however, may be very much worthwhile and should be accepted graciously.

68

9.   Teacher-Pupil Conference.   Before a teacher arrives at a conclusion regarding a pupil's misconduct and certainly before sending the pupil to the main office, the teacher should confer privately with the pupil.   This private conference serves two highly important purposes: It gives the teacher and the pupil an opportunity to come to a mutually acceptable understanding, and it provides an atmosphere in which valuable rapport between the teacher and the pupil can be established.

10.   Office Assistance.   To the extent that they are able to do so effectively, teachers should handle disciplinary cases without asking assistance from the office.   With occasional exceptions, teachers should not ask for assistance in a disciplinary problem unless the teacher has first made a sincere effort to settle the matter without such assistance.   However, if the problem is serious or if the teacher is in danger of losing control, the pupil should be sent to the office.   The teacher should notify the office immediately and submit a written description of the situation to the office.[8]

Perhaps a sense of humor is a teacher's most valuable weapon for control. Conversely, "punishment," if used indiscriminately with many norm violators, may only prove to be so destructive that its end is entirely defeated, as is indicated by the following excerpt from an article by a psychiatrist.[9]

Children who have not known understanding, social acceptance, significance, friendship, or love, or who have misinterpreted or misused them when offered in an overprotective and unchallenging way will often experience, as they grow up, frustration, insecurity, anxiety, and tension which explode into aggressive, antisocial behavior.   Unguided guilt feelings, following such behavior, provoke still more insecurity, still more anxiety and tension, which in turn explode into vengefulness and more aggressiveness at their hopeless frustration.   Punishment will only aggravate the frustration which has produced this pattern of disturbance or delinquency.

"Punishment (by the teacher) is regarded by the child as confirmation of his feeling that he does not belong in school.   He will want to avoid school and look for means of escape, not means of meeting the difficulty." [10]

A deviate, a disobedient child, a so-called juvenile delinquent,

69

a criminal "will interpret punishment only as a sign that society is against him, as he always thought. Punishment does not deter him. Even the electric chair can not act as a challenge to this sense. The criminal conceives himself as playing against odds; and the higher the penalty, the greater is his desire to show his superior cunning. It is easy to prove that many criminals think of their crime only in this way. A criminal who is condemned to be electrocuted will often spend his time considering how he might have avoided detection: 'If only I had not left my spectacles behind!'

"From the psychologist's standpoint, all harsh treatment in prison is a challenge, a trial of strength. In the same way, when criminals continually hear, 'We must put an end to this crime wave,' they take it as a challenge. They feel that society is daring them and continue all the more stubbornly. In the education of problem children, too, it is one of the worst errors to challenge them: 'We'll see who is stronger! We'll see who can hold out the longest!'

"They see their contact with society as a sort of continuous warfare, in which they are trying to gain a victory; if we take it in the same way ourselves, we are only playing into their hands." [11]

To help the teacher, school, and community the California Teachers Association has adopted a policy and procedural statement concerning discipline and the pupil.

THE STATE OF CALIFORNIA: Discipline of today's children and youth is a matter of serious public concern. Discipline is of particular concern to the teaching profession when behavior problems limit the effectiveness of instruction and the learning opportunities offered to pupils.

Teachers are aware that they are asked to assume increasing responsibility for establishing and teaching standards of behavior for children and youth. The Commission on Educational Policy believes that cooperation between home, school, and community must be strengthened, and that pupils, parents, teachers, administrators and members of governing boards need to have a clear definition of their obligations and responsibilities in regard to pupil behavior. Such a definition, stated in school policies, can provide an understanding of what is expected and can eliminate confusion about lines of authority and disciplinary action.

70

Local policies cannot be determined externally. In each school district and community, those involved must decide together what is workable and appropriate in their own situation. Because of the importance of the discipline problem and its effect upon the total educational program, the teaching profession is urged to initiate local study for this purpose.

The Commission makes these recommendations for the development of local school policy regarding pupil behavior.

1. All people affected by the policy should be represented in its development. The study group should include pupils, teachers, parents, administrators and members of governing boards. Valuable contributions can also be made by representatives of law enforcement, social and family agencies, and by business and civic leaders with particular interest in education.

2. The study group should have a common body of background materials as a basis for its work. Sample policies from other school districts, excerpts from the writing of experts on school discipline, and provisions of California law relating to pupil behavior should be available.

3. All agencies of the California Teachers Association, including Field Service and the Personnel Standards Commission, should encourage and assist local chapters of the association to initiate such a program of policy development.

4. Policy should permit some flexibility. Extremely rigid regulations could handicap the teacher in doing a creative job and prevent him from using his professional judgment in the treatment of individual cases.

5. Stated policy should be developed to include the following:
   a. expected standards of behavior
   b. responsibilities of pupils, parents, teachers, administrators and governing boards in relation to defined standards
   c. procedures to be followed when discipline problems arise:
      1) lines of authority and communication within the school system
      2) communication with parents
      3) use of counseling and guidance services
      4) use of physical punishment
      5) basis for suspension and expulsion

d. legal requirements of the Education Code and the California Administrative Code.

6. When the policy statement has been approved by the governing board, wide publicity should be given to its adoption. Pupils, all members of the school staff, parents and the community at large should be informed about the policy. Support for the policy should be sought on the grounds that it will improve the effectiveness of the school program by guiding pupils in developing patterns of responsible behavior, protecting the learning opportunities of the majority of students, and providing help for pupils with learning or behavior problems.

7. At regular intervals, policy should be again interpreted to staff, students and parents to insure continuing understanding.

8. Once policy has been established, it should be regularly evaluated, and modified when necessary by a representative group.

Stated policies alone will not solve problems of student behavior. Progress in developing and maintaining high standards of conduct is made when the people involved have opportunity to study the problems and, together, reach understanding of their mutual responsibilities.[12]

Fortunately, the teacher's responsibilities and opportunities as a group leader have been recognized and accepted recently by an ever-larger number of people. But, first, the teacher must understand her class group; the following comment provides useful insights into how she may take the first steps in this process.

LOS ANGELES COUNTY, CALIFORNIA: While the deliberate use of group forces to motivate learning is relatively new in classroom teaching, teachers always have been aware of the tremendous variation among groups. A first-grade teacher said recently, "I don't have a group; I just have a bunch of exotic individuals!" Or a fourth-grade teacher may say, "This would be a pretty good group except for these two boys who are inclined to sabotage!" Another teacher may say, "If I leave the room for one minute, this class goes to pieces!"

The teacher may well ask: "What makes one group so different from another?" "What gives this group its special personality?"

Factors which influence the structure and personality of groups include:

1. How well the children know each other. Are many children in the class new to the school, to the community?
2. How much diversity is there in ethnic, social, and religious backgrounds?
3. Is this a highly competitive class? Are there marked cliques? Are these prejudiced and hostile toward one another?
4. What has been the group-experience background of these children? Have they previously been in classes with a highly authoritarian teacher? Have they had experience in decision-making, in cooperative teacher-pupil and pupil-pupil planning?

The teacher will realize that the degree of group belonging and performance will vary with all these factors and that it changes with social maturity. For example, the individualistic tendency in preschool children shifts to a sensitivity toward group standards as the peer culture emerges.

The moment a teacher begins to assess her class as a group and wonders how she can organize it into a working unit which develops and enhances individual competencies, she has taken the first step toward action research in group dynamics.[13]

Discerning and well-trained teachers can make frequent use of group dynamics in attempts to bring about desired changes when working with youngsters who have social or emotional problems.

DEARBORN, MICHIGAN: Following the administration of a sociometric test the identification of a number of isolates led to the formation of a special art project class to prepare materials for a veterans' hospital. Composed of these isolates who were invited to participate in a service opportunity, a similar test administered a few months later to the same groups found many of the patterns changed. There are many similar activities which a school can foster in a special class or group situation.

In one school all newcomers are received by one teacher. The child remains with this teacher for the entire semester. Other classes are not disrupted and the newcomer has fewer adjustments to make.

In the modern school, teachers and administrators use the latest techniques to aid the pupil in achieving his classroom goals. But too often research has revealed that many schools are much too slow in using practices and adaptions which have been experimentally validated. A school's adherence to timeworn practices that should be replaced by more effective methods may spell the difference between help and hindrance for the norm violator.

Los Angeles County, California: The research study disclosed five critical school situations which were found to have definite interrelatedness with the delinquency of students. The first two of these have implications for administrative responsibility in the delinquency problem; while the remaining three have implications for classroom teachers' responsibilities for reducing delinquency.

1. Knowledge of a student's record of repeated failure and frustration in school subjects without adjustment of the school program to meet his abilities, interests, and needs.

Record data showed that in a large number of cases the failure to provide a curriculum suited to individual abilities, interest, and needs was basically the reason certain students had found truancy and other serious forms of misbehavior and maladjustment more interesting and challenging than their unhappy school programs through which they had experienced their history of failure and frustration. Where efforts had been made and proved unsuccessful, they seemed to have come too late, and after certain well-developed bad habits had been formed.

2. Enrollment of a student in courses selected arbitrarily for him without reference to guidance information about him.

It was shown that this situation existed in only a few schools, but where it did exist it proved to be serious. It was learned that the schools where the situation existed were, in the main, the same schools which lacked adequate cumulative records, lacked a constructive testing program, and where there was not a full understanding of guidance services and techniques on the part of the administrator and his staff. These schools were shown to be also the same ones, generally, which had more than an average share of students with problems not being met. Disciplinary methods, as such, rather than the functioning of an effective guidance program, appeared in these schools as having definitely failed to bring about a solution of the problems or to reduce the number of delinquents or serious, maladjusted cases.

3. Employment by the teacher of only one teaching method, i.e., talking, thus depending only upon a student's auditory impressions as medium of learning, rather than including also his visual impressions and his manipulative contacts.

The study results showed that there was a definite relationship between the serious behavior and maladjustment of certain students and the fact that in almost two-thirds of the recorded cases, classroom teachers had failed to differentiate their teaching methods to stimulate student reaction not only to auditory impressions (hearing) by their talking, talking, talking, but also to include stimulation by visual impression (seeing), and by manipulative contacts (doing). This situation was most serious in those cases where the first method only was used, especially with some students having a dual-language background, or a reading or language handicap [hearing or vision or coordination difficulty]. In such cases, very little improvement resulted as long as that teaching situation continued. In some cases, only a change of program involving enrollment in a different teacher's class was the solution. In other cases, it was too late, and there was no solution.

4. Failure of the classroom teacher to be able to distinguish between poor achievement, requiring remedial instruction in the fundamental tool subject, and limited intelligence, requiring modification of the curriculum; and failure to provide the correct type of program indicated.

The study results indicated that many teachers do not have the training and ability to distinguish between the need for remedial instruction and the need for a modified curriculum, nor are they able to provide the correct type of program after the true condition has been diagnosed. Evidence disclosed the fact that several teachers were of the opinion that a number of students were mentally retarded, when more adequate diagnosis later proved that they were really in need only of remedial instruction in the fundamental tool subjects, mainly reading. Other cases were described where teachers were attempting to provide remedial instruction to certain students, when their real need was a modified curriculum. Such students were already achieving approximately at capacity, but noticeably below grade norm.

75

The purpose of the remedial program had been to raise their achievement up to grade norm, but because of limited capacity of such students, the remedial instruction had not been very successful.

The real clue to adequate diagnosis of the situation was shown to be in the selection of intelligence tests which measure non-language or performance factors as well as language factors or verbal ability. In most cases, diagnosis based on verbal tests only was shown not to be correct. In many other cases, no diagnosis, whatever, had been done, remedial instruction having been attempted without any objective data other than poor grades in subject-matter.

Many students were shown to have been failed because they had been working far below grade norm, even though that accomplishment had been at their own capacity level. This relationship existed in regard to students who really had better ability than was indicated by their poor achievement grades or by the results of a purely verbal test. Lack of interest in school and truancy were two of the resulting factors pointed out by the counselors as being definitely related to this problem.

5. Failure of the teacher to provide a permissive classroom atmosphere where mental health principles and democratic practices are observed.

Study results showed that a definite relationship existed between the serious misbehavior and maladjustment of certain students and the fact that they were enrolled in classes where teachers failed to provide a permissive classroom climate with mental health principles and democratic practices being observed. In reality, some of these teachers were known to be definitely austere and even antagonistic to delinquent students, and this fact greatly aggravated the situation. Inservice training was shown in a few cases to have brought about some improvement, but in others, the only solution was change of program for the student to permit his enrollment with a different teacher. The teachers who failed to provide a mentally healthy classroom atmosphere were shown to have been unable to entertain the concept of a student as an individual, worthy of kindness, consideration, and respect, separate and apart from his misbehavior. Such teachers, rejecting the misbehavior, held the concept of the student and his behavior as all one entity, and rejected the student with no reservations.

76

Situations described by the counselors showed the existence of more cases of maladjustment and misbehavior in the classrooms having the more austere emotional climate and not practicing democratic procedure; and fewer cases in the classrooms having the more permissive emotional climate and demonstrating good mental hygiene practices.

Adjustment techniques utilized successfully in the correction of predelinquent tendencies and the prevention of their developing into actual delinquency included the following:

a. personality adjustment techniques
b. remedial instruction in the fundamental tool subjects
c. modification of the curriculum to meet individual limitations
d. adjustment of the total school program to meet the full range of individual student differences, interests, capacities, and needs
e. provision of inservice training for the school staff in guidance techniques, and opportunities for professional growth
f. elimination of criticism, failing marks and grade or subject repetition, and giving of passing marks and encouragement to students working up to capacity but below grade norm
g. use of extra-curricular activities
h. establishment of a permissive rather than an austere classroom atmosphere
i. assignment of school responsibilities and duties to a student within his abilities to perform
j. understanding and capitalizing on special interests of students
k. the use of mental hygiene principles and democratic practices in the classroom
l. capitalizing on a student's psychological assets and minimizing his liabilities
m. assisting a student to participate in wholesome and constructive group activities
n. providing psychotherapy by a recognized psychologist or psychiatrist
o. arranging a flexible school program
p. working with parents to secure their cooperation in overcoming either domination, neglect, or ineffectual home conditions
q. using group guidance techniques

r. providing satisfying situations and experiences that supplement an inadequate home situation

s. devising specific ways to help develop a sense of school loyalty in individual students

t. proving to be a good listener

u. giving worthy and judicious praise to students who have experienced a history of failure, frustration, and criticism

v. changing teacher attitudes from critical and condemnatory to understanding, permissive, and encouraging

w. treating a misbehaving or maladjusted student as a respected individual worthy of courtesy, kindness, and personal attention

x. understanding adolescent characteristics and psychology.[14]

All that has been said hitherto about the teacher's effectiveness in dealing with the potential and actual norm violator is predicated on sound teacher education programs, the hiring of the best instructors by administrators, and the administrator's continuing support of the teaching staff through inservice training and adequate supervision.

The wholesome concern of a citizen advisory committee in a large urban center for initial assignment, orientation, and inservice training of educational personnel is reflected in the following recommendations, with their accompanying discussions.

DETROIT, MICHIGAN: Recommendation: It is recommended that the assignment of new personnel be the responsibility of the personnel department consulting with the supervisory staffs, district administrators, and principals to insure the best possible placement of each new teacher and to the end that each school be staffed on an equitable basis. New teachers . . . should be placed in schools and in a reasonable ratio to experienced teachers and where the working climate will permit optimum professional growth and development.

Discussion: The assignment of educational personnel is of vital importance to the success of a school system whether it be a new teacher or a seasoned veteran. Under the present operation, all assignments are made from a central source, and this has been traditional over many years. With a teaching force of over 10,000, it seems impossible for such an operation to succeed in fitting proper personnel into the places where both the teacher and the individual school will be best served.

Recommendation: It is recommended that there be established a strong, planned program of orientation for two groups: (1) new teaching personnel and (2) teachers, supervisory personnel, and administrators assigned to districts where changing conditions of population, ethnical groups, or other conditions require new viewpoints and new methods from the teaching staffs.[15]

When the school administrator plans an inservice training program that has implications for delinquency prevention and control, he will frequently need to join forces with other community resources such as the courts, police, mental health agencies, social welfare groups, and college and university centers.

Illustrations of inservice programs, one spearheaded by the Massachusetts Department of Education and the other by the staff of the Illinois Youth Commission working with the University College of the University of Chicago, provide two approaches. The Institute on Youth Problems, a teacher-training program, has stimulated the development of a program that involves voluntary service of youth to the community in varied worthwhile and meaningful tasks. A parallel, but different, development can be seen in the Chicago area. Here workshop experience has led to the development of active participation of teachers in an organization formed to provide direct help to delinquents.

BOSTON, MASSACHUSETTS: The Civic Education Division of our state department of education has conducted a six-year program also deliberately designed to acquaint teachers throughout the state with ways and means to assist other youth-serving forces in their communities in the prevention and control of delinquency. By means of university extension courses called "Institutes on Youth Problems," this division has reached nearly one thousand teachers in this time period. The finest resource people in these communities and in the state, including mental health experts, police, clergy, librarians, probation officers and judges, recreation workers, parent-teacher organization leaders, and social welfare representatives, have exchanged views and working techniques with these teachers. Additionally, special provision has been made for the exchange among school people of effective materials and practices to assist youngsters with problems.

Recognizing that inservice courses and familiarity with resource people and their services hardly constitute a complete pattern, our Division of Civic Education and others have purposely encouraged on-going programs, and set out to create new ones which focus on the development of a sense of social responsibility in youth. Essentially these programs stress forms of community service to the aged, the mentally ill, and others. They are carried out in general hospitals, settlement houses, playgrounds, nursing homes, and mental institutions.

In many of these situations, school personnel are involved in friendly relationships of Kiwanis "Key Clubs," Explorer Scout units, Junior Red Cross, Girl Scouts, and Campfire Girls. Some school people, like some other adult leaders, are delegating more and more responsibility to youth, and are encouraging more pupil-managed programs. Teachers, like others, are benefitting from research findings, and many have learned from the experiences of detached workers that even the energies of our most troublesome street corner gangs can be shifted to wholesome, constructive service activities which can be mutually satisfying.

No better illustration can be given to demonstrate the feasibility of a school-community partnership in civic education, which has built-in delinquency controls, than the School Bureau community service programs sponsored by the United Community Services of Metropolitan Boston and directed by . . . a former school teacher. School administrators and youth agency workers who witnessed the Junior Volunteer "Recognition Day" ceremony last September in honor of one thousand youngsters who gave 65,000 hours of free service during the summer to this program sensed that herein lies one very solid pathway to the prevention and control of delinquency.[16]

[A student volunteer program is organized through the Bureau of School Projects in Boston.] During the school year students generally volunteer two or more hours a week. Summer assignments are one-half to one day or more a week:

The Job	The Place	The Task
Directing activities for children	Settlements, day nursery	Assist in games, sports, story telling. Supervise arts and crafts.
Helping the sick	Hospitals	Perform messenger and escort service. Assist in flower and mail delivery, in snack bars and gift shops.
Having fun with people	Museum of Fine Arts, Museum of Science, The Children's Museum	Assist in children's tours, courses, work, and assembling projects.
Assisting in office	Agencies, Visiting Nurse Association, United Community Services	Filing, assembling, answering telephone calls.
Working at a day camp	Day camps	Assist in hiking, games, trips, and tours.[17]

CHICAGO, ILLINOIS: During the past few years members of the staff of the Illinois Youth Commission have been in touch with approximately 400 public school teachers in Chicago, all of whom have taken several courses in the treatment of delinquents in the Sociology Department of the University College of the University of Chicago. . . . Workshops have been offered and designed to acquaint teachers with the range of facilities, services, and programs available for the treatment of delinquents and the prevention of delinquency. The assumptions, philosophy, techniques, and procedures of the treatment agencies discussed and analyzed include those of law enforcement, custodial institutions, special schools, probation and parole systems, group-work institutions, community organizations, and special pilot projects under way in the city.

Many of the teachers who have taken these courses have become genuinely interested in the problem and, upon completion of their studies, have offered to volunteer their services in sponsoring delinquents and in supporting the work of the Community Services program of the Illinois Youth Commission and the Chicago Area Project. In order to coordinate the efforts of these teachers, a new organization was launched in the spring of 1959 —The Association of Teachers for Delinquency Prevention. While this is an independent organization, its activities are related to the Board of Education, the Illinois Youth Commission, the Chicago Area Project, and the University of Chicago.

Teachers who have taken these courses have expressed an interest in assuming responsibilities in the following tasks: (1)

81

make special efforts to work with and encourage parolees in their school work; (2) secure part-time after-school employment for such youths; (3) cooperate with families and community leaders in better meeting the needs of youthful offenders; (4) encourage and financially support neighborhood organizations for delinquency prevention; (5) cooperate in studies and investigations of the problems of adolescents and related social studies.

Special projects were launched recently in three high schools and in one elementary school. In one of these schools fifteen teachers have already begun to volunteer their services in sponsoring a delinquent child, usually a parolee from the training school. Under this arrangement a teacher will give special attention to one child, maintaining contact with him at least every day and assisting him in dealing with his needs on a day to day basis. Assigned to function with each of these schools is a Community Worker on the staff of the Illinois Youth Commission, who will collaborate with the teacher in meeting the needs of the child and follow through in those instances where the family and other neighborhood institutions are involved in this effort.

In assuming its share in delinquency prevention along with the other community agencies and institutions, the school can make its most valuable contribution by employing the best qualified teachers. Those responsible for the training of teachers will need to scrutinize the selection of candidates. At the same time, teacher-training institutions will need to broaden their programs so that the teacher trainees will acquire both self-knowledge and skills in interpersonal relationships as well as a deeper understanding of the cultural backgrounds and value systems of their students. In addition, the program should also provide a greater variety of learning experiences in working in direct contact with all types of youngsters.

References

[1] Welfare Council of Metropolitan Chicago. "Hard to Reach Youth." Bulletin No. 8. Chicago: the Council, 1958. p. 26-27.

[2] Board of Education of the City of New York, Curriculum Council and the Division of Curriculum Development. "Ways in Which Schools Aid

in Juvenile Delinquency Prevention." *Curriculum and Materials* 11: 1-2; November-December 1955.

[3] Saint Paul Public Schools, Office of Secondary and Vocational Education. "Dealing with the Maladjusted Pupil." Curriculum Steering Committee Workshop Series, 1957-58. Saint Paul: the Office, 1958. p. 17.

[4] Office of the Los Angeles County Superintendent of Schools, Division of Research and Guidance. "Preliminary Materials: Guidance Handbook for Elementary Schools." Los Angeles: the Division, 1956. p. 5.

[5] Detroit Public Schools, Department of Special Education. *Ungraded Classes for the Socially Maladjusted.* Detroit: the Department, 1953. p. 20.

[6] Office of the Los Angeles County Superintendent of Schools, Division of Research and Guidance. *School Factors Related to Delinquency.* Los Angeles: the Division, 1951. p. 33.

[7] Board of Education of the City of Detroit, Citizens Advisory Committee on School Needs. *Findings and Recommendations of the Citizens Advisory Committee on School Needs.* Detroit, the Board, 1958. p. 22, 24.

[8] Saint Paul Public Schools, Advisory Committee on Pupil Problems. "Policies and Practices Regarding Discipline in the St. Paul Public Secondary Schools." Saint Paul: the Committee, 1951. p. 1-4.

[9] Papenek, Ernest. "The Role of Reward and Punishment in Education and Correction." (Reprint of article in *Federal Probation Magazine,* June 1958.)

[10] *Ibid.,* as quoted from: Adler, Alfred. *Education for Children.* New York: Greenberg, 1930.

[11] *Ibid.,* as quoted from: Adler, Alfred. *What Life Should Mean to You.* Boston: Little, Brown & Company, 1931.

[12] California Teachers Association. "Developing Student Behavior Policy." State Council of Education Minutes, April 10-11, 1959.

[13] Office of the Los Angeles County Superintendent of Schools, Division of Research and Guidance. "Preliminary Materials: Guidance Handbook for Elementary Schools." Los Angeles: the Division, 1956. Section III, p. 1-2.

[14] Office of the Los Angeles County Superintendent of Schools, Division of Research and Guidance. *School Factors Related to Delinquency.* Los Angeles: the Division, 1951. p. 4-9 *passim.*

[15] Board of Education of the City of Detroit, Citizens Advisory Committee on School Needs. *op. cit.,* p. 87.

[16] Massachusetts Department of Education. *School Practices to Prevent and Control Delinquency.* Boston: the Department (n.d.). p. 11.

[17] United Community Services of Metropolitan Boston, Bureau of School Projects. "Be a Student Volunteer." Boston: the Bureau (n.d.).

chapter 4 PROVIDING HELP THROUGH CURRICULUM ADJUSTMENTS

basic principle: THE SCHOOL PROVIDES A COM-PREHENSIVE CURRICULUM TO ENABLE THE FULL REALIZATION OF EQUALITY OF EDUCATIONAL OP-PORTUNITY FOR ALL CHILDREN, INCLUDING THOSE YOUNGSTERS WHO REFLECT SPECIAL EMOTIONAL AND/OR CULTURAL NEEDS. THE ENTIRE SCHOOL STAFF LOOKS UPON SCHOOL EXPERIENCES AS A DAILY OPPORTUNITY IN MILIEU THERAPY FOR PREDELINQUENT AND DELINQUENT YOUNGSTERS.

Only the school which attempts to insure equal educational opportunity for all youngsters, irrespective of their varying abilities, special talents and disabilities, interests, and cultural backgrounds, can hope to achieve the democratic tradition's promise of truly universal education and equality of opportunity. Good schools do not mass-produce identical products; good schools begin with youngsters who are already quite different and enable each to achieve according to his talents; good schools maintain and encourage individual differences. The school program which provides only a narrow one-track academic curriculum that squeezes out all but college-going and academically able students tends to deny equal opportunity for all youngsters; by exclusive focus on academic prestige and objectives, it may also make "second- and third-class citizens" of the less academically inclined students, and it may precipitate and stimulate manifestations of delinquent behavior.

The curriculum of the school includes all the experiences which are planned and provided by the school agency in an effort to achieve stated objectives. Instruction involves motivating and guiding the learner through skillfully planned activities calculated to bring about new modes of behavior or to improve or change older and less effective ways of behaving. The pupils in the school do not live and work in a vacuum; they operate in a special learning environment, and that environment is the school curriculum.

Attending school and participating in the learning activities provided by the school should make a difference. This difference should be visible, broadly speaking, in the behavior of the learner. Such changes may be seen in his ability to think more clearly and critically when faced with real-life decisions, in his ability to add a long column of numbers correctly, in his ability to prepare and explain a committee report, in his ability to read literature with discrimination and enjoyment, and in his capacity for further learning. Unless the pupil's behavior has been modified and improved or unless new and desirable behaviors have been established, learning (here defined as a product involving changes in behavior) cannot be said to have taken place.

Essentially, the teaching process attempts to motivate and guide youngsters into certain activities through which established goals will be attained as well as to help evaluate the extent of the youngster's growth toward these objectives. Faced with the ever-present problem of individual differences, the school will need to provide a variegated curriculum with suitable individual goals and learning experiences to serve all those who come to school. This means that the first step in the teaching process must include the study of all members of the class. It may be platitudinous to repeat, but it is nonetheless true, that the teacher must "learn the learner" before beginning the instructional process *per se*. This calls for careful and directed observations, diagnostic testing, parent conferences, and personal interviews with the youngster himself. Instruction that is provided in undifferentiated fashion for all members of the class, regardless of their individual abilities, achievements, interests, and value systems, will penalize either the bright and talented or the average learners or the slow and less academically favored. Pouring all students into a single academic mold causes many predelinquents to suffer frustration, failure, and conflict, which, in turn, beget aggression that frequently eventuates in patterns of norm-violating behavior. Early school drop-out—a frequent forerunner of delinquency—is also closely related to the failure of the undifferentiated curriculum to stimulate or hold the student whose interests and capacities are not academic.

There are many reasons why expected learning may not take place, and these will always vary with the individual pupil. Sometimes causes for failure in school learning can be traced, as indicated above, to the nature of the limited or restricted school offering; in other cases failure to learn may be traced to factors in the youngster himself, such as low IQ, physical impairment, poor health, or emotional disturbance; in still other cases failure may be traced to home and neighborhoods where there is a lack of parental interest or where contradictory value systems take their toll in interest and motivation. The unsuccessful pupil, as many research studies have pointed out, can become vulnerable and susceptible to the "way out" that is offered by an illegitimate means to achievement and success.

Lacking special diagnostic and remediation services, a school will generally fail to help many children who, in the business of the school day, may become bankruptcy cases. In such situations the delinquent act may sometimes be used to prove to peers and adults that the nonlearner or nonachiever is not as dumb as the report card suggests and that he is good at something—even though it be stealing, breaking windows, or carrying on gang warfare.

Improving and modifying the curriculum will demand the constant attention of school administrators, school staff, and even lay citizens in the community. The total school staff should be actively engaged in curriculum study and revision, and the school system that does not do this will very likely fail to help many youngsters, especially those who are pre-delinquent and delinquent.

Guidelines

* Whenever possible, the objectives and goals of the school curriculum should be structured in terms of desirable behavior so that classroom learning makes a favorable difference in everyday living. Curriculum planning should include both knowledge and attitudes as factors supporting desirable behavior.

* An optimum-functioning curriculum presupposes a differentiation of instruction, with due regard to the individual's abilities, special talents, interests, prior achievements, value systems, goals, and aspirations. Such adaptations are made in the basic communication skills and in all subject-matter fields.

* Measuring and evaluating techniques to appraise individual differences in growth and achievement are judiciously employed so that effective curriculum planning is assured for each youngster.

* The teacher's methods in providing learning experiences directed toward chosen objectives reflect adaptation of practices validated by research.

* A meaningful curriculum is provided for lower-class students, including the norm-violating.

* The effectiveness of the total school experience for the norm-violating youngster is increased through the operation of the school guidance program which does not overlook the significant problems of any one social class.

* The school gives direction, develops interests, provides experiences in worthwhile leisure-time pursuits for the youngster now and in the future.

* The curriculum provides remedial instruction either through special services or regular classroom teaching.

87

* The curriculum is tailor-made and planned to fit the general and special social, cultural, and economic needs of the local school-community.

* Schools organize play, study, and work experiences for children from minority groups and for broadening all students' cultural and social understanding.

* The school programs and experiences intended for all youngsters—student government, athletic events, cafeteria, assembly, school patrol, outdoor or camping education, and all other school-sponsored activities—may be strategically employed to help the potential and active norm violator.

* The school provides learning experiences in citizenship that are meaningful to the youngster, regardless of class status, and aims both by example and by precept to inculcate a law-abiding attitude in all youngsters.

* The training for the responsibility of modern marriage and parenthood is offered by the school through an articulated program; in view of his generally unfavorable home and family background, this aspect of the curriculum is particularly important for the norm violator.

* For those youngsters who show school maladjustment and who intend to drop out before graduation, the school establishes a terminal pre-employment curriculum.

* The school curriculum provides opportunities for supervised work-study programs at the secondary-school level. These programs are worked out jointly by the school, labor, industry, and child welfare organizations.

* If possible, the school rules and regulations are drawn up with the cooperation and support of the student body or its representative on the student council. School authorities try to avoid establishing arbitrary and perfunctorily enforced rules and regulations that may invite frequent and inevitable violations on the part of many students.

88

* The school evaluates its educational and sociological effort to help the norm-violating youngsters by means of valid and reliable techniques of appraisal.

Practices

Throughout this document two central and closely related ideas recur thematically: provision for the needs of the norm-violating *individual* and provision for the needs of the norm-violating *group.* The materials submitted to the Project which were concerned with practices in the area of curriculum, repeatedly emphasized these themes. Thus in the following item the California Teachers Association discusses the school's general obligation to establish a curriculum capable of meeting the needs of the youngster "handicapped by delinquency" and the necessity of the school's resolving, within its means, the problem of the "few" versus the "many."

SAN FRANCISCO, CALIFORNIA: In the case of every child, it should be remembered that the indispensable function of the school is to promote intellectual growth. Further responsibilities to the child are shared with other agencies . . . .

To the school, "delinquents" are individuals with major social disabilities. They are as rightfully a concern of the school as pupils with other physical, mental, and environmental problems.

The obligation of the school is to contribute to the fullest possible development of the child; we conclude, therefore, that the public school is committed to the limits of its resources to meet the individual needs of boys and girls—but that when the school is unable to meet fully the widely varying needs of the children it serves, the contributions of the school to the lives of its many pupils should not be sacrificed to the problems of a maladjusted few.[1]

Sometimes a student's problems are such that special adjustment of the curriculum is necessary in his case. The rationale for such adjustments and the means whereby these may be achieved are discussed in two following statements.

89

SAINT PAUL, MINNESOTA: Despite efforts to provide a curriculum which meets all needs, it is nevertheless true that the curriculum is still relatively limited and too inflexible to function effectively for some children. We must be ready to adjust the curriculum radically when a situation requires it. After careful, intelligent consideration by the persons who work with a maladjusted student, special plans or exceptions can be made, when such are believed to promise the greatest benefit to the student.

In such cases it is possible to:

Make exceptions to required subjects
Define a subject broadly and provide an alternate course
Shift classes
Give special work within a class.

Insecurity and anxiety regarding achievement may be present even though a student is achieving at his potential level. A child may be overly anxious and feel insecure about what he is accomplishing. Effort should be made to give the student a chance to find an area where he can work securely.[2]

HOUSTON, TEXAS: Believing that one of the deterrents to juvenile delinquency is success in school, the staff of the Houston schools makes every effort to adjust the curriculum to the individual needs of each student. Sometimes this adjustment is made by placing the pupil in remedial reading or arithmetic classes; in other instances the pupil is placed with a slow-moving group or, if indicated, a fast-moving group; in still other instances a special program is planned for the pupil in light of his special interests. Materials within the range of the pupil's achievement level and interest range are carefully selected. In addition, each school has a wide variety of before-school, in-school, and after-school activities which will challenge the interest of many students.

In reply to an initial letter of inquiry about programs to combat juvenile delinquency, the following comment was submitted:

SAINT PAUL, MINNESOTA: Our program started approximately 20 years ago with the establishment of a guidance program on a small scale, and as the guidance counselors analyzed their many problems which confronted them, they discovered it was necessary to attack the problem on many fronts. It was apparent that many of the delinquents became early drop-outs because they were unsuccessful in school work. Our first approach then was to develop a curriculum which was more meaningful and interesting to them and one in which they would have a realistic chance to succeed. This has led to a much broader curriculum than existed formerly. . . . Another front on which the problem has been attacked has been in the field of student activities. During recent years, we have overhauled our junior high school program and incorporated within the school day a very excellent activity program. . . .

Since the reply quoted above indicated existence of a curriculum adjustment program and made particular reference to the junior high-school level, the Juvenile Delinquency Project sent a follow-up request to the school system for additional information on these topics. The report, which appears below, describes how this city was adapting its curriculum program at this level; it provides a very helpful example of how a curriculum may be varied to meet the needs of a particular group, in this case a "difficult" age group. It is also a reminder of a point stressed in Document 1 of this series: Work with juvenile delinquency must be concerned not only with the individual, but also with group characteristics.

SAINT PAUL, MINNESOTA: If [junior high schools] are to meet the needs of young adolescents to deal with problems that are unique to their age group, [they] ought to be something other than senior high schools, junior grade. . . . a rigid limited program patterned after that of the senior high school precludes exploration and is not the answer to the physical, psychological, and social needs of the junior high age group. There is agreement among recognized educators in the junior high field that the junior high school curriculum should provide opportunity for students to broaden their scope of interests, explore their talents, and increase their self-knowledge—so they will make wise choices in determining the further course of their lives.

To make this philosophy effective, the committee proposed a broader curriculum which would overcome the rigid time and subject schedule program. The original proposed curriculum has undergone some modification, and this modified form is in

91

existence at the present time in the three new junior high schools which were built in Saint Paul from 1955 to 1957. Several basic departures from usual practices may be noted:

1. Students are programmed in seven subject areas, instead of the usual five or six, so that they may participate in a broader program for strengthening fundamental skills and for exploring and discovering individual interests and needs.
2. All students participate in a special interest activity, which meets one hour per week. Activities change three times during the year.
3. All students participate in a regularly scheduled club and assembly program. Assemblies are conducted every other week; class meetings, interest club meetings, or service club meetings are held on alternate weeks.

Two other alterations are the requirements of one semester of speech during each of the seventh and eighth grades, and one semester of personal typing in the ninth grade. In order to accommodate the additional subjects and the activities in the program, an adjustment was made in time scheduling, and as a result all classes meet four times weekly. Seven classes, meeting four hours weekly, account for twenty-eight school hours per week; an additional hour is spent in a special interest activity, and another hour in a club or assembly program—a total of thirty hours per week. . . .

Curriculum improvement is a continuous process. A curriculum is not developed once and for always; nor is it revised once and for always. School people in Saint Paul do not contend that these changes which have been effected in the junior high school day, in the content of the curriculum, in the kinds of learning experiences that are provided, constitute a prototype of the "ideal junior high school" for all time. They do feel, however, in the light of what is presently known about the physical, psychological, and social needs of the junior high age group, that this program better meets those needs than others which have come to the attention of our local committee. Continued experimentation, expansion, and growth will be needed if our educational program is to keep pace as the needs of our society change.[3]

Saint Paul's junior high-school curriculum just reported was planned to meet the needs of the group. In contrast, the next report discusses a curriculum designed to meet the needs of an individual who is in a detention center for delinquent boys—observe how the boy, and not the group, is the center of the planning.

Los ANGELES COUNTY, CALIFORNIA: We have often heard of efforts to teach the academic skills in vocational or shop classes. This is not often successful for each individual in the class. In Los Angeles County, we have for the past eight years tried the converse; that is, the teaching of vocational skills, prevocational skills and habits within the academic classroom in an individualized academic program. This guarantees success for each individual in the class, and . . . [indicates that] behaviors demanded in vocations can be learned.

We are not saying this method is universally accepted in Los Angeles County. It requires, like all methods, administrative endorsement and enthusiasm. . . .

The children at the Reception Center are boys who have not responded to efforts of their parents, their elementary school teachers, their high school advisors, the clergy, the police, the court, and their probation officers to guide them in social living. . . . Thus the children are to learn a new set of habits, understandings, purposes, goals, ideals, feelings, and attitudes. . . .

The teachers are skilled in the teaching of behaviors and habits which society demands as a condition of personal freedom. These behaviors are [27] in number and the boy learns:

To listen
To remember
To observe objectively
To take correction
To do what it is time to do
To depend on himself
To ask permission
To do jobs promptly, willingly
To take turns in reciting, speaking, drinking
To respect others
To take care of property
To give and receive help
To put things away
To finish a job—every job
To talk quietly

To walk quietly
To be on time
To be in the place assigned
To dress properly for work and interview
To sit properly
To stand properly
To take care of books
To leave self, tools, and place clean
To respect fellow workers
To respect tasks of others
To endure tedium and self-direction and self-control
To [accept] supervision willingly.

[Likewise, with opportunities and favorable conditions provided by the teacher, the boys learn, through mutual helpfulness, *not* to do the following:]

Arguing	Heckling	Spitting
Back talk	Agitating	Hurting
Loafing	Butting in	Angering
Quitting	Whistling	Scaring
Smart alecking	Fighting	Horse playing
Stealing	Undressing	Tattooing
Chumping	Shopping	Marking books, etc.

Since some boys do not respond to suggestions or direction, the teacher uses other boys [who have experienced success] to evaluate the penmanship, spelling, sounds. . . . The newcomer now encounters the social and vocational values of his peers. He is now reflecting a resentment, inadequacy, and disappointment toward fellow students rather than his teacher. He must return to the teacher for help, for reassurance; he must accept help from others, and he must learn to give help to others. . . .

He learns that most boys lose 28 jobs on the average before they learn to hold on to one. He learns that people do not discharge people for lack of skill or lack of experience, but for lack of responsibility in memory, listening, following directions, and seeing. This must be told, illustrated, told in story, dramatized.

Military service, too, requires these basic vocation skills. Our training in this sense is not removed too far from boot camp.

The price paid for disability [in these skills] or behavioral immaturity or lack of training is discharge, loss of time, loss of money, self-depreciation, unpaid bills, trouble in the home, repeating of union initiation dues, and loss of freedom.

Whether a boy learns the names of the letters of the alphabet or whether he works problems in geometry, all assignments given are developed into jobs.

This is more than a transfer of terminology—job instead of assignment. Jobs must be planned in terms of the boys' ability, in terms of boys' interests, in terms of academic skills known and to be learned, so a job for a dull boy requires no more effort expenditure, than a job for a very exceptional boy with 150 IQ.

Thus all subjects are set up with varied levels of jobs—and their appropriate tools. [For example, in United States history courses each of the five ability levels has its own set of texts and materials, which are organized into appropriate jobs.]

The academic content of jobs must also be equal so that Job 1 is equal [to Jobs 12, 13, 14] in time, effort expenditure, success factor for each boy, dull or bright. . . . This enables the boy to look upon school and academic efforts with a new attitude, new motives, new values and motivation. It is his job.

The teacher plays the role of a foreman—for the boy. The boy's jobs are assigned on an achievement level . . . no boy is asked to do a job in which he fails; his jobs are to be a guarantee of success. The level and number of jobs required is determined on basis of achievement test and mental age or ability expectancy levels. Children progress at their own rate of speed, with equal satisfaction and success—a planned personnel management in planned production procedures.

Setting up jobs for all subjects at once looks difficult and is almost impossible. But by developing jobs, say, in spelling, first, then in penmanship, arithmetic, etc., the task becomes easier. In . . . three to six months teachers acquire real skill, experience, and knowledge which become effective in future . . . job planning.

Once the boy sees his set of jobs and regards his teacher as his foreman, school is altered attitudinally. The boy accepts responsibility for learning. The teacher provides conditions and opportunities for learning both academic skills and vocational or on-the-job skills and behaviors.

This is not teaching as conceived by the populace, or the boy. Once the boy accepts responsibility for a given job there is no longer a "try and teach me" attitude. The provision of jobs, guaranteeing success and no failures, and provision of opportunities and conditions for learning academic skills . . . is a different kind of teaching both skilled and satisfying. It is not spouting off information to unwilling recipients, where only teachers are active and others are passive or lethargic. . . . The teacher instead must learn to listen. . . . This is most difficult . . . but teachers must listen to the boy's moment of triumph.

The boy must tell the teacher what he has learned, why he learned it, and must demonstrate his skill. This develops self-expression and confidence. The continuous feeling of success is the most successful motivational device known to psychology; it is his moment of triumph. Thus, after a boy has finished three to five jobs, his taste for success [overcomes] . . . apathy and antipathy toward academic skills or subjects. . . . boys become eager to work at academic subjects although they have opportunity to escape to motion pictures, TV, games, arts or shop activities . . . . success is a sweet foreign taste to these boys. . . .

Instruction or learning must be so individualized that one boy learns by remembering; another by seeing; another by doing; another by listening; and another by reasoning, judgment, and understanding; and a normal boy by all methods.

Boy A learns Job 1 in spelling by listening to a tape recorder. Boy B learns the same job by seeing—writing the name of each letter in a word, such as "home" eitch-oh-em-eeh; another boy looks for similarities or differences between such words as "come," "some," "home." The boy's particular and individual method of learning is discovered in the mental maturity test, which also indicates his general ability.

In this manner an intelligence test and an achievement test become professional tools in the hands of a teacher. The tests supply procedures and individual methods for the child's needs rather than the teacher's curiosity. All procedures up to this point do not guarantee success.

A test of comprehension of each and every job goes a long way. This test is simply giving each boy an opportunity to feel how much he has learned rather than think how much he has learned.

First the boy must pass his test, say, in Job 7 . . . [at which time he is examined by a boy] at the same achievement level who has already passed Job 7 and may be working on Job 9. This boy who "hears" the lesson learns to help others as an accepted responsibility. He learns to review what he has learned. He learns honesty—often rigorously demanding all the standards demanded by teachers, but with a great deal less leniency. He exacts higher standards more often than otherwise.

The teacher can observe both boys for helpfulness, race feeling, antagonism—which might have escaped detection were this opportunity and condition not provided.

The boy reciting learns he need not hide inadequacy; he will not be laughed at; he will not be ridiculed or felt sorry for. This allows the inadequate, sullen, silent boy to learn to tell what he has learned; he learns to explain, to feel he can explain and talk as well as feel.

Now he is ready to look forward to helping another boy with Job 7. . . . He knows the boy can learn, he can help him, and he feels he need not cheat for him. He learns integrity, responsibility, reliability—very saleable vocational skills.

The boy at this time learns to accept the correction, the help and point of view and sense of values from other boys in an academic way. He can also learn behaviors from other boys in the same manner. The teacher will explain the habits a boy must learn, but each boy will be given an opportunity to act as row monitor and call attention of boys to behaviors he is to learn or unlearn. . . . Often a boy cannot accept social inhibitions for himself. If such a boy is given opportunity to act as a monitor of behaviors, he will learn them and exact them from other boys after his day or week of service as a monitor expires. . . .

The job lists on the wall indicate each one's turn, each one's job. . . . We provide conditions and opportunity for each boy to make a schedule of each day's work in school. If he only learned the discipline of a schedule, this would be great; but he learns to make positive plans for each day and to look back at his plan. It helps his teacher and the monitor . . . they often ask: "Is that on your schedule?"

Boys learn to work to retain a position and to secure satisfactory grades for attitude, work, school, group living, and respect for rules and people.[4]

A prominent concern of the researcher, guidance worker, and curriculum director focuses on the drop-out. Meeting the problem of the school drop-out constitutes an initial step in forestalling potential delinquency for many youngsters. The development of job-oriented programs providing economic hope or success for the student is one way of preventing drop-out and thus increases the potential of the norm violator to find an acceptable position in society.

NEW YORK CITY: New York City schools, like those in most large cities, offer several types of high-school curricula: there are curricula for the gifted and the talented; there is the college-preparatory academic curriculum; the commercial course; a variety of vocational courses; and an omnibus curriculum called the "general course." The largest group of maladjusted students is found in the latter course, and the drop-out rate in it is very high; large numbers of the students in this course leave school in the tenth year (the first year of senior high school) and shortly

97

after their sixteenth birthday. When followed up after school leaving, they are frequently unemployed, change jobs often, are paid lower salaries than high-school graduates, and express many more dissatisfactions with their life prospects.

In the effort to lessen the maladjustment of this group, a new terminal pre-employment tenth-year course was established in five junior high schools for vulnerable students, providing intensive guidance services, remedial assistance in reading and arithmetic, occupational information, supervised part-time employment, and job placement after junior high-school graduation. Those who wish it may continue in senior high school, but most of the group have expressed their intention of leaving school at age 16.

This program, recommended after long study by the Youth Board, which is the official organization established to combat juvenile delinquency in our city, is in its first year, so that its effectiveness is not yet known. It is being watched with considerable interest.[5]

The following program for overcoming drop-out, which is now being tried, was based upon long-term study. Ideally, all such school programs should be based upon the careful study exemplified in this program.

SAINT PAUL, MINNESOTA: Continuous study has been made of our drop-outs in order to determine how we may better meet their needs. [A recent study was made but not filed.] Every professional member of the staff was asked to study it and make recommendations as to how they might better improve their procedures in order to prevent these drop-outs. Principals, assistant principals, counselors, visiting teachers, and other teacher groups have come up with many recommendations which they can follow in order to improve their procedures and lessen the percentage of drop-outs. . . .

Another thing we have done in order to eliminate a hurdle which causes students to drop out of school is this matter of hidden tuition costs. We have made a consistent and successful effort to cut down and eliminate student fees for class and activity programs.

One common curriculum adjustment or development for reducing the number of drop-outs is the supervised work

98

opportunity and/or job-skill training program (
part of the regular school program and with r
personnel. These programs may be found both
senior high schools.[6]

Perhaps one of the best known programs is t
apolis' plan for employable skill training within the regular
school day. The school studied the market area and set up
those programs for which a market demand existed. Here,
then, is a constantly developing curriculum based on neighborhood needs and student interests.

INDIANAPOLIS, INDIANA: . . . the Wood High School maintains
multiple track learning routes. It operates a junior-senior high
school division which provides opportunities for pupils living in
the regular school district to earn a high school diploma from an
accredited school. Wood High School also offers an educational
program oriented to the special needs found among the gifted or
slow learners. Then, too, it has a program of occupational
courses for persons who elect to train for certain types of employment. In fact, Wood High School is a three-in-one school.
Junior-Senior High School Division

The junior-senior high school division offers a complete six-
year program of academic courses for grades seven through
twelve. This division serves the immediate neighborhood as
district high school. . . .

Each department offers many courses, so Wood High School
pupils may select programs tailored to their individual needs.
All pupils have additional opportunities for participation and
self-development in the extended school program. This program
includes athletics, clubs, all school sponsored projects such as
plays and concerts and class dances, along with other social
events. . . .

The exceptional child division of Wood High School has
accented instruction with a personal appeal for the exceptional
child's needs. Many pupils with an IQ range within 50-80 are
referred to this school from all sections of the city. Individual
assignments and class progress are strictly held to pupil performance levels. A low teacher-pupil ratio and diversified training in this area promote a pupil success climate for study and
learning. An understanding staff of special licensed teachers

and a pupil personnel service augmented by a psychologist, guide these pupils toward obtainable goals.

Pupils with an IQ of 130 or above are also referred to the Wood High School from different sections of the city. They are grouped with Wood High School gifted learners. The exceptional child division has an answer for instruction of this group too. It lies partly in an enriched program. But the real answer again is in teaching the person and keeping teaching at the personal achievement level. Assignments, counseling, and study projects in this area have a challenging ring. Their purpose is to tap maximum pupil effort—test pupil capacities—and yet be manageable within pupil abilities.

Occupational training courses for certain types of employment make up the third Wood High School division. Persons eligible for high school and not attending any school at present may enroll in occupational training courses, and if desired, complete the academic work required for high school graduation at Wood High School. Pupils may take occupational training along with the regular work required for high school graduation. Pupils attending Indianapolis Public High Schools may take occupational training courses at Wood High School and continue the academic work required for high school graduation in the school in which they are now enrolled.

Training opportunities at the Wood High School include many occupational courses which are not available at other Indianapolis high schools. Two credits may be earned in each of the courses per semester. These credits will be accepted toward graduation by the high school in which the student does most of his work. All occupational training courses require a full half-day's attendance at the Wood High School. Morning classes are scheduled from 8:15 a.m. to 11:15 a.m. and afternoon classes meet from 12:15 to 3:15 p.m.

Some of the courses are for one semester only, some for two semesters, and some require four semesters.

Arrangements can be made through the student's homeroom teacher whereby the student can be given a program in his or her own school which will allow the pupil to attend that school for a half-day and spend the other half-day in the Wood High School.

Time will be allowed in the pupil's program for the pupil to travel between his own school and the Wood High School. The transportation costs (at the pupil rate) will have to be paid by the pupil.

Although a high school diploma may not be required for employment in all the occupations for which training courses have been developed, it is highly recommended.

Occupational training certificates will be awarded all persons who successfully complete the work outlined in any job preparation course.

Advisory committees, made up of experienced men from business and industry, assisted in the development of these courses and will assist the Wood School in job-placement of students who successfully complete the occupational training units.

Graduates of the eighth grade, regardless of their age, may take the courses in:

Auto Body Repair	Cleaning and Pressing
Commercial Foods Preparation	Shoe Rebuilding

and receive their academic work in English, mathematics, social studies, science, and other subjects at the Wood High School.

Pupils who wish to commence occupational training in their junior or senior year may do so and, if necessary, complete the work after they have graduated from high school.

[Other special courses, which require age or grade qualifications, offered, include: barbering, beauty culture, dental assistant, practical nursing. Other special courses are offered as the need arises.] [7]

The earlier that programs to reduce the number of dropouts get under way, the more effective they will be, for they must start before a youngster's desire to leave school has become a decision to leave school. In New York State a "Check List Identifying the Potential Drop-out" has been worked out.[8]

Factor	Vulnerable to Dropping Out	Favorable to Retention
a. Age	Old for grade group (over 2 years) _____	At age for grade group _____
b. Physical size	Small for age group _____	No size demarcation _____
	Large for age group _____	

101

Factor	Vulnerable to Dropping Out	Favorable to Retention
c. Health	Frequently ill ＿＿ Easily fatigues ＿＿	Consistently good health ＿＿
d. Participation in out-of-school activities	None ＿＿	Planned and reasonable ＿＿
e. Participation in school activities	None ＿＿	Planned and reasonable ＿＿
f. Grade retardation	One year or more retarded ＿＿	At grade or above ＿＿
g. Father's occupation	Unskilled ＿＿ Semiskilled ＿＿	Professional ＿＿ Semiprofessional ＿＿ Managerial ＿＿
h. Educational level achieved by: Father Mother	Grade 7 or below ＿＿ Grade 7 or below ＿＿	Grade 10 or above ＿＿
i. Number of children in family.	Five or more ＿＿	Three or less ＿＿
j. School-to-school transfers	Pattern of "jumping" from school to school ＿＿	Few or no transfers ＿＿
k. Attendance	Chronic absenteeism (20 days or more per year) ＿＿	Seldom absent (10 days or less a year) ＿＿
l. Learning rate	Below 90 IQ ＿＿	Above 100 IQ ＿＿
m. Ability to read	Two years or more below grade level ＿＿	At or above grade level ＿＿
n. School marks	Predominantly below "C" ＿＿	Predominantly "B" or above ＿＿
o. Reaction to school controls	Resents controls ＿＿	Willingly accepts controls ＿＿
p. Acceptance by pupils	Not liked ＿＿	Well liked ＿＿
q. Parental attitude towards graduation	Negative ＿＿ Vacillating ＿＿	Positive ＿＿ United ＿＿
r. Pupil's interest in school work	Little or none ＿＿	High ＿＿
s. General adjustment	Fair or poor ＿＿	Good ＿＿

In originating any program designed to increase vocational skill or employment opportunities for youth in a community, certain essential steps are required. Yet, even before these steps are undertaken, the school authorities must decide whether the program will be "within the school day," as were those programs just cited, or an "out-of-school" program, similar to many of those which will soon be discussed. Another preliminary decision to be made concerns what kinds of youngsters will be served: Will they be inschool youth, academically talented students, or school drop-outs? Once these and related questions have been answered, the school is ready to take the initial step of identifying and studying the child-labor law applicable to the community, thus, apprising itself of the employment opportunities of school-age youth in the community.

Calling on the experts for information about what is or is not permitted under child-labor laws would dispel many mistaken notions about the stringency of the laws. Last spring a national magazine carried an article by a juvenile court judge citing all kinds of ridiculous provisions in the child-labor law of his State which he said should be changed. Actually, none of these examples reflected provisions in the State child-labor law. The same sort of objections were raised at a meeting in Washington, D. C. Analysis showed that in this case it was the school attendance law which was apparently the obstacle. Many times sheer inertia leads employers to set an 18-year minimum age so that they will "stay out of trouble." If we are trying to provide constructive opportunities for employment, we ought to be willing to take the time and trouble to find out exactly what the provisions of the law are and under what conditions youth may be employed.

Some State labor departments issue popularly written folders explaining the provisions of their child-labor laws so that everyone, including boys and girls looking for jobs, can understand them. More should be done to get accurate information into the hands of counselors, social workers, placement officers and all who are interested. Then we will know whether it is the laws that are blocking employment or whether lack of opportunity results from other circumstances. Then if some kinds of placement that are prohibited seem desirable, we can consider what specific provisions ought to be changed.[9]

If a school, court, or community group has already compiled and published a booklet on all laws concerning youth, including those dealing with employment, much of the groundwork for this initial step has already been laid. San Diego County's Department of Coordinating Councils, for example, published a booklet containing "summaries and interpretations of laws of major concern to youth and their parents living in the City and County of San Diego." If, however, the community lacks such a helpful resource, it is necessary that the school identify and obtain interpretations of the laws relevant to the school employment program; in the course of this work, it may be possible to assess the effect these laws have had on the community and whether modifications are necessary.

When the laws of the community pertaining to youth employment have been thoroughly understood, study of the local industrial and economic community is the next essential step. The nature of the economy and industry—the opportunities afforded for employment and the resources available —will be vital in determining the scope and emphases of the out-of-school program. In Pittsburgh a guidance textbook, "Work Opportunities in Greater Pittsburgh," was published as a part of that community's bicentennial project; representatives of the Rotary Club, the Chamber of Commerce, the schools, the university, the legal and medical professions, and the industrial employment service cooperated in its preparation. The introduction from this book provides an overview of the study itself and indicates the scope of the publication.

PITTSBURGH, PENNSYLVANIA: "Work Opportunities in Greater Pittsburgh" is designed to meet an important need in the guidance of students in the secondary schools of the Pittsburgh area. As a textbook for students of occupations and as a guidance tool for counselors, this handbook provides an abundance of local information not previously collected and made available in printed form. Teachers in all fields should find it invaluable in showing the relationship between subject fields and occupational life in the Pittsburgh metropolitan area.

104

The handbook includes information about specific occupations and professions, and it makes frequent references to local and national trends. Such materials make the publication useful as an independent textbook as well as a supplement to the general textbooks on occupations already available.

Chapters I and II set forth the characteristics that make Greater Pittsburgh unique in the abundance of its natural resources, in the dynamic quality of its people and institutions, and in the richness and diversity of its cultural and economic life.

Chapters III through IX present specific and detailed information dealing with the important aspects of occupational life: the nature and character of the employment, job opportunities in terms of numbers employed, the skills or preparation required, personality factors involved, and available resources for obtaining needed preparation.

Chapters X through XIII deal with industries that do not lend themselves to the usual occupational breakdown. Here, employment in transportation, communications, government agencies, and public utilities is discussed.

The final chapter presents information which counselors, through their years of experience, have found most useful to young people.

While most of the statistics that are included in this handbook apply to the metropolitan area of Allegheny, Beaver, Washington and Westmoreland counties, "Work Opportunities" should prove useful to schools outside this immediate area.[10]

The next necessary step for the school curriculum planners is that of designing the out-of-school program itself. The Job Upgrading Program of Detroit, which was structured to meet the needs of out-of-school youth, provides the first example of this phase.

DETROIT, MICHIGAN: . . . A flexible voluntary and informal program for young people 16 to 21 years of age who are out of school and unemployed . . . is sponsored by the community and the Detroit Public Schools.[11]

Training includes: (a) learning how to apply for a job; (b) classes in regular school for job preparation, if desired; (c) proper grooming for the job; (d) help with your problems.

105

Paid work experience lets you: (a) earn while you learn; (b) obtain job reference for the future.

A full-time job is your final goal, and you will be assisted in every way possible to attain your objective.

Follow-up service provides you with help while getting started on the job.[12]

[The Detroit Job Upgrading Program] serves unemployed school drop-outs through counseling, individualized instruction, and supervised work, all focused on the dominant motivation of this group—to get and hold a job.

The unique features of this program are:

Self-improvement and development of sense of responsibility is the objective. There are no academic standards to meet, no grades, no penalties for absence or tardiness.

Job-Upgrading Centers are informal, job centered. Youngsters work on their individual job sheets, at their own rates of speed, keep their own records of their progress.

Counseling is, central. Each teacher-counselor is available for individual work with boys and girls at any time. Group guidance through discussion helps youngsters gain confidence in self-improvement.

Supervised work experience is arranged for those who need it. Training stations in real job situations are found with understanding employers who will focus primarily on the youth's development and put production in second place. Some job upgraders are ready for regular jobs after varying periods in the program at the Job-Upgrading Center, without the supervised work experience. Careful placement and follow-up is provided until the young people are able to carry on in regular jobs without it.

The community finances the supervised work experience. Funds are provided from several sources to pay job-upgraders while they are in their training stations. They are paid on the job just as other employees are, but employers are reimbursed—private employers from funds provided by Rotary, and public and social agencies from the other community funds.

Representatives of the Detroit Council for Youth Service and the Board of Education, original sponsors of the Job-Upgrading

106

Program, suggest these pointers for other communities undertaking similar programs:

Go slowly and carefully.

Find a source of income for paying young people for their supervised work-experience.

Find enough employment spots for training.

Get the right kind of teacher-counselors, genuinely interested, patient and understanding.

Have a committee from the community working with school people to develop the broad community support and cooperation needed for success.

Accept the boys and girls as worthwhile individuals just as they are.

Operate 12 months without vacation interruption. . . .

The Detroit Job-Upgrading Program is now a regular part of the school program, under the direction of the Divisional Director of the Department of Guidance and Placement. The staff is most gracious in receiving visitors at the Centers where the program may be seen in operation.[13]

A copy of the Progress Chart used in the Detroit program follows.

I. GETTING STARTED
Counseling Record
Student Record Card (1007)
Folder for Materials
Bus Card
Student Irregularity Permit
Locker
Rules
Birth Certificate
Social Security Card

II. MAKING MYSELF
  EMPLOYABLE
Getting Acquainted with
Application Blanks:
  Learning about Application
    Blanks
  Personal Data Sheet
  A.T.&S. Restaurant
  Best Buy Supermarket
  Detroit Motor Company
  Downtown Department Store
  E. Z. Dime Store

Public Service Company
Speedy Messenger Service
Sure Cure Hospital
Checking Your Knowledge
  about Application Blanks

Minding My Manners
  Put Your Best Foot Forward
  Manners in Public
  Courtesy Comes to Town
    (Movie)

Using the Telephone
  Use of Telephone Directory
  Answering the Telephone
  Taking a Telephone Message
  Telephone Courtesy (Movie)

Learning How to Get the Job
  What Employers Want
  How to Get a Job
  Choosing Your Job
  Discovering Possible
    Employers

107

108

A program, likewise orientated to aid out-of-school youth operates in New York City. This program, in which the emphasis is on guidance in helping the out-of-school youth assess his strengths and weaknesses and plan his own future, is not a skill-training program.

NEW YORK CITY: Our two guidance centers, established in 1951 and 1955, respectively, have continued to offer educational and vocational guidance to out-of-school youth. While most of our applicants are in the 17-21 age group, we have never turned away a client because of age. The problems of the middle-aged or older worker, who wishes to return to school in order to complete his education, improve his vocational skills, or secure a better position, are also of concern to us. . . .

Clients are either self-referred or are sent to us by their schools, agencies or the board of education. Many come because they have heard of our service from friends. Interviews are held by appointment only. There is usually a wait of one to five days, although in some cases interviews may be scheduled immediately (when a cancellation occurs).

The client is first asked to fill out a brief interview form calling for personal data and employment history. His assignment to a counselor is made in accordance with the type of problem presented. One, two, or more counseling interviews may follow, depending on the clients' needs. Referrals for individual or group testing are made where indicated. Individual tests are given by the psychologist. Group tests (which may include intelligence, achievement, aptitude, interest, and personality tests) are administered, rated, and interpreted by counselors experienced in testing procedure. Group testing is always followed by an interview for the interpretation of test results.

Clients are helped to assess their strengths and weaknesses, to secure current factual information pertinent to their vocational and educational objectives, and to develop plans leading to a solution of their problems.[15]

The two previous examples were primarily of services offered to out-of-school youth, but the following article reports help offered during out-of-school hours to youngsters enrolled in school. This program, which supplies work opportunity, places particular stress on encouraging youngsters 14 to 18 years of age from the city's two highest delinquency areas to complete high school.

CINCINNATI, OHIO: A volunteer, citizen effort, YES was formed as a result of a study group on juvenile delinquency conducted by the YWCA and the Council of Jewish Women. They studied the causes and came to the conclusion that one area of delinquency prevention in which very little was being done was in job placements for deprived youth. Joined by five other women's organizations, Woman's City Club, Federation of Colored Women, Link's Inc., Council of Church Women, Cincinnati Council PTA's, YES was inaugurated.

In the year and a half it has been in operation, 350 high-delinquency-area youths have been placed in part-time jobs. It places those 14 years of age and older who are (1) recommended by teachers and counselors, (2) checked as to performance, and (3) prepared for their designated jobs.

Here's how it works:

Volunteers at the Service Office receive the job orders and channel them to the school counselors. The teeners also get jobs from satisfied employers who either hire them or refer them to acquaintances or friends. . . .

When operated through the school, the youngster is sent to the YES office for an interview with the volunteer to get facts about job requirements, pay scale and hours. (The service has a minimum wage scale for the different occupations.) Then he (or she) gets a referral card to take to the employer.

The volunteer phones the employer to tell him about the student and find out the interview (or the start-to-work) date. Then a call-back is made to the employer several weeks later to get his reactions and check on the possibility of more openings.

For youths who don't get hired, special counseling sessions are arranged to give them help in overcoming interfering problems the employer might have with them. [The CCY executive director] attributes the high batting average of YES to the fact that the Service doesn't take direct applications from the teenagers, but gets the job order from the employer FIRST, and then requests referrals.

The special training sessions set up by YES, in these Cincinnati schools, include one on gardening for boys, child care and homemaking service for girls and one for florists' helpers.

110

Disadvantaged youngsters . . . often need very special job help, which betters them and also the community. Without this assistance many will be unable to find their place in our working society. For them, YES provides a learning process to get to understand what the world will be like when they go into it. YES also helps them to know how to go out and look for full-time jobs later on. In many cases, the jobs they get influence their life's work. . . .

YES also sends out pamphlets to the teeners telling them ways to get jobs and advising them on the "do's and don'ts of job hunting." The pamphlets remind the youths that it pays to go to school—that income and education move together.

In like manner, YES sends out pamphlets to business and industry, where the "sell" job to employers is much harder, since it must convince them that it is a wise move to take a chance on these youngsters. In fact, it asks the community to become involved in an experiment to help the teeners help themselves. It thereby gives people the chance to share in a constructive project. The employer pays no fee, yet obtains a screened, willing employee.

And YES gives the reasons for hiring teen-agers:
1. They are better suited to some jobs than are older persons.
2. They will generally work harder for a reasonable wage.
3. They are quick to learn, have sharp eyes and are loaded with energy.
4. The employer, as a civic-minded citizen, can encourage teen-agers to develop ambition, dependability and learn the value of work.

What are the results of this service?

It is difficult, if not impossible, to evaluate at this time the effect these jobs have had on each youth. However, in the year and a half the Youth Employment Service has been in operation, more than 30% of the placements have resulted in semi-permanent or permanent employment. Many teen-agers sent out on one day jobs received additional employment because of this contact.

Employers are happy with the service too. One wrote: "The boy referred to me made a very fine impression on me, both first and continuing. He worked well, fast and carefully. I would say he washed walls and woodwork as well as any professional

111

cleaner I've had. He did not pretend to know yard work, but there he followed instructions well and was satisfactory to me. His conduct at all times was excellent. He seemed to be intelligent and ambitious. I am enthusiastic about the work of YES and will call on you again when I need help."

Can jobs be found which will benefit both employer and teen-agers from a high delinquency area? In Cincinnati, the answer is YES![16]

Another effort designed to give continued academic opportunity for youngsters from low socioeconomic areas may be found in a Community Talent Search program.

WASHINGTON, DISTRICT OF COLUMBIA: Community Talent Search, as a nation-wide project, is now one year old. It began as an idea, but now everyone concerned with it believes in it as a living organism. Washington, D. C., has approved a CTS-inspired project scheduled to begin in September 1958. Thirty other cities are in various stages of consideration, ranging from deep enthusiasm to casual indifference. . . . The profound concern of school superintendents for their deprived children has stirred up great interest in methods of searching out the hidden talent among them.

A CTS project attempts to help a community bring about the concentration, in junior and senior high school, of additional and special testing, guidance, instructional, and auxiliary services, together with cultural exposure and a more intensive program of parent involvement, to pupils living in a low socioeconomic area, pupils deprived of the cultural advantages of pupils from the middle classes—regardless of race, creed, or sex. . . .

Community Talent Search helps communities to tap those underprivileged groups which—through no fault of their own—are not contributing their fair share of superior students to our pool of trained manpower, which is in such short supply today. In doing so, CTS also helps communities achieve the cherished American ideal of equality of educational opportunity for all.[17]

A day work-camp program was jointly established by the Fuld Neighborhood House and the Essex County Park Commission in New Jersey as a means of supplying summertime earning opportunity to teen-age boys. The following report

112

on this experimental program deals with its second year of operation.

NEWARK, NEW JERSEY: In the summer of 1958, a slightly different approach was tried. Since the staff of the first project had recommended smaller groups and a more realistic duration of the work day, two leaders were assigned ten boys each. Work was to be conducted during four hours in the morning; three afternoon hours were to be used for rest and supervised recreation. While all this had been discussed with the boys and agreed to by them, the program was less liked than that of the previous year. Supervised daytime recreation in the woods, far from their usual companions, was not what these boys cared for. Their pride in being hired workers and earning an income of meaning was hurt by the smaller pay, as well as by the demonstrated fact that they were primarily considered "kids" who had to play part of the day.

The summer was successful in terms of regular attendance and carrying out of assigned work, but the previous year's joy and enthusiasm were missing. The recreation aspect of the project had to be abandoned in the course of the six weeks.

Nevertheless, according to reports received, the boys returned to the agency in the fall, are participating in the teenage program, and are all doing well in school. They hope that a work camp functioning on the terms of the 1957 project will be conducted this summer.

A project of this kind combines the important features of (1) work from which the community profits, (2) increased status and self-respect for the campers, and (3) integration of teenagers into the world of adults. The project gives, furthermore, important insights into the emotional needs and reactions of the young people involved, clues about: their personal and vocational counseling needs, the length of workday they can comfortably carry, and their own feelings about appropriate recreation.

Based on the New Jersey findings, it is recommended that similar projects: (1) stress individual guidance and counseling so as to make the summer experience into a preparation for adult employment, (2) consider salary as a means to gain status, independence, and a feeling of responsibility toward personal and family needs, (3) determine length of the workday by the youngsters' physical fitness as well as their psychological need to work "all day," and (4) give compensation in accordance with psychological needs as well as the work load. It is furthermore recommended that work projects be carried out independently from recreation programs, so that working teenagers may gain a real feeling of growing up and being a true part of the world in which they live.[18]

However, a caution based upon the experience of the previous year must be recorded.

No one was prepared, however, for the aftereffects of the project. When the boys returned after the four weeks of vacation, during which the House was closed, they had exploited to every possible degree, the high status gained through the Work Project. They had become neighborhood models as well as neighborhood bullies. Every youngster within a radius of several blocks wanted to join the club and many claimed to have done so. Cocky behavior and minor delinquencies committed by real and by self-appointed members of the club had irritated adults, police, and school officials, and had caused much friction. . . .

Then, suddenly, the fantasy . . . broke down. . . . The club went wild. . . . Under great protest, the whole club was then expelled from the agency. . . . The boys were told that they could return as individuals after their parents had been visited by staff members and informed of the breaking-up of the club.

This plan was carried out and eventually all members of the former club returned to the House. The situation was, however, not a happy one. The resentment at having been betrayed and deprived of status never died down. . . . However, each of the boys maintained a certain measure of loyalty to the House and confidence in individual members. A rule not to fight in or near the agency was made by the boys themselves and was obeyed. Help from staff members was still sought when any member of the group found himself in trouble. A process of disintegration had, nevertheless, set in and could not be stopped.[19]

An employment committee in the nation's capital is part of a larger organization created to prevent and control juvenile delinquency. This committee has attempted a wide program offering vocational education, listing employment opportunities, and organizing youth employee groups. This committee which acts as a coordinator of an all-community effort, pro-

114

vides the final example of a possible school role in the occupational life of its community.

WASHINGTON, DISTRICT OF COLUMBIA: The Commissioner's Youth Council is composed of volunteers who are community leaders in the field of youth activities. They constitute the over-all planning and policy making group of the Council. One of the Council's most active committees is the Employment Committee. The Committee membership consists of D.C. Schools personnel (including the Superintendent of Schools); representatives of organized labor; the Director of the U.S. Employment Service for the District; members of the Federation of Businessmen's Associations, Junior Chamber of Commerce and the Washington Board of Trade and civic-minded individuals who have a particular interest in youth employment. The Committee both initiates projects and supports programs which originate with the Council's Area Boards.

The Area Boards are neighborhood committees composed of volunteer neighborhood leaders who are identified with the neighborhood either by virtue of their residence and/or employment. They carry out programs tailored to fit the needs of their neighborhood. Of course, youth employment is basic in the programs of all these Boards.

The Council's Employment Committee has concentrated its deliberations and programming on the following main topics. . . .

1. Revision of the Child Labor Code for the District

Several years ago it became apparent to us that the D.C. Child Labor Code was outmoded in a number of respects. The original code was drafted in 1926 and since that time technological progress altered employment situations. We are interested in making changes pertaining principally to the occupations prohibited and hours of employment and not in altering the code substantively. For example, the code reads "no person under the age of 18 shall operate an elevator in the District of Columbia" also, "girls under 18 are prohibited from working after 7 p.m." The latter automatically prevents girls under 18 from working in lunch rooms, restaurants, department stores, etc. This practically shuts out employment at these sources because at 7 p.m. they are just reaching their peak period of business. Baby-sitting for girls under 18 becomes illegal after 7 p.m. also. However, since it is impossible to enforce this, a ruling exempting baby-sitting has been allowed by the D.C. Corporation Counsel.

For this project we cooperated with a committee of the District Bar Association who enlisted the services of the Harvard Law School Reference Service. They drafted a national Child Labor Code using the District of Columbia as a model. When this was completed, we realized that substantive changes had been made that were not acceptable to us and, therefore, we are back to the point from which we started. We have not discarded this project, however, even though it is in a quiescent stage.

2. Pamphlet for Employers Hiring Minors

As a result of several employer surveys, we learned that employers are reluctant to hire teen-agers because they are unsure of the law, what is legal and what is not. They also criticized the fact that information is not available in a positively stated manner and so, rather than take a risk of violation, they desist from hiring minors altogether.

With the cooperation of personnel of the U.S. Department of Labor, the D.C. Schools Department of Attendance and Work Permits and the U.S. Employment Service for the District, a pamphlet has been prepared, entitled "You May Employ Youth." It has been distributed to some 2,000 employers by the U.S. Employment Service and we hope to have their suggestions for constructive changes after they have used it for a period of time.

3. Brochure of Instructions for Minors Seeking Employment

We have learned that procedures for obtaining a work permit are generally unknown to the majority of minors seeking employment. They are required to have the prospective employer sign an "intent to hire" card, [and are required to have a] birth certificate and physical examination when they are under 16, etc. Many are completely ignorant of the procedures as well as the offices and addresses for processing.

As in the employers' pamphlet, we are working with personnel from the U.S. Department of Labor, U.S. Employment Service for the District and the D.C. Schools Department of Attendance and Work Permits. At this point we are compiling the data to be contained in the brochure and following its approval by all agencies involved, it will be printed by the U.S. Employment Service and placed in strategic locations such as schools and recreation centers.

4. School Drop-Out Program—Job Conditioning Center

We observed that there is a need for such a program from the findings of a survey which indicated that 50% of the 4,000

116

out-of-school youth, between the ages of 16-18, in the District were unemployed. This really concerned us greatly, particularly since it is related to juvenile delinquency as pointed up in the cliché "idle hands are the devil's workshop."

Now after many months of deliberations the program will be introduced in the schools [when personnel becomes available].

5. Youth Employment Week

This project takes place annually the week following the close of the school year in June. We believe this to be the best time to focus the attention of employers on the fact that teen-agers need constructive and remunerative activity for the summer vacation period. All efforts are geared for publicity of this project for this week. The Commissioners of the District of Columbia cooperate by issuing a Proclamation which officially announces Youth Employment Week. This is followed with publicity in the press and spot announcements on radio and television during the week. The Odd Jobs Program goes into high gear and the various agencies involved, mainly the Recreation Department and the U.S. Employment Service, plan their staff activities accordingly. The telephone number of the Youth Council office is publicized and the number of telephone calls from employers during the week points up the effectiveness of the project. We feel that we have merely scratched the surface here and with more time for better organization, we can do a far better job in the promotion of this idea.

6. Odd Jobs Program

Background information leading up to the present operation of the Odd Jobs Program is as follows:

At the close of the school year in June, 1954, one of the Area Boards developed and carried out a successful plan to provide teen-agers with neighborhood jobs of mowing lawns, raking leaves, cleaning attics and basements, painting furniture and, in general, any job casual to the home.

Publicity was achieved by distribution of flyers throughout the neighborhood—door-to-door, organization mailing lists, super-market placement in grocery bags, posters in strategic spots, etc. The flyer advised householders of the availability of teen-agers for work around the home and suggested certain types of jobs that might be handled. It also made known the compensation schedule of 75¢ an hour.

Teen-agers, learning of the program, registered for jobs at the neighborhood recreation center.

A job form was devised which included date, job number, employer, address, phone number, job description and assignment. A bulletin board was made available in the recreation center for posting information about each job that had been called in. With assignment of the job, a postcard return addressed to the Center was given to the youth to take to the employer. The information on the card provides for the name and address of the employer; a check of the hours worked and "remarks." The card also includes a statement of wage rates.

Since that first center, which got underway in 1954, other Area Board Odd Jobs Programs were started and, this summer, there are 25 Centers operating, with at least one Center in every neighborhood in the city. Each Board sponsors its own "Odd Jobs Program" with publicity and support to the Centers where the program operates. There is a uniform pay rate in the city of 75¢ per hour and every year, in the fall, there is a city-wide conference held where Area Board members meet with personnel of the Centers, counselors from the U.S. Employment Service and Youth Council Staff to discuss the program and to resolve problems arising in its operation.

Last summer for the first time U.S. Employment Service offered the services of their counselors. These counselors service the public schools during the school year and they are particularly well qualified to participate in this youth program. They accounted, in large part, for the degree of success that was achieved because, not only did they assist with the placement of the youth, but they made contacts throughout the neighborhood in promoting the program and were also most helpful to the young people in counseling on careers and employment in general. We are delighted to have these counselors with us again this summer.

Last summer we had some 3,000 placements in the city. This is a minimal count because, frequently, the youth have repeat jobs and other jobs in the same block and the Center is not informed. This summer we estimate that there will be many more than last year's 3,000.

The Youth Council has been successful in achieving excellent cooperation from the press. All of the city's newspapers have printed stories with pictures from time to time, particularly during the summer months. Another most helpful means of publicity has been movie trailers which are shown in all the neighborhood theatres every summer during the month of August, which we have found to be the time when the program needs "a shot in the arm." The Area Boards continue their neighborhood publicity throughout the season with blurbs in church bulletins, posters in frequented neighborhood spots, neighborhood newspapers and frequent circulation of their flyers.

Business has boomed to a point where, in some Boards, they have engaged the services of a commercial answering service which relays the calls once a day to the Center.

In analyzing the success of the program we note:

1. It meets a community need.
2. It strikes a responsive chord with the youth.
3. It is carefully devised to operate as simply as possible.
4. It is wholly voluntary on the part of the youth.
5. It demonstrates the effectiveness of coordinated agency services.
6. It has changed the attitude of householders from reluctance to . . . acceptance in the employment of youth.

Of these factors, the responsiveness of the youth, we believe to be of the utmost importance. The program appeals to youth because they can earn some money and can select the time they desire to work. Thus, they become willing workers and the chances are better for learning satisfying work attitudes.

The factor of coordinated agency services results in mutual benefit to the agencies involved as well as to the youth. As an example, the program brought an increased number of youth to the Center. While waiting for jobs to be called in, they participated in the Center program. It also helps to establish a close and better relationship between Staff and the youth.

The benefit of the project to the community is obvious. To the youth, it is not only beneficial financially but educationally as well. For the first time some of them took on the responsibility of a job, worked for a stranger, accepted the discipline of a job. They were received seriously; they grew up a little more. Some earned money for the first time. It is a net gain all around.

7. The Carrier Boys Program

Well-organized groups of supermarket package carriers operate under a city-wide Coordinating Committee. From the time of the first club, which was organized in 1956 under the guidance of a Staff member at a neighborhood recreation center, the program has now grown to include approximately 25 clubs, most of which are sponsored by the Youth Council's Area Boards and are a natural adjunct of the Odd Jobs Program. The clubs operate out of supermarkets where there is a need for organized package carriers.

Before organization of Carrier Boys Clubs, the store became a problem area for loitering, foul language, fights, thefts, disfiguration and damage of property and a place where unacceptable social patterns were learned and practiced.

In addition to the city-wide Coordinating Committee, composed of representatives of each sponsoring group of every Carrier Boys Club, there is a coordinator for the program who is a counselor of the U. S. Employment Service. Meetings of the Coordinating Committee are held monthly at the USES where problems of mutual interest are resolved. At these meetings there is also an opportunity to share experiences and learn of activities of all the clubs.

This type of remunerative activity (the boys receive tips from the customers) appeals to the youngsters under 14 years of age who are too young for the Odd Jobs Program. In addition to the remuneration, there are indirect benefits. The clubs are well organized and there are weekly meetings with the adult sponsors. Each club has a "captain" and plans for the week-end business are laid at these meetings. More than package carrying is involved. Efforts are made to raise the cultural standards of the boys by having inspiring speakers, recreational activities, social events, etc.

This report, then, is the essence of the youth employment picture of Washington, D. C., insofar as the Youth Council is concerned. General, indeed, for there are many aspects which do not lend themselves to analysis on paper.

One very important aspect is the Special Unit for youth that operates at U.S. Employment Service. Here in one visit there is aptitude testing, counseling and hopefully, placement. Theirs is a job magnificently done. . . .[20]

The employment-oriented program is only one of the many specific types of action that schools can develop to initiate and support a plan for juvenile delinquency prevention. The following summary attempts to classify in some detail specific curriculum adjustments designed to help the slow learner.

NEW YORK CITY: Educators have discovered that school discipline problems grow in part out of a curriculum which does not make sense to the learner. They have found that the classroom in which subject-matter content bears no relationship to the needs or interests of the learner is a source of difficulty.

The incidence of delinquency is four and one-half times higher among children with low IQ's than among those with high IQ's. School is a source of constant failure and frustration to the slow child. As a result, he learns to feel that the world is pitted against him. He may respond by rebelling or by withdrawing into a world of fantasy.

As a first step in setting up a program for very slow pupils, homogeneous classes are often provided. Here, arbitrary standards of achievement are replaced by realistic standards based on the child's ability. In heterogeneous classes, the child tends to develop aspiration levels from his brighter peers; and frustration often results. Under the homogeneous class arrangement, pupils are encouraged to work to their potential—and tension is reduced.

In the high schools, curriculum offerings have been extended in many areas. Art, industrial art, home economics and music departments have been expanded to provide for these children. Special classes in leadership, dramatics and dance also make provisions for them. All school activities—assemblies, G.O., service squads, student courts—seek to involve all pupils.

Simultaneously, the courses of study have been modified for pupils of lower ability. Applied science and general mathematics have replaced the more abstract disciplines in the high schools.

In social studies also, emphasis is placed on aspects of the work that are especially meaningful to the slow: democracy; economic citizenship; current affairs; international relations. Thus, for the tenth or eleventh years, the Committee on World History for Non-Regents Students recommends four units: Democracy and Dictatorship; Economic World; Colonialism; War and Peace. In American history, stress is given to the growth

121

of political, social and economic democracy; to the technological revolutions; to labor, business and consumer problems; to problems of foreign policy.

In language arts, too, the course of study is modified for these children: basic language skills are taught functionally; reading is encouraged through the use of easy-to-read materials, including adventure, romance and abridged classics; experience as well as subject-matter units are taught—teen-age problems, family life, getting and keeping a job, all of which may involve letter-writing, interviewing, speaking, reading and thinking.

Throughout, the traditional approach has been supplemented by a wide variety of instructional materials and experiences through which these children learn. Thus, audio-visual programs have been expanded; pamphlet and magazine materials purchased; trips, panel-forum discussions, charts, bulletin-board construction, pupil-teacher planning and evaluation are encouraged.

The core program is used extensively for these children. The special emphasis of the core program is the all-round development of the pupil as a human being, family member, consumer, producer and citizen. In the double-period arrangement, the curriculum is flexible and geared to the child's needs; and the teachers are guidance-oriented.

The junior high schools, too, are adjusting the curriculum to the varying needs of the pupils. Included are experiments with the core, an increased use of committee and unit procedures, and modifications in the materials and experiences through which pupils learn. In addition the junior high school program involves exploratory work in special shops; art, music and remedial reading classes; and special orientation classes for Puerto Rican children.

Thus teachers of teen-agers in all types of secondary schools find that behavior problems are reduced as learnings are related to students' needs and interests, and as students participate in learning experiences which are meaningful to them.[21]

[Because there are so many items in a description of school programs or procedures found worth while in preventing delinquency they have been classified for convenience as follows:]

122

Curriculum

A. Methods
1. Class grouping with modified assignments within each group. Adaptation to needs, abilities and interests of children, homes and communities
2. Flexible curriculum
3. Individualization of instruction
4. A program of continuous progress
5. Opportunity for self-expression

B. Administration (programming, etc.)
1. Enriching curriculum through audio-visual aids
2. Comprehensive program of excursions
3. Clubs, hobbies, development of talents

C. Remedial program
1. Special instruction in reading and/or arithmetic
2. Special tutoring for retarded children

D. School climate
1. Esprit de corps engendered through participation in assembly exercises, school and class activities
2. Mental hygiene approach emphasized
3. Democratic discipline developed

E. Working with parents and agencies
1. Teacher-pupil-parent contacts
2. Friendly relations maintained with parents and school agencies [22]

Other programs to help the potential or active delinquent have also been reported. Emphasis has been placed most frequently upon citizenship education. This emphasis may be expressed through imitative example presented by the teacher, as in Philadelphia; through courses designed around student problems, as in Jamestown; through courses planned to structure habits, as in Pittsburgh; through courses and activities stressing our lawful heritage, as in Massachusetts; or through courses based upon teaching core values, as in Saint Louis.

PHILADELPHIA, PENNSYLVANIA: The public schools of this city traditionally have assumed important responsibilities for character education, teaching the difference between right and wrong,

123

and teaching the fundamental elements of civic responsibility. These important instructional elements are sometimes organized in a formal manner, but more often the inculcation of these values depends on informal and incidental contacts between teacher and child—the helping hand, the kind word at the proper moment, and the correction of undesirable behavior when it appears.

JAMESTOWN, NORTH DAKOTA: We have a unit in each grade of the social studies courses which attempts to acquaint students with sound basic conceptions in citizenship and personal behavior. In grade 10 we offer a special unit on mental and physical hygiene, correlating these units with special problems pertaining to the Senior High School level. An extensive extracurricular program is maintained.

PITTSBURGH, PENNSYLVANIA: One of the major goals of the public schools, the development of good citizenship, permeates the entire school program, and constitutes the school's most important contribution to the prevention of delinquency. The Pittsburgh public schools have accepted responsibility for building desirable habits of conduct and for changing, when necessary, the habit patterns of children. Respect for personal, private, and public property; respect for the rights of others; and respect for authority occupy prominent places in the program.[23]

THE STATE OF MASSACHUSETTS: Schools have done much that is commendatory in sustaining Our Lawful Heritage. Each system has its share of teachers whose personal conduct represents the finest kind of teaching. It is a statement of fact that the vast majority of our teachers view their jobs as a public trust and conduct their personal lives accordingly. Good personal behavior is most praiseworthy, but it is not enough. Maximum effectiveness involves more than that; it includes the school's philosophy, teaching content, teaching methods, pupil experiences, and community relationships.

Many schools do concentrate on some of the kinds of teaching I have been stressing. Some schools, such as Quincy, Massachusetts, supplement the work of the home by teaching aspects of family living which involve the recognition of the place of moral and spiritual values. Other schools, including Beverly and Dedham, Massachusetts, encourage young people to share in planning codes of behavior. Many schools invite their youngsters to

124

engage in a multiplicity of community services which provide tangible evidence of acceptance of social responsibility.

All these things are desirable, and we recommend to school authorities that they become a part of a total school program which adds greater strength to one's acceptance of the vital objective—"An understanding of the place of law in our lives and the will to oppose delinquency in its observance." The Boston public schools are to be commended for considering this objective of civic education in its totality. So, too, is the smaller neighboring town of Westwood, Massachusetts, which has endeavored to anticipate incidents of delinquency. Particular reference should be made to the programs in the elementary schools of Holyoke . . . and at the Tripp School in Fairhaven, Massachusetts.[24]

SAINT LOUIS, MISSOURI: The Community Planning Committee of the St. Louis Board of Education, a committee composed of three board members, has been studying, with the Executive Officers of the St. Louis Public Schools, the prevention of vandalism. It has been decided to approach the matter with an educational program and supplementary units of study on the subject of "Respect of Public Property" have been prepared for the elementary and secondary schools.

A statement reported from a conference of health workers held in Washington, D. C., emphasizes the relationship of family education and sex education to the general problem of juvenile delinquency.

NATIONAL HEALTH CONFERENCE: Health personnel do not have a primary responsibility for family life education in the public school system. Since such education is part of the total curriculum, ultimate responsibility rests with the educational authorities. Health personnel, however, can and should participate in the family life program and should take special responsibility for certain facets of it.

The conference participants recognized that the assignment of primary responsibility was of considerable import, since health personnel do not want to do anything to further compartmentalize the high school student. Conferees stressed the importance of having one member of the high school faculty carry responsibility as advisor to each pupil and to all other school personnel who participate in the pupil's educational program. This key individual should be responsible for interpreting pertinent information to the pupil's classroom instructors, physical education supervisor, administrative personnel, and others concerned with him. Such information should concern the youngster's needs and problems in relation to school program, his physical and emotional health, and his personal and family problems as they affect his ability to participate fully in the activities of the school. The person responsible for the individual student should aid others in planning modifications in the school program that may be indicated because of the student's particular problems, capacities, and potentialities.

Such individualization of the school program is basic to family life education, for although it does not provide specific information, discussion, and guidance related to family life, it does provide the climate in which youngsters can grow toward maturity and eventually assume their proper role as family members. While specific family life education material may be offered at the high school level, education for family living actually starts in the kindergarten when teachers help children to share and forego immediate pleasure for later reward. The entire curriculum needs to be examined to see wherein family life education material may best be placed. The American Social Hygiene Association has been aiding the school system in a number of states in performing this task and has prepared specific material of value to teachers in developing family life education content.

Such material must, of course, be adapted to the need of different groups of youngsters. One needs to be aware, for example, of the cultural background of the children. Sometimes family life education in schools may conflict with what youngsters learn at home. Teachers need to be aware of the possible problems engendered by such a situation. Occasionally the family traditions, customs, and mores may be so far from the practices reflected in the curriculum that the beginning must be made in parent education rather than in family life education. . . .

The importance of sex education as part of the total preparation for family living through the school system cannot be overemphasized. The United States Public Health Service reports that the incidence of primary and secondary syphilis shows a marked increase beginning at eleven to twelve years of age and reaches a peak at nineteen years. It is also found that the reported cases of gonorrhea begin to increase sharply at eleven to twelve years. We are forced to recognize that a definite venereal disease control program exists in this age segment of the population. With another recent study of the Public Health Service indicating a definite positive correlation between one index of delinquency (the number of defendants in criminal proceedings tried under the Juvenile Delinquency Act in United States district courts) and the incidence of venereal disease, the idea is suggested that not only are some young people having sexual experience at an early age but that this is particularly true of those who are prone to be delinquent. Obviously, therefore, health personnel must be concerned with the preparation which young people receive to deal with the sexual aspects of life.[25]

Special courses, special grouping, special guidance, special interest, all are used by some schools to aid in prevention and control; for example, a special course for elementary-school pupils that uses high-school facilities has been developed.

WATERBURY, CONNECTICUT: The "Opportunity Program" is for boys of approximately 14 years of age and over, who are still in elementary school (ours is a K-8, 9-12 system) and having difficulty with the regular academic program. (It is not a special class for retarded pupils.) Boys eligible to enter the program come to one of our high schools four afternoons each week, after the regular high-school pupils have been dismissed. At all other times, these boys attend their regular school.

The requirements for admission beyond the age factor are:

1. The boy himself must be willing to come.
2. The parents must approve.
3. The school principal must feel that the program will benefit the boy.
4. The boy must take some "tests" for admission. These are usually mechanical reasoning or spatial perception tests which we use more to gain knowledge of the applicants than for selection, but the boys take their entrance examinations very seriously.
5. The person in charge of the program must approve the boy for admission.

No qualification is made with respect to mental ability other than the fact that the individual must have enough intelligence to avoid danger of shop tools and machinery. Most of the boys are of average mental ability. IQ's of the group have ranged from a low of 68 to a high of 115.

The program consists of three or four shops (woodworking, electricity, printing, machine) depending upon availability of qualified teachers, and a "citizenship class." Each week, the boys attend shop three days and the "citizenship class" one day. One period of physical education (swimming or gym) is provided when a teacher is available.

Approximately 15 boys are assigned to each class. The primary concern of each teacher is the boy and his attitudes rather than the shop skills. The shops are considered to be a means to an end. The "citizenship class" is used to crystallize and extend the development of sound attitudes, of a sense of responsibility, and of social skills. This particular class has possibilities which we have not yet explored.

The person in charge of the program takes a personal interest in each boy, and problems in and out of school are brought to her by them. They respond strongly to the acceptance and warmth that is shown them.

A number of these boys have problems over and above the academic. If we come across a boy with a serious behavior problem in one of our elementary schools, we invariably look for a place for him in the "Opportunity Program," and almost invariably he responds.

We find an exceptional brand of loyalty to the program and to teachers involved, particularly to the person who heads up the program. There appears to have developed a code of ethics in the program which the boys themselves help to maintain. A number of the boys who went through this program continued in high school although they had been inclined to leave school at age 16.

Each year we have many more applicants than we can accept. It is considered a privilege to be selected.

Special grouping and assignment to class sections—the first using reading, the second using general ability as criteria for such grouping—have been successfully utilized by a small South Carolina town and by our nation's capital.

GAFFNEY, SOUTH CAROLINA: Each child is grouped according to his reading ability. It is surprising to find how much one's reading ability reflects his ability in all other subjects. When the teacher begins to work with her group in any subject, the subject matter is presented in a flexible manner so that quick learners will not be bored, and no child will be unable to achieve. This practice tends to help the pupils keep busy and feel the joy of accomplishment; it has a definite bearing on preventing problems in behavior during class periods. We feel that the amazing decrease in drop-outs was brought about by this type of grouping. Drop-outs have decreased approximately 50 per cent since this plan was installed.

WASHINGTON, DISTRICT OF COLUMBIA: In the areas where we have the "lower class" children, we have large numbers of low ability children. In the junior high school, they can no longer be in "ungraded" classes, operating in a corner of a building. . . .

We have nine special classes, where we are trying to provide an education for these children in keeping with the pattern of the junior high school. We are departmentalized—three special teachers working together, and teaching the "academic" subjects to each of the other sections. Many discipline problems are handled through the cooperation of these three teachers. In teaching a very slow child to adjust to a modified junior high school program, he learns to adjust to people and groups.

My own section has 26 ninth graders, all below 70 IQ when they entered. (There are two such sections in our school.) They are now 15-17 years old, most of them reading at fourth to sixth grade level, and most of them on the way to becoming pretty good people.

In New York City an experimental project has been undertaken. Instead of changing the curriculum in hopes of meeting student desires and interests, an intensive guidance effort has been made to raise the levels of aspiration and interest of the students.

NEW YORK CITY: The Demonstration Guidance Project, which is being carried on in two schools, was begun at Junior High School 43, Manhattan, in September 1956, in the seventh, eighth, and ninth grades to identify and stimulate able students from a deprived area to reach higher educational levels and to help as many as possible to enter college. It was extended to George Washington High School in September 1957, when the first

129

project class from the junior high school was admitted to the tenth grade.

The plan is to continue the project for six years from its introduction so that all three groups of students will have the opportunity to complete high school under the project program. At the end of the six-year period a final measure of the success of the program will be obtained by determining how many more students complete high school or enter college than did so in previous years.

The responsibility for conducting the study is shared by the Bureau of Educational and Vocational Guidance and the Bureau of Educational Research of the Board of Education. The direction and implementation of the project are the responsibility of the principals and guidance administrators in the two schools. An advisory committee headed by the superintendent of schools determines general policy. The main support for the project is provided by the Board of Education, with some additional funds and planning support from the College Entrance Examination Board and the National Scholarship Service and Fund for Negro Students.

A major purpose of the project is to raise the levels of student achievement and aspiration by compensating for the limitations of cultural deprivations. It is a nation-wide problem that students from deprived socio-cultural areas tend to do less well on intelligence and achievement tests and in school achievement, and tend to leave school earlier than those from more favored areas. Only a very small percentage go on to college. In failing to achieve their potential, these boys and girls are depressed educationally and vocationally, and their talents are lost to higher education and to the skilled technical and professional manpower pools. In many instances, the student's family and the social groups with whom he associates have not had a tradition of higher education so that neither the parent nor student thinks in terms of such ambitions for the student. In some instances, students with superior academic potential seem to lack interest in attaining academic success or further education. Thus, an important aim of the project is motivation and raising the educational and vocational goals of these able students.[26]

Last but not least is that section of the curriculum which is sometimes called extracurricular or cocurricular. Here is a valuable area of learning experience where many attempts can be made to aid in the adjustment of, and to offer opportunities for school success to, the potential or active norm violator. This is particularly true whenever the sports offered coincide with the focal concerns of excitement and toughness (e.g., football, boxing, and wrestling).

DES MOINES, IOWA: The entire program of social and extra-curricular activities in the 13 junior and senior high schools deserves attention as an important part of our program which tends to reduce delinquency. Our junior high schools carry on a very large and quite extensive program of special interest groups and intramural game activities. Our five senior high schools run a full program of varsity sports including swimming, wrestling, tennis, and golf in addition to the football, basketball, baseball, and track. In all of these we provide for large squads. Our high schools will average about 100 boys out for football during the season.

Thus, through constant evaluation of the school curriculum, (here defined as including all planned school experiences), the teacher and administrator may discover ways to aid the potential or active norm violator through organization of his daily activities as well as those of his peer group. Supplementing or complementing the teacher, the administrator and the curriculum are the integrated special services whose special functions will be discussed and illustrated in the next chapter.

References

[1] California Teachers Association, Youth Activities and Welfare Committee. "The School and Juvenile Delinquency." San Francisco: the Committee, 1958.

[2] Saint Paul Public Schools, Office of Secondary and Vocational Education. "Dealing with the Maladjusted Pupil." Curriculum Steering Committee Workshop Series, 1957-58. Saint Paul: the Office, 1958. p. 17.

[3] Saint Paul Public Schools, Office of Secondary and Vocational Education. "The Organization and Curriculum of the New Junior High School in Saint Paul." Saint Paul: the Office, 1958. p. 2-3, 16.

[4] Los Angeles County Special Schools, Reception Center. "Teaching of Vocational Skills in Academic Classes for Emotionally Disturbed Children." Los Angeles: the Center, 1959. p. 1-14 *passim*.

[5] Krugman, Morris. Paper presented to the Panel on Juvenile Delinquency at the meeting of the Council for Exceptional Children, Atlantic City, New Jersey, April 10, 1959.

[6] Reports of job-skill training programs within the regular school program were submitted to the Project by Hobbs, New Mexico, and Madison, Wisconsin.

[7] Indianapolis Public Schools. *The Wood High School*. Indianapolis: the Schools, 1957. p. 1-17 *passim*.

[8] Reproduced by permission of the University of the State of New York.

[9] Beyer, Clara M. "Youth Employment: Opportunity and Protection." (Reprint of article in *Social Action*, February 1957.)

[10] Pittsburgh Chamber of Commerce. *Work Opportunities in Greater Pittsburgh*. Pittsburgh: the Chamber, 1959. p. 2-3.

[11] The Detroit Council for Youth Service. "Detroit Helps Unemployed Youth Through the Job Upgrading Program." Detroit: the Council, 1958. p. 1.

[12] Detroit Public Schools, Department of Guidance and Placement. "The Job Upgrading Program Helps You Become a Successful Worker." Detroit: the Department, 1958. p. 2-3.

[13] U.S. Department of Labor, Bureau of Labor Standards. "Job-Upgrading for Detroit's Out-of-School Youth." Washington, D. C.: Superintendent of Documents, Government Printing Office, 1957. p. 1-2.

[14] Detroit Public Schools, Department of Guidance and Placement. "Progress Chart: Job Upgrading Program." Detroit: the Department, 1957.

[15] Board of Education of the City of New York, Bureau of Educational and Vocational Guidance. "Bureau of Educational and Vocational Guidance Annual Report, 1957-1958." New York City: the Bureau, 1958. p. 47-48.

[16] Glaser, Marian. "Jobs for Teenagers from High Delinquency Areas." (Reprint of article in *American Child* 41:6-11; March 1959.)

[17] National Scholarship Service and Fund for Negro Students. "Community Talent Search: First Year's Report, 1957-8." New York City: the Service, 1958. p. 1.

[18] Fried, Antoinette. "Day Camp for Working Teenagers." *American Child* 41:10-11; May 1959.

[19] Fried, Antoinette. "A Work Camp Program for Potential Delinquents." *Prevention of Juvenile Delinquency: Annals of the American Academy of Political and Social Science*. 322:38-46; March 1959.

[20] Commissioners' Youth Council. "Youth Employment Report—August, 1958." Washington, D. C.: the Council, 1958. p. 1-6 *passim*.

[21] Board of Education of the City of New York, Curriculum Council and the Division of Curriculum Development. "Ways in Which Schools Aid in Juvenile Delinquency Prevention." *Curriculum and Materials* 11:2; November-December 1956.

[22] Board of Education of the City of New York, Association of Assistant Superintendents. *Juvenile Delinquency and the Schools*. Report of the Assistant Superintendents of Schools, 1950-51. New York City: the Association, 1951. p. 21.

[23] The Board of Public Education, Committee on Schools and Instruction. "Report on Discipline in Relation to Juvenile Delinquency." Pittsburgh: the Committee, 1954. p. 17.

[24] Massachusetts Department of Education, Division of Civic Education. "School Practices to Prevent and Control Delinquency." Boston: the Division, 1958. p. 5.

[25] U.S. Department of Health, Education, and Welfare, Social Security Administration, Children's Bureau. *Health Services and Juvenile Delinquency.* A Report on a Conference on the Role of Health Services in Preventing Dissocial Behavior. Washington, D. C.: Superintendent of Documents, Government Printing Office, 1955. p. 17-19.

[26] Board of Education of the City of New York, Demonstration Guidance Project. "Progress Report 1957-1958." New York City: the Project, 1958. p. i.

chapter 5 PROVIDING HELP THROUGH INTEGRATED SPECIAL SERVICES

basic principle: THE SCHOOL DEVELOPS AN INTE-
GRATED SYSTEM OF SPECIAL SERVICES, ADEQUATE-
LY AND PROFESSIONALLY STAFFED, TO HELP THE
NORM VIOLATOR. THESE SERVICES GENERALLY
ARE DESIGNED TO ASSIST THE INDIVIDUAL CLASS-
ROOM TEACHER AS SHE WORKS WITH ANY PUPIL
NEEDING HELP. THE SCHOOL PERIODICALLY AS-
SESSES ITS UNIQUE NEEDS FOR SUCH SERVICES IN
THE PRESENT AND FUTURE, AND IT ADOPTS LONG-
RANGE PLANS FOR MEETING THESE NEEDS.

The classroom teacher should not try to be all things to
all pupils. There will be occasions when the teacher will
need to lean heavily upon special service personnel for aid
and guidance in understanding and helping certain pupils
and certain parents. These youngsters with special problems, of which the incipient or persistent norm violator is a
good example, may often be retained and helped in the regular classroom through the skillful and timely use of auxiliary
services. They may often be helped only by means of the
child-study, diagnostic, and treatment resources which are
available through the special competencies of guidance
workers, psychometrists, school nurses and doctors, psychologists, caseworkers, speech therapists, remedial reading experts, and psychiatrists. There are real limits to what the
average classroom instructor can be expected to do by way of
child study, diagnosis, and treatment. Specialized professional personnel are needed to supplement and re-enforce
his role.

The availability of many of these services will not relieve
the teacher of his classroom responsibility, but judicious use

134

of such services can make his work as a teacher more effective, especially in regard to those youngsters who present incipient or severe learning, emotional, or social difficulties.

The teacher and the principal will need to know how to tap the special services that are accessible to them in the school setting. They will need to be able to comprehend the recommendations of the specialist and to cooperate as teamworkers in carrying out the recommendations which are pertinent to the classroom learning-teaching situations.

Not all systems are aided equally by the variety of special services that could profitably be incorporated into the school operation. However, as the illustrative materials in this chapter bear out, many of the larger school systems, particularly those in the more heavily populated urban centers where the bulk of norm violators is found, have reported many different kinds of teacher aids in a complex network of special services. From time to time, school administrators in systems where coordinated programs of special services exist will need to study existing gaps and to establish a priority of needed facilities and personnel. Such planning should be done with due reference to existing services in other local, county, and state offices.

Obviously, special services demand heavy initial outlay of funds, but in the long run they should insure more valid or scientific approaches in diagnosing the nature of the pupil's difficulties and in pointing out those corrective, remedial, or rehabilitative measures that will relieve the basic problem. Only in this way can the community hope to cut down on what is generally even more costly, a trial-and-error approach toward helping the youngster who may be forced to carry his physical, social, or emotional problems into adult life because of the amateurish or inadequate help that he has chanced to receive. What is most impressive to one who studies the national scene in terms of the array of services that may or may not be available to a youngster is the importance of geographic accident; the area or community in which a youngster lives will often determine whether or not special help will be forthcoming for him.

When a school system is too small in size or population to justify the hiring of certain specialized personnel on a full-time basis, the school should obtain part-time help, or plans should be made to fill such needs on a regional, county, or state basis.

There are many problems arising in the classroom that will extend beyond the competencies of the teacher. When these appear, the system that provides special help and aid to the teacher along the lines set down in the following operational guides will be the one that has a better working chance to help the predelinquent and delinquent youngster.

Guidelines

* The school plans for a program of special services that reflects the particular needs and problems of the community and neighborhood which it serves.

* The school has ready access to, or provides medical services for, physical examinations that supplement routine sight, hearing, and dental check-ups and follows through to see that the necessary medical treatment is carried out.

* The services of the school nurse who has established a helpful and positive image in the youngster's mind are used strategically in dealing with the family of a norm-violating youngster, who often entertains a hostile and negative attitude toward other school helpers.

* The physical education staff may skillfully play a special service role to the lower-class norm-violating youngster who sets store by athletic prowess and feats of toughness; these can be capitalized on in the physical education program and channeled into positive group activity.

* Diagnostic testing and evaluation is provided for all youngsters who have difficulty in the basic skills as well as in subject-matter areas. To support the work of the classroom teacher, remediation services for students with weaknesses in speech, reading, arithmetic, sight, and hear-

ing are made available in the form of help to individuals or small groups.

* An articulated guidance program is provided at both the elementary- and secondary-school level, with intensive service for the potential school drop-out.

* The school maintains a reasonable guidance load for the counselor working with norm violators on an individual or small-group basis. The case load handled by this worker will need to be much lower than the usual counselor-pupil ratio.

* Community and casework service for potential or actual norm-violating students is provided by members of the school staff with a background in social work or by equivalent workers from community agencies.

* The school provides or has access to the diagnostic and therapeutic service of the psychologist and psychiatrist.

* The school provides therapeutic tutoring service in the home for selected cases of emotionally disturbed, physically handicapped, or socially ineffective youngsters who cannot function in the regular school organization.

* All special services should be coordinated with the total school environment and instructional program and should operate on the "team" approach with the teacher and representatives of the various special services cooperating in a coordinated program of sharing information, diagnosis, planning, and treatment.

Practices

The previous chapters have recognized the central position of the teacher in preventing and controlling norm-violating behavior. Few persons would claim, however, that the school's role in the delinquency problem is limited to the classroom or that it lies solely within the teacher's jurisdiction. The present chapter offers examples of what some schools have done in adopting certain commonly accepted special services to help a pupil, especially the norm-violating pupil, within the framework of the school. No attempt will be made here to outline or describe the total functions of a given service; only those factors which are thought to have a direct bearing on norm-violating behavior will be presented.

The special services available in today's school program were not, as a rule, created specifically to combat the delinquency problem. They should, however, be developed to fit the needs of each school's pupil population or neighborhood. If and when such services become available, they will automatically benefit the potential and active norm-violating pupil.

Los Angeles County, California: Inevitably problems arise with reference to the kinds and numbers of specialists to employ in a district program of pupil-personnel services. The answers to these problems must be sought by studying the nature and needs of the district. One district may require the services of several school nurses, while another may need only one. Likewise, a district may need, for example, two school psychologists and one school social worker, while another may need one school psychologist and two school social workers. In any case, the kinds and numbers of specialists employed in the program of pupil-personnel services depend primarily upon the needs of the district. Consequently, study of district needs should precede decisions of such importance. Some clues may be found, however, in the estimates which have been made in informal studies of the proper ratios of specialists to pupils. The studies are in essential agreement, although not all specialists are included in all the studies. Roughly, the ratios suggested for the elementary level are these:

> Director of pupil-personnel services: One for each district
> Psychologist or psychometrist: One for each 2000 pupils
> School social worker: One for each 2000 pupils
> Counselor: One for each 1200 pupils
> Physician: One for each 5000 pupils
> Nurse: One for each 1000 pupils
> Child welfare and attendance worker: One for each 2500 pupils
> Special teachers: Determined by survey of pupil needs.[1]

Although the special health activities represent one of the most generally accepted and best established of the school's special services, they still are confronted with the problem of providing maximum help with limited means. As both of the following statements indicate, the family physician can do much to lighten the burden of the school. A non-school physician in Illinois furnished an interesting comment on what the family doctor may do through parent education to prevent those family situations which give rise to delinquent behavior even before the child is enrolled in school. Likewise, it should be noted, school health officials who see the youngster in preschool, nursery, or kindergarten settings have an opportunity to work with parents in overcoming incipient family problems. The responsibility of the school health service, as a national health conference pointed out, is to follow-up any correctable student health problems known to school personnel; the conference, moreover, proposed expansion and improvement of school health programs for adolescents as an important measure for the prevention and control of delinquency.

URBANA, ILLINOIS: The pediatrician and general practitioner have access to many mothers and children during the pre-school and early school years. In these formative years the subject of mental health and delinquency may be discussed with the mother. Emotional instability in a child and problems of delinquency should be discussed frankly. The physician should have adequate information about community resources to assist the delinquent and his family. Parents should be advised of these available services, and the physician should arrange suitable contacts from among them. As the physician instills basic concepts of proper diet, sleep habits, and good hygiene, he should emphasize the need of the child for love, consistent discipline, and recognition. Such service by the physician requires determination, patience, and dedication to this responsibility.[2]

NATIONAL HEALTH CONFERENCE: The periodic examination given a school child obviously does little good if it is found that a condition noted for correction in one examination has still not been corrected at the time of the next examination. It is not surprising that school physicians who are confined in their work

139

to simply making such examinations often suffer from a sense of futility and frustration. The reason why the child's condition has not been corrected can be one of several, it was pointed out. His family may not have a physician, being unable to afford one. The condition may be one that calls for services and facilities that do not exist in the community and for which the child would have to be taken to another community. Sometimes personal factors complicate the situation. The parents of the child may fail to take any action about their child's condition even though services are available to them. In some cases the child's family physician may disagree with the school physician's diagnosis.

One way in which the burden of the health problem for schools might be lightened, it was suggested, would be to discourage parents from depending so much on the periodic health examinations given under school auspices. In order to use their limited health services more effectively, some school systems are now encouraging parents to have their children examined periodically and treated by the family physician. With the major part of the student body thus taken care of, the school can then arrange for children whose families do not have a physician to be both examined and treated by the school physician, in his private office or through appropriate community agencies. Thus the school is able to do the maximum good with the limited services it is in a position to offer. In communities in which the school physician is limited to screening the children, it becomes his responsibility to work out a plan whereby those whose families do not have a physician can obtain the treatment they need. . . .

Community health services for adolescents are in many places conspicuously lacking. Diagnostic and treatment services are generally needed; convalescent facilities for adolescents are rare. Such health supervision as the adolescent gets is apt to be incidental—an occasional school health examination, for example. Obviously, if health services are to make their maximum contribution to the delinquency control effort, programs addressed to the care of the adolescent must be strengthened, expanded, and improved.[3]

Guidance and counseling services are perhaps the most universally provided special services in today's school. Because they can reach all enrolled pupils, there are many specific ways in which guidance services may be utilized to aid the potentially or actively norm-violating pupil.

First, the guidance program must be ready to aid the youngster as soon as he is identified as a potential or active norm violator. This means extension of guidance services to the elementary schools. The importance of guidance services at this level and the type of services to be offered are discussed in two comments from large metropolitan centers.

NEW YORK CITY: [Guidance services which are commonly provided for most students at the secondary school level are much too late for the delinquent, the potential delinquent, and the otherwise maladjusted young person.] By adolescence, personality and life patterns are fairly well set—so much so, that many psychiatrists hesitate to do psychotherapy with this age group. If fundamental changes are to be made in behavior patterns, efforts must be made earlier. This makes a guidance program essential at the earliest school levels.

In the New York City schools, an elementary school guidance program was started experimentally about 10 years ago. Since there was very little known about guidance services at that level then, the program evolved slowly through experimentation with a great variety of techniques. Emphasis was placed on teacher education in mental hygiene and child development; early identification of children likely to show learning, behavior, and adjustment problems; classroom procedures facilitating learning; parent education; objective, subjective, and projective methods of personality evaluation in young children; individual and group counseling for very young children; and other aspects of a rounded guidance program.

DETROIT, MICHIGAN: The guidance program in the elementary school needs to be educational and personal rather than vocational in nature. Accordingly, every teacher on the staff of a school has a contribution to make to the guidance program. It is proposed that an adequately trained person give direction to a sound guidance and counseling service in each building as needed.[4]

Another responsibility of guidance personnel is to act as the coordinator for the special services needed by the youngster. Such coordination is required whenever a norm-violat-

141

ing youngster's problem is extended beyond the immediate classroom. It may take the form of aiding the family in obtaining help from the community, as in the first example, or, as exemplified in the second report, it may represent aid to the family within the network of the school's resources.

PHILADELPHIA, PENNSYLVANIA: As the counselor works with the pupil and his parents, he does not take over or duplicate the help offered by other school resources. Rather, he coordinates the efforts of all school personnel concerned with the child. Many of these handicapped children and their families can also profit by specialized help from community agencies which offer family, child care, psychiatric, and recreational services In such instances the counselor helps the family make use of the appropriate resources.[5]

HOUSTON, TEXAS: A major function of the Guidance Department is counseling with individual students and their parents. As with visiting teachers, only a small group of those children referred because of emotional and social problems could be considered delinquent or predelinquent. However, they exhibit the kind of antisocial, aggressive tendencies that frequently result in delinquent behavior. . . .

Every effort is made to discover early those students who have emotional and personal problems and to provide intensive counseling service. If the child has been known to the visiting teacher, pertinent information is transmitted to the counselor in order that no break will occur in service. In addition, of course, teachers, principals, parents, community social workers, and others are continually locating adolescents who need such counseling service.

In addition to working with individual children, the counselor serves as a consultant to parents as well as to the school staff and faculty, helping them to become more sensitive to and aware of those behavior patterns which are indicative of insecurity, rejection, immaturity, aggression, and anxiety, and helping them develop techniques of meeting these attitudes successfully. . . .

Individual studies become helpful, not only to the specific child, but also to other members of his family; to other children as his relationships affect them; to adults . . . who also have or work with other children.

The relation of guidance to discipline is admittedly very close. Yet, in what way may guidance personnel proceed so that they may work most effectively in the area of discipline? One school has formulated a very practical answer to the problem.

PONTIAC, MICHIGAN: Good discipline is closely related to the total guidance program. The goals of both are to help students achieve self-direction and to change misbehavior into socially acceptable conduct. When discipline is perceived only as punishment, the way the student feels about his problem is overlooked. Counseling can lead to an understanding on the student's part of his own hard-to-handle feelings and to a more acceptable means of dealing with them.

This similarity of purpose, however, does not mean that the counselor himself should be the disciplinarian. Educators generally agree that he should not be directly responsible for administering disciplinary measures, but should serve as a "consultant" to the disciplinarian. Cases of misbehavior should be referred to him for counseling, and the counselor should interpret the school's discipline policies to the student, helping him to understand and accept the necessity for such policies.[6]

Guidance personnel through their evaluative and testing services may aid in curriculum planning and in establishing procedures that increase the school's effectiveness. The following report tells how a guidance department, acting at the request of a group of elementary teachers, helped formulate a more successful school operation.

LOS ANGELES COUNTY, CALIFORNIA: The teachers' repeated requests for help in evaluation have resulted in closer articulation in one elementary district and the neighboring high school. With the help of guidance and curriculum coordinators from the county superintendent's staff, eighth-grade teachers formulated statements of curriculum objectives. Several techniques for evaluation of children's knowledge and understandings, attitudes and skills were devised and used. Findings were reported and analyzed in a series of meetings with ninth-grade teachers. From these meetings have come suggestions for the records sent to the high school, orientation and visiting days for elementary-school

143

students, and other ways of helping boys and girls make a successful transition to high school.[7]

The guidance counselor playing an adult authority role may use his special training and skill in establishing a therapeutic relationship with the potential or active norm violator within the school structure. A New York study provides one example showing how such intensive guidance changed the expected results for a group of students who were potential delinquents and school drop-outs. The second report, submitted by a member of the National Invitation Conference, tells of another plan to extend the services of a counselor to a selected group of deviant boys from several schools in an attempt to supply a needed adult relationship.

NEW YORK CITY: In an effort to learn whether very intensive guidance services will reduce early school leaving, 1000 students in four high schools showing the well-established characteristics of early school leavers and potential delinquents, were divided into two matched groups. One group was in the normal guidance stream of the school, while the experimental group was assigned to one full-time teacher-counselor to 125 students. Both groups were in the same subject classes.

The experimental group remained in school until graduation at a higher rate than the comparison group, but both groups stayed much longer than similar groups in other schools. This was attributed to the fact that the teacher-counselors worked with the teachers of both groups, thereby bringing about better adjustment for both. The rate of graduation of the experimental group was as good as that of the total school average, whereas formerly it had been very much lower.

Follow-up a year after graduation showed sustained adjustment for the experimental group in higher education, in vocational adjustment, and in personal adjustment.

The second report stated that:

One school system in the northwestern United States may consider using a counselor working with a total of 45 deviant youths from three separate high schools. This counselor would support each youth psychologically and academically. Then face-to-face association and liaison with his teachers and parents, and plan-

144

ning career future to point of finding a job for each at or before graduation. School credit could be earned through satisfactory job performance. Major point: to give youth a good relationship with one adult. Secondary point: to ease teachers' burdens and counselor load in the high schools.

The guidance personnel within the school building may also be expected to render immediate emergency aid. Their accessibility—not just availability—to any youngster has beneficial results. That any disturbed norm-violating youngster needs help at the time of crisis is an implication that cannot be ignored. In the school situation this means that he should have access to the person in the school who is most qualified to provide effective help; in the majority of schools this would be the guidance worker, who is skilled in counseling techniques.

Help to offenders must often be immediate and treatment must proceed by small steps. Merely "holding-the-line" may prevent further antisocial flare-ups and thus keep the patient from being lost to treatment from the start. Indeed, holding-the-line until normal maturational processes supervene would seem to be a valid and realistic goal in working with many adolescent delinquents. By this means, recurring stressful situations could be handled, even though not too much change in personality might be expected at the time. This consideration would suggest a re-evaluation of the types of agency programs intended for delinquents. While there is the need for intensive treatment facilities, with their usually elaborate set-ups and procedures, it is also essential to provide psychotherapeutic "first-aid" with a minimum of formality and a maximum of concrete, on-the-spot service.[8]

A conference of authorities on health, in its comments on "spot" help for parents, reaffirms the importance of the timing of help in crisis situations.

NATIONAL HEALTH CONFERENCE: The parents whose children are in difficulty need help right away. The anxiety engendered at such times is acute. It is often the presence of anxiety that makes it possible for individuals in a crisis situation to use a small amount of help in a most constructive fashion. Recent experience in military psychiatry, for example, has demonstrated

145

that first-aid mental hygiene rendered to a soldier right behind the lines is more effective in restoring him to function than psychiatric assistance rendered long after the acute crisis has passed.[9]

Every school should take appropriate measures to provide a service that makes available time and personnel for working with parents, family, or community agencies as an essential part of its program. This service may be offered on several different professional levels under many different titles, each having its own approach and each reflecting differences in responsibility, authority, training, and techniques of operation. The titles employed by schools across the country vary widely and include attendance officer, attendance counselor, home visitor, home and school visitor, psychiatric social worker, school adjustment counselor, school social worker, social counselor, visiting counselor, visiting social counselor. However, despite the diversity of titles and professional levels all these services share a common technique —casework—and a common function; they provide liaison for school, parent, and community in a three-fold effort to help the individual youngster in trouble. The outline of responsibilities of the school superintendent, principal, and teacher, suggested by the State of Illinois, can be applicable to many of the services that operate under different job titles.

THE STATE OF ILLINOIS: [Establishment of a special counselor* service.]

It is the responsibility of the school superintendent:

    a. to understand the special counselor service and what it offers to help maladjusted children, parents, the school faculty and the community,

    b. to interpret the service to principals of schools,

    c. to select qualified personnel who meet professional standards established by the state.

It is the responsibility of the principal

    a. to understand the work of the special counselor and give

---

* This statement was adapted by substituting the less restrictive job title, "special counselor," for the Illinois title, "visiting counselor."

full support to the service in interpreting it to the faculty and the community,

b. to make the special counselor a member of his faculty. This can be done by having the . . . counselor receive all regular faculty notices, inviting the . . . counselor to faculty meetings and to serve on appropriate faculty committees, having the name appear on faculty lists, etc.

c. to establish with the faculty and special counselor eligibility of pupils and referral and working procedures so they are clearly understood by all,

d. to establish a regular working plan between himself and the special counselor.

It is the responsibility of the teacher

a. to refer to the special counselor children who are having difficulty participating in the group process of the classroom, or are indicating in some other way social and emotional maladjustment in school,

b. to use the special counselor for consultation regarding children about whom the teacher is concerned, but for whom the teacher feels case work service is not currently required.

The success of the efforts of the special counselor to help the child who has social and emotional difficulties to use the school experience is dependent on the cooperation of the superintendent, the principal and the school faculty. This factor of school cooperation must not be underestimated.

The effectiveness of the service depends to some extent upon the sympathetic understanding of the teacher. The teacher's understanding of a child—of the nature of the child's problem in school, of his use of the classroom experience, of his relationships to others in the class—will be of great assistance to the special counselor.

The teacher and the special counselor, as well as all other school personnel, share responsibility for helping parents learn how they can work together with the school for the child.[10]

In the reports submitted to the Project on programs for preventing and controlling norm-violating behavior, it was found that references to the important role of the liaison caseworker recurred with noticeable frequency.

NEW HAVEN, CONNECTICUT: We still have one attendance officer who handles all children who violate the law. This year we have attached a school social worker to this department to handle such cases where rehabilitation is possible without referral to Juvenile Court.

LONG BEACH, CALIFORNIA: Our attendance counselors are far beyond the old "hooky cop" type of personnel. They work on a constructive basis with the parents and with the youngsters in an effort to keep the youngsters in school. There is close cooperation among the attendance counselors, the school counselors, vice-principals, Juvenile Bureau, Probation Department, Court, and California Youth Authority.

MADISON, WISCONSIN: The major function of the visiting teacher is to make home and school calls regarding school attendance. Through a social casework method, emphasis is placed on the discovery and correction of causes that lead to non-attendance and related problems. Visitation is conducted to secure information which may be used to the mutual benefit of the school and parents to encourage better school attendance and better pupil adjustment generally. Cooperation with various social, legal, religious, and police agencies is undertaken in the interest of individual children to aid in a program of prevention and treatment.

HOUSTON, TEXAS: The major function of Visiting Teacher Service is direct casework service to the child and his parents. Although the majority of children referred are not seen as delinquents or even predelinquents, their varying disturbances are the kinds of conditions that could give rise to delinquent behavior.

Visiting Teacher Service has been based in elementary schools. Those associated with this program know that the earlier problems are recognized and treated, the greater the possibility for a good adjustment and less likelihood of more complex problems developing later. Visiting Teacher Service is largely a preventive service. . . .

Visiting teacher, school social worker, school adjustment counselor, psychiatric social worker, each has his own professional skills and techniques, his own personal strengths and weaknesses, but each serves the norm violator in the area of school-family-community interrelationships. The

148

work of the visiting teacher is discussed in the two following items.

THE STATE OF GEORGIA: Visiting teachers are members of the local system staff. They are educated as teachers and have either taught or have been given an orientation period in school policies, curriculum offerings, responsibilities of the different staff members, usual problems of administrators and how handled, etc. However, to warrant additional personnel to lay people and even educators, this additional staff person should have additional knowledge, skills, and techniques to supplement the help a child can receive in the usual classroom and principal's office situation.

DETROIT, MICHIGAN: The need for mental health services for children and adults is becoming increasingly evident.

Detroit has 38 visiting teachers: 26 are assigned to the elementary schools; 9 are assigned to the junior and senior high schools; 3 are assigned to the Special Centers.

At present 1 visiting teacher is assigned to approximately 7,500 elementary school children; 1 visiting teacher is assigned to approximately 8,500 high school students.

Experts say that 1 visiting teacher should be assigned to every 3,500 students. [12]

School social worker is a title frequently used to describe a job category with functions similar to, though not necessarily the same as, those of the visiting teacher.

MADISON, WISCONSIN: The primary function of the school social worker is to assist the individual child to a satisfactory school adjustment by working with the child, the parent, the school, and/or other community agencies. Of great importance is the interpretation of the home to the school and the school to the home, so that mutual respect and understanding may result. Parents may be helped to understand more clearly their children's attitudes, behavior, capacities, and adjustment to school, and to cooperate with the school for the benefit of the child.

The social worker has used group therapy (counseling) as a means of reaching a number of children in grades 5 to 11. Approximately 90 children were seen in groups during the 1955-56 school year. Currently 18 are active in groups of this kind.[13]

The school adjustment counselor program which draws upon state support, provides casework services to the elementary school.

NEWTON, MASSACHUSETTS: The functions of the school adjustment counselor became chiefly these:

1. To work with those cases in which it appeared that a family approach in the long run might be the more promising plan for an effective solution to the child's problems in the school.
2. To work with multi-problem families not already receiving casework services.
3. To serve as resource person for the Newton Judge Baker Guidance Center Unit.

The underlying purpose in this approach might best be expressed by stating these questions which the worker asked herself in regard to all cases:

1. How can this child, this mother, this father, this family, whatever the case might be, develop inner strengths to meet the problems to be faced?
2. What persons and/or agencies within the city of Greater Boston can be utilized to help bring about this development?

As the reader might guess from the above paragraph, the team approach was used in most instances. Persons called in to serve on such a team frequently included well-trained remedial educators to work with an individual or small group, paid either by the family and/or some other authorized source. Volunteer workers with varying degrees of teacher or social work training and experience assisted in individual cases on a regular basis. In some instances the clergy or student training for a clerical post was called in for special services or counseling. Recreational agencies in the city were called upon for the help which they could give—not only their group activities, but in a number of instances, the personal interest which specific workers could take. Three Neighborhood Clubs, under the direction of the Boston Children's Services, were in weekly operation under trained and supervised leadership, with specific goals in mind for particular children. Big Sisters were found for two girls in these families, who will carry on relationships voluntarily for two years on a weekly basis, under the supervision of the Big Sister Association.

150

Three graduate student interns (Boston University and Brandeis) took on specific cases for counseling.[14]

In still other communities and states the liaison casework function is carried by a psychiatric social worker.

MADISON, WISCONSIN: A psychiatric social worker has been placed on a County Child Welfare staff in a very rural county and is functioning as a school social worker. He is serving eight school districts throughout the county, which involves a student population of about 6,000. Early reports are that his service has been readily accepted by the teachers and that his efforts to assist children showing signs of poor adjustment in the classroom have been very successful.

MILWAUKEE, WISCONSIN: The services of the Psychiatric Social worker were utilized in three ways for the school year of 1956-57.

The first area of service was that of psychiatric staffings with . . . the school's part-time Psychiatric Consultant. Cases are referred to the [Psychiatric Consultant] either by the Welfare or Psychological Counselor when their studies indicate emotional disturbance as the basis for the child's difficulty. The Psychiatric Social Worker reviews the Welfare Counselor's social histories prior to the staff meetings, coordinates and attends these meetings and sends a resumé of the staffing to the School Welfare Department, Psychological Services, Special Education and a copy of the recommendations to the schools. In most cases, the Welfare Counselor in the district assumes responsibility for carrying out the recommendations made, but in a limited number of cases the Psychiatric Social Worker was given this responsibility. There were a total of 74 psychiatric staffings this year, including 15 restaffings.

The second area of service was in connection with the Guidance Class at the Wisconsin Avenue School, where casework responsibility has been a major function of the Psychiatric Social Worker. The Psychiatric Social Worker acted as a liaison person between the home and the school, and also between the parents and the therapist treating the child and his family. Twelve applicants were screened for the class and five were accepted for placement in the class. During the year five boys were removed from the class, four of them were transferred to other school placements and one was placed in an institution. There were nine meetings of the Wisconsin Avenue Guidance Class Committee to plan and evaluate the class.

The third area of service was that of exploration of cases referred to the Psychiatric Social Worker either by the Assistant Superintendent of Special Services or the Director of Pupil Personnel. After an exploration, the Psychiatric Social Worker continued to give casework service or the case was referred to the District Welfare Counselor.[15]

One of the discussion groups at the NEA's National Invitational Conference on Juvenile Delinquency expressed a prevalent point of view when it said in summary:

The job of all of us in special services is to have the child in the classroom in the best possible mental and physical condition to undergo a learning experience. Without assistance by all possible facets of community-school-home relationships, we are failing to do an adequate job. The above applies to all pupils and especially for the child with a problem.

Psychological and psychiatric services are the next group of integrated services to be considered here. These services deal with "factors under the skin," and they can provide invaluable help to the teacher who is confronted by a youngster manifesting a suggestion of pathological behavior. Often the outer manifestations of the internal forces disturbing a youngster can represent a real threat to the teacher. Teachers have no difficulty in accepting the youngster "who doesn't know any better," but they are properly worried about the student who "acts crazy." They can and are willing to work with the youngster caught "experimenting with sex" but often hesitate to work with the youngster with "perverted sex tendencies." The boy who is described as "needing a masculine identity" does not represent an overwhelming problem to the teacher, but the boy characterized as "effeminate or psychosexually disturbed" is an entirely different matter. The teacher of norm-violating students may accept a youngster who carries a knife if he uses it only for whittling or if he carries it only as a symbol, but when he uses it to imply a threat or as a weapon, he represents real trouble. In short, the psychologist and the psychiatrist are special resource persons to whom the teacher can turn for help in identifying the degree and type of psychological disturbance involved in the problem of a particular youngster. The initial referral to this service on the part of the teacher should always be for study and diagnosis.

DES MOINES, IOWA: It has been found that teachers and other adults working with children need to know facts that are not readily learned through the regular channels. Therefore, the Des Moines Public Schools employ five school psychologists who work very closely with the schools in dealing with the maladjusted child. Requests for the services of this worker may often come from the visiting teacher but may also be received directly from the school principal or boys' and girls' advisers.

In nearly all cases this referral is made in writing on forms furnished by the Department of Pupil Adjustment. This referral includes a complete description of the child's behavior and problem, what is known about the child's family and home, and a description of the different techniques used by the teacher or other school personnel in an effort to help alleviate the child's problem. Included in this report is also a copy of the child's Standard Test Record card (group achievement tests), his Health Record card, and his previous school records.

The psychologist, with this information as a frame of reference, then works with the individual child using a wide and varied repertory of skills and techniques for the psychological examination. A number of different tests are administered and evaluated by this worker. He is perhaps best known for his work with the standard intelligence tests such as the Stanford Binet, the Wechsler Intelligence Scale for Children, and the Wechsler-Bellevue Intelligence Scale. These tests provide a quantitative measure of the child's intellectual ability which may be expressed in a numerical score or IQ. They also offer an opportunity for the psychologist to observe the child under relatively standard conditions. This observation of the child's behavior is often more important than the numerical score. From the responses the child makes to the test items, the psychologist evaluates success or failure and secures a numerical score, but many responses even when the child fails may give valuable information. The child's behavior and reactions to the whole examining situation are significant. Often such behavior is very suggestive in leading to the discovery of the etiology of the particular problem.[16]

After a youngster has been assigned to a psychologist, the following steps are usually in order:

MADISON, WISCONSIN:

1. Consultation with the principal and teacher to obtain a description of the child's adjustment difficulty
2. Observation of the child in class, an interview with the child, and psychological testing and evaluation
3. An interview with the parents to obtain background information on the child, acquaint them with the findings, evaluate the potential ability of the parents to cooperate in helping the child, and to make recommendations
4. Writing up the results and discussing them with the principal and teacher, with suggestions and recommendations.[17]

A detailed account of the school psychologist's work is furnished by a school system in an Eastern community.

NEWTON, MASSACHUSETTS:

1. Consultation with Parents. Examples: Discussion of psychological factors involved in a pending decision as to whether parents who are separating should have their son go with his mother or with his father. Discussion of issues involved in the question of whether or not a sex-play incident constitutes evidence of a serious psychological disorder in a school boy. This boy was also examined psychologically. Referral of parents to outside agencies for treatment of their own emotional problems interfering with a healthy rearing of their children.
2. Consultation with School Administrators. Examples: Evaluation and discussions relating to the admission, suspension, or expulsion of children to and from the public-school system. Evaluations and discussions in regard to transferring children from one school to another. Discussions of techniques in handling discipline problems. Evaluation for grade placement, promotion, retardation, grade level transfer and special class placement.
3. Consultation with School Counselors. This is a thoroughly symbiotic relationship, with regular monthly meetings, in which there is mutually profitable give and take between

154

Division psychologists and secondary-school counselors. Both groups have significantly different views of the students, due to difference in function and contact, and these sessions prove to be indispensably valuable in maintaining and increasing the effectiveness of our service to the children. In addition to the monthly meetings of the two combined staffs, counselors and psychologists confer a great deal on the handling of individual children, both before and after referral. These counselors also constitute one of our main lines of communication to both parents and school personnel.

4. Consultation with Teachers and Other School System Personnel . . . . Examples: Explanation to teachers why no child can be automatically expected to like his counselor and appreciate his therapeutic experiences. Seeking valuable classroom data from the teacher on a child's reaction to failure. Freeing a teacher to be less emotional with a child by pointing out that the child's reaction to him is not personal but neurotically over-generalized.

5. Cooperation with Professional Groups from Outside the School System. Examples: Conferences with outside experts, individuals, and groups; doing action (in this case, treatment) research with Newton School children; *e.g.,* Judge Baker Guidance Center in regard to School Phobia and Learning Problem studies, Dr. Edward Daniels in regard to his group therapy work at the junior high-school level, Judge Baker Guidance Center-Pilot Program, etc. Administrative, supervisory, and consultative functions in regard to the training of school psychologists from neighboring universities—in this latter work we effect an exchange of a relatively small amount of our time for a much greater amount of service for our school children.

6. Direct Service to the Children. This work takes up the bulk of our time and energies. In the main, it involves therapeutic or counseling work of one kind or another and often includes observation and/or diagnostic testing as a preliminary step. Here we attempt to use our particular training and experience to get at and eliminate—or at least reduce—the key stumbling block, the anxiety, that prevents ordinary learning and correction in regard to both classroom and life experiences. Sometimes a child is seen indi-

vidually from time to time as the need is indicated. Some children are worked with on a regular weekly basis—in individual sessions. Still others are members of therapeutic or counseling groups which meet regularly once each week. . . .

7. Adjunctive Service to Parents. Ideally, almost all parents whose children are being counselled should themselves also enter into psychological treatment. Actually, most parents are not effectively convinced of this necessity. Practically, we are not equipped, in either number of staff or work space, to provide this extensive service. However, a few parents do request this service each year and in those cases where we feel it imperative for the successful treatment of the child and when we can find the time, we do provide this service. This service may be on an individual or group basis.

8. Screening, Referral, Placement Service. Some children present problems we are unable to work with because they fall outside of our sphere of training, facilities, and so on. In these cases we have a responsibility to screen, make the appropriate referral and follow through—so far as we can —to see that the proper placement takes place.

Examples: Assistance in the hospitalization of a child who carried out a suicidal gesture and the placement of the child in a foster home after release from the hospital. Referral to Children's Hospital for neurological examination of a child suspected of having suffered brain damage. Placement in Catholic Boys' Guidance Center of a boy so disturbed as to require in-patient treatment. Referral to the Newton-Wellesley Hospital Out-patient Clinic of a senior in High School who needed protracted, continuous treatment.[18]

The psychiatric services operate in a fashion similar to that of the psychological services, but a different level of professional skill is required. Two brief statements from New England indicate the nature and functioning of their operation.

NEW HAVEN, CONNECTICUT: We now employ a psychiatrist two days per week. He does diagnosis, treatment on short-term cases, and works with teachers, principals, and special personnel for a better understanding of children, both the sick ones and the well ones.

HARTFORD, CONNECTICUT: At present, the department has available four hours of psychiatric service a week through the Institute of Living. Two hours are set aside for evaluations of children actually seen by the psychiatrist. Two hours are available for conference with the psychiatrist to discuss the more serious or puzzling problems. Teachers and principals are particularly welcome to participate in these conferences. The psychiatric service is scheduled and coordinated by the chief social worker, but it is available to all Bureau personnel.[19]

Two excerpts from the annual reports of psychiatric consultants give a very detailed picture of the functions pertaining to this specialist. In the first report the psychiatrist acts as a consultant to the teacher, but he may not directly contact the youngster in question. The second report describes a consultant service in which the psychiatrist does work directly with the youngster, a situation which raises the question of the school's responsibility and its opportunity for therapy.

NEWTON, MASSACHUSETTS: It has seemed best again this year for me to use my time largely as consultant, available to the counselors for help with their cases, in the areas of diagnosis, treatment, and referral. Sometimes it is necessary to only talk over the child and his problem to arrive at a plan, sometimes it is necessary for me to see the child or parent, usually both. The procedure varies with the individual case. The amount of time spent on each case also varies, depending upon the situation, the plans made for handling it, the progress being made, etc.

I. Diagnosis. The counselor brings to me the background material: reasons for referral to the Counseling Center, evidences of maladjustment, complaints of school or family, early life history, reports of home visits or parent interviews and parental attitude, psychological test results, etc. We talk all of this over and try to fit the pieces of the puzzle together. If it seems indicated, I see the child and parents. The counselor and I then discuss the accumulated findings and try to make a diagnosis following which we can make plans for disposition of the case.

II. Treatment. Sometimes treatment involves something as simple as manipulating the environment. More often, it requires changing attitudes and undesirable patterns of behavior which necessitates frequent interviews by the counselor. These interviews may be discussed with me if the counselor feels any need of supervision or help. Some of these cases have to be referred to intown clinics for more intensive treatment than a school Counseling Service is prepared to give. However, we continue, as in past years, to try to give treatment to such cases as need immediate help when it seems as if delay would too greatly increase the chances of exaggeration of the child's problem. Some of these cases are handled by the counselor and some are seen by me. . . .

III. Referral. All cases too disturbed for handling by the Counseling Center or appearing to be in need of long-term therapy have to be referred to private psychiatrists or psychiatric clinics for children. These clinics continue to give us the utmost cooperation insofar as their long waiting lists permit. The work which the Newton Counseling Center has done in preparing the case for referral does facilitate the referral sometimes making earlier acceptance possible.

MILWAUKEE, WISCONSIN: During the school year 1956-57 the psychiatric consultation service continued to function much as it has in the past. There was a slight increase in the number of cases referred for this service, but if one considers the number of children referred to the department of pupil personnel and other special services in whom personality and behavior problems appear to be a major factor, one might question why there has not been a greater increase in the use of the psychiatric consultant. It must be remembered, of course, that the use of psychiatric consultation is sharply limited by the fact that it is a half-time service only.

In almost every instance, the children who were referred for psychiatric consultation represented serious mental, emotional, and social problems. The degree of disturbance present in these children made it highly unlikely that modification of their school programs and environments alone would have any marked therapeutic effect. In some instances, more understanding of the personality structure and dynamics of an individual child helped school personnel understand that child and help him make a more acceptable adjustment within the school. Even with this kind of understanding and adjustment it must be remembered that this child is still a seriously disturbed child who is in need of services beyond those presently offered by the school system. He is in need of individual psychotherapy. Unfortunately such service is frequently not available to him or his family. This is especially true for the child who comes from a family of average or better income which probably makes the family ineligible for care at the Milwaukee County Guidance Clinic, but at the same time they cannot afford private care. Last year, 60% of the referrals for psychiatric consultation came from average or better income homes.

Since the school appears to be more concerned about these disturbed children than anyone else, the question might be raised whether the school should, in the future, offer a clinical or therapeutic service. This is a question that should be examined very critically. These children are problems to the school, but they are not problems of the school. In physical illnesses the school offers nothing beyond first-aid and turns the responsibility for "major surgery" over to the family and the community. The same should probably apply to mental and emotional illnesses.

The psychiatric consultation service could probably be more effective if it were expanded but this expansion must be kept within the confines of school responsibility as compared to home and community responsibility.[21]

Schools may offer their psychological and psychiatric services through the organization of child-guidance or child-study clinics. Three patterns of such school organizations are described herein. The Houston Child Study Clinic serves as the central resource agency for all the schools of the city school system. By contrast, in New York the diagnostic and treatment functions are both carried on by clinics functioning within a regular school as a permanent part of their daily program. The third clinic, the Educational Diagnostic Center of Los Angeles, is itself a school for a small number of students on the basis of short-term placement.

HOUSTON, TEXAS: Another division of the Houston Public Schools which contributes to the prevention of delinquency is the Child Study Clinic. The director of the Clinic is a child psychiatrist who not only works with individual children on a referral basis, but who also serves as consultant in the in-service training of school staff. In addition to the director, the clinic staff includes a psychologist, a social worker, and a group of pediatricians interning in psychiatry.

NEW YORK CITY: The original design for professional personnel of the [child guidance] clinics [within three schools] was as follows:

Elementary School—8 clinicians, including 2 psychiatrists serving on a part-time basis, 2 psychologists, 3 caseworkers, and a casework supervisor. Later a caseworker replaced a psychologist.

Junior High School—10 clinicians, including 2 psychiatrists (part time), 2 psychologists, 3 caseworkers, 1 vocational guidance worker, and one employment placement worker in addition to the casework supervisor. One psychologist and the employment worker were later dropped.

Senior High School—10 clinicians. No changes were made in the original clinical staff set-up consisting of 2 psychiatrists (part-time), 2 psychologists, 3 caseworkers and a casework supervisor, a vocational guidance and an employment placement worker.

The supervisor of a clinic is an important factor in the school-clinic working relationship as is the principal of the school. One of the unique features of these clinics was that social workers were chosen as the key persons in each school, responsible for the intake and for the orientation of the clinic staff to an educational program. This social work orientation is a significant characteristic because most guidance services in educational settings are under the direction of a psychiatrist or a psychologist.[22]

LOS ANGELES, CALIFORNIA: The resulting paramount recommendation called for the establishment, within the school framework, of an institution where a limited number of these atypical pupils could be observed, studied, evaluated and, hopefully, some positive, realistic plan could be developed for their educational future. The spring of 1958 saw such a facility opened in the South Elementary District of Los Angeles, and this pilot project was designated as the Educational Diagnostic Center. Inherently the title defined the function. Serious cases of scholastic maladjustment were here to be analyzed or diagnosed in a "Center" setting rather than a clinical situation inasmuch as its ultimate purpose was to be advisory rather than therapeutic. . . .

160

From its inauguration the enrollment at the Center has been held to a maximum of twelve pupils at a given time, six to each classroom. Furthermore, efforts have been directed to limiting the period of attendance to twenty school days. Considerable attention was also given to maintaining some semblance of chronological homogeneity as well as avoiding the bringing together of children exhibiting too radically different patterns of behavior.

The success of such a venture as the Educational Diagnostic Center obviously would be dependent upon its active, professional personnel here assigned. Efforts were made to recruit a staff from various fields and disciplines in the belief that it would be possible in such a group to foster an eclectic approach that would not only make valuable contributions to the scholastic scene but also bring a measure of assistance to unhappy children.

The Center was staffed with an administrator, two master teachers, a Child Welfare supervisor, and a secretary, as full time members. In addition, a school doctor, school counselor and school nurse were on fractional assignments. After the children had been enrolled in the Center for some four weeks and individual case studies completed, these staff members were joined by the district superintendent's administrative assistant, the assistant medical director, the guidance supervisor, and a psychiatric social worker to function as a Case Conference Committee to formulate and adopt specific recommendations on behalf of the individual child.[23]

A caution must be observed when youngsters are isolated or referred for special service by a psychologist or psychiatrist; the need for caution has been spelled out in the Report of the Subcommittee on Juvenile Delinquency of the Senate Committee on the Judiciary.

Boys and girls who participate in an individualized treatment program with a school psychologist are often subjected to severe pressures and criticism from their colleagues. Any boy who leaves his group for an extended period of time with regularity to work with a psychologist is regarded as a possible "ratter" or "nut" by his school associates. The mores and cultural patterns of the correctional school population are regulated frequently by the boys, and their view of life is transferred to the

161

institution from the city streets. They are suspicious of anyone who has sustained an intimate contact individually with the school administration. Therefore, using the standard techniques of individualized treatment, which isolate youngsters from their cottage group with regularity for psychological consultation, is often more damaging than helpful to the boys involved.[24]

All special services should be coordinated and tied in with the instructional program. Personnel representing these services should operate as a "team" in an effort to share information in a systematic child study and treatment process.

STRATFORD, CONNECTICUT: We hold regular monthly meetings at which time we discuss our problem cases. All of the information is considered as strictly confidential, and we do not receive any type of publicity. . . . It is a team approach—we feel very strongly that we need each other's support in order to help these problem children. The group feels no one of us can work in a vacuum, but each needs to share information with the others.

Some idea of the number of people and the complexity of services that are necessary to a team approach is provided for a school system of 8500 students and for one of 228,000 students. Obviously, coordination in either small or large communities will not be possible without careful planning and supervision.

GREENWICH, CONNECTICUT: Division of Research and Guidance serves children at all grade levels and in all the public schools. . . . Some idea of the extent and nature of the service may be gained from a description of its staff. Approximately 8,500 students are served by the following professional staff:

1 director	4 secondary guidance counselors
6 school social workers	4 remedial teachers
2 psychologists . . .	3 special teachers for physically
3 speech therapists	and mentally handicapped.

PHILADELPHIA, PENNSYLVANIA: [Attendance officers, counselors, doctors, nurses, psychologists, psychiatrists, remedial and adjustment teachers are some of the personnel involved]. . . . Special classes have been established for the physically as well as the mentally handicapped children. By way of example, in the Philadelphia school system there are 115 attendance officers,

290 full-time counselors, 19 psychologists, and 2 psychiatric consultants on a part-time basis. These special services make it possible for the schools [to cope with the problem more effectively].[25]

Summary of Special Education, Philadelphia Public Schools

	No. of Teachers
Classes for Educable Mentally Retarded	423
Classes for Trainable Mentally Retarded	24
Classes for Socially and Emotionally Malajusted	36
Shallcross Residential School for Truant Boys	5
Orthopedic Classes	26
Classes for Hard-of-Hearing and Deaf	23
Classes for Visually Handicapped and Blind	16
Hospital Classes	13
Home School	27
Speech Correction	41

The teacher does not stand alone in planning and carrying out a satisfactory educational program. He has many consultants to whom he may turn for help. In some areas—orthopedic, hard-of-hearing, visually handicapped, disciplinary classes, residential school—an advisory committee is set up to review each case that is referred. The purpose of these committees is to insure the best possible placement of each pupil. Medical and educational records are available to the committees and such information is transferred with the child to the new school.

For all children who enter classes for the mentally retarded and for many who go into the other special classes, psychological examinations are given by public school psychologists. A thorough battery of tests is administered. The report which is made available to the receiving school includes, among other things, such help for the classroom teacher as information about present levels of achievement in basic school subjects, assets which the particular child possesses, and any emotional factors which need to be considered. Careful study and interpretation of the psychological reports gives the teacher much help in planning the curriculum.[26]

This conviction as to the powerful role of our schools has been sharpened by our experience in the Philadelphia School System with the Case Review Committee which was organized in 1949 by the superintendent of schools to consider cases of potentially dangerous children. The organization of the Committee was prompted by the murder of a fourteen-year-old boy by a boy of sixteen. The unusual circumstances panicked the entire city. The boys had met in a movie for the first time in their lives, and the older one invited the younger one to his home on the pretext of showing him his chemistry set. . . . The repercussions on the city prompted simultaneous meetings. The police, the courts, the Department of Welfare, and our schools were deluged with requests for pre-emptory action. In establishing the Committee, . . . [the] superintendent of schools at the time indicated that he wanted more than a case conference; that he felt it was important to have top echelon persons involved. As a consequence, the Committee was made up of the directors of the Division of Medical Services, of Pupil Personnel and Counseling, of Special Education, and a district superintendent, with the superintendent of the Philadelphia School System serving as its Chairman. School principals concerned about children who were potentially dangerous to themselves or to others were invited to submit summaries including classroom, counseling, medical, and psychological information. Since 1949, 758 cases have been considered and each has been followed for months or for years until some kind of appropriate solution was achieved. . . .

Our schools are vested with both a direct and a derived authority which should be used more fully and more constructively. By way of illustration, we are now using suspension from school more purposefully and responsibly as a means of alerting and involving parents when a child is defiant of school regulations. We are also using our derived authority in that we are filing petitions with the Juvenile and Magistrate's Courts asking for probation or placement of children who do not respond to our services and requesting fines be imposed on parents who neglect to see that their children get to school. Parents are invited to district office interviews, and a preliminary notice is sent in advance of prosecution in court. Since we established this procedure three years ago, our attendance rate has been sustained at the unprecedented high point of 91 per cent.

If we are to prevent "hard-core cases," not only must we

identify the problems early, but we must also follow through with appropriate action to the point of commitment to an institution, if this be the answer. Schools have been much too patient with children with chronic patterns of mal-adaptive behavior with the result that the learning pace of the so-called normal child has been jeopardized and children with distinctly delinquent patterns have been permitted to continue unabated. All too many troubled and delinquent children are in our schools by default. Although their disturbed, hostile, and violent behavior cries out for specialized residential care, our facilities have not kept pace with the need. We cannot afford to have our schools become a dumping ground for disturbed children for whom our Juvenile Courts cannot find appropriate facilities. The attitudes of those youth who are not held accountable for repeated and flagrant violation of probation are contagious and affect adversely the morale of all children. We must at one and the same time strengthen and expand our school services while we establish more definitive and firm limits as to what we shall tolerate as acceptable behavior. Otherwise, we cannot fulfill our primary function of education. . . .

Our schools can be even more effective when we are ready to provide sufficient money and personnel. For example, experiments with the school-work program to prevent premature drop-outs and small classes for emotionally disturbed children and slow learners hold great promise. We should look ahead to providing trade training for the youth who will become the semi- or unskilled worker; sheltered workshops for the handicapped; residential camps for youth who cannot profit by further academic education but who cannot find jobs; . . . more intensive testing, occupational and vocational guidance; and education for family living.[27]

The core of team cooperation is to be found by the case conference where professional workers from every discipline meet to focus their attention on a single youngster. The following excerpt shows how the case conference works as a planning authority in a procedure for dealing with norm violators.

NEW BRITAIN, CONNECTICUT: A committee . . . was appointed to make a study and recommend uniformity of a procedure in dealing with children exhibiting atypical conduct.

In approaching the problem, the Committee states:

1. Atypical conduct has been a concern to educators since the inception of public education. Problems of this type must be handled every school year.
2. Many methods have been tried to bring about solutions to the type of problem—from severe corporal punishment to modern methods of handling such cases.
3. Heretofore, school principals, with the assistance of their staff members, have handled the majority of such problems with a measure of success in many instances. However,
4. Modern education has broadened to such an extent that a number of specialized fields are now considered an integral part of the total function of education. Among these fields are psychology, psychiatry, guidance, social work, remedial reading, speech and hearing, health, and physical education.
5. Hence, quite frequently, the principals must seek assistance from these resources to resolve some of the more serious problems facing them.

The following plan of action was proposed and is hereby endorsed as regular procedure:

1. A problem falling within the definition of *serious atypical conduct** stated below comes to the attention of a classroom teacher. The teacher, with the assistance from available resources within [himself] and in the schoolroom, handles the problem to the best of his ability. In many cases the teacher is able to handle the problem satisfactorily. Or,
2. The problem is of such a serious nature that the teacher is unable to cope with it and refers the problem to the principal.
3. The problem is identified by the principal. The principal, working with the teacher, other staff members, and parent contacts when advisable, studies the problem carefully, and some possible solutions are proposed and

---

* The Committee considers serious atypical conduct as marked deviation from the desirable and expected conduct of children—the slow, the quiet, the emotionally disturbed, etc. Causes for this type of behavior usually stem from four sources: intellectual, health, emotional, or social, either singly or in combination.

implemented. Considerable success has been attained through this process. In other cases, the principal feels the need of assistance from other school sources, such as the Attendance Department, the Department of Research and Testing, the Guidance Department, or other departments.

4. The principal then confers with a representative of one of the departments mentioned above—the nature of the problem at hand will determine which one—and together they discuss the problem and plan the next step. Jointly, they may (a) bring about a solution to the problem, or (b) decide that a case reference is in order, and one is called by the school principal.

5. The case conference study groups should comprise:
   a. The school principal
   b. The teacher or teachers involved
   c. The directors of the Attendance, Research, and Guidance Departments
   d. Other administrative staff members when necessary
   e. When advisable, a representative of an appropriate state or community resource (previous joint determination)

6. Based upon the deliberations and findings, the case conference study group may: (a) make some recommendations to continue working with the case—this might include referrals to such agencies as the Child Guidance Clinic, the Diocesan Bureau, the Family Service Bureau, and/or others; and (b) in the event that the combined efforts of this group fall short, the case, with the stated recommendations, may then be referred by the principal to the superintendent of schools for further action.[28]

In a larger school system it is often necessary to hold case conferences, not as problems arise, but on the basis of regularly scheduled and frequent meetings.

SAINT PAUL, MINNESOTA: It is generally agreed that while circumstances and conditions may alter this plan, most effective results are obtained when:

Meetings are held regularly, once a week, at a definitely specified time, in a room permitting privacy and uninterrupted conference

The assistant principal serves as chairman

Accurate records of the proceedings are kept by a secretary selected by the group and serving regularly

Preplanning has been done

There has been a limited screening of the apparently minor cases by a designated member of the committee (Because such minor cases may later develop into major problems, records of screened cases should be kept.)

An agenda has been prepared and distributed to committee members prior to the meeting

All available, pertinent data have been assembled previous to meeting time. Such available data may consist of Form 40, health file, counselor's records, attendance cards, teachers' evaluations

The teaching staff has been informed of the cases to be considered

Meetings are open to teachers interested in a particular case

Minutes of previous meetings are reviewed, follow-up reports made, and new cases brought up for discussion, and disposition

All members of the committee as well as all staff members have been impressed with the need for confidential treatment of information discussed at these meetings

Provision has been made for informing faculty members concerned regarding proceedings of the meetings. [29]

After the committee has conferred with the pupil and has thoroughly studied all of the available information, a plan must be formulated whereby, it is hoped, the pupil may be rehabilitated. To help the committee avoid the common tendency to rely on a few ordinary adjustment techniques, the following suggestions are offered:

A. Adjustment of the pupil's school program
B. Grade placement of over-age pupil
C. Transfer to a different school (request for transfer to be made to Inter-School Advisory Committee on Pupil Problems)
D. Correction of physical deficiencies or treatment of illness
E. Improvement of economic status through employment of financial assistance
F. Placement in a foster home
G. Placement on probation, on a "big brother" basis, under one of the following:

1. A teacher with whom the pupil has good rapport
2. Student council member
3. Another pupil
4. Juvenile Division of the Police (informal basis)
5. Juvenile Probation Office (informal basis)
6. One of the committee's members. . .
H. Submission of weekly or biweekly reports to a person under whose probation the pupil has been placed
I. Referral to Inter-School Advisory Committee on Pupil Problems.[30]

The provision of adequate help to the normviolating youngster is always dependent on the nature of the youngster's contact with the teacher or with the special service personnel. But it must also be kept in mind that the channeling of help and the study and planning which precede the actual work with the youngster also depend upon the quality of the relationships existing among members of the regular and special school staffs.

FARMINGDALE, NEW YORK: Staff relationships influence teacher behavior. What and how teachers feel about existing programs and personnel affects the acceptance and utilization of special services.

NATIONAL HEALTH CONFERENCE: Essential for the team effort is a mutual understanding among the various professions. For example, health workers who have occasion to work with schools must understand the school as a social institution. The worker who gives consultation to a school must be aware of such small details as the close schedule on which schools run and the importance of being prompt for appointments. There should also be an awareness of the pressures under which a school operates, of the fact that everybody wants to tell the teachers what to do and how to do it. Some individuals go into schools with a chip on their shoulders because they have not examined their own attitudes toward authority and at one time in their lives schools represented authority. Self-knowledge and knowledge of the other person and the setting in which he works is necessary for good team work.

Capacity for joint effort cannot come suddenly when professional responsibilities which require it are assumed. Experience in joint effort is needed and should be provided as part of professional education. To give social workers, health personnel, and educators the common core of knowledge they require, the walls between graduate schools should be broken down so young people in training for these professions can learn to work together by learning together. The various forms of apprenticeship used in training for these different professions should include planned team experiences.[31]

An appropriate conclusion to this chapter is provided by the State of Illinois, where a state enabling law has been most effective in stimulating the development of a wide range of integrated school services.

THE STATE OF ILLINOIS: In 1945 [the most recent amendment to the special education law of Illinois enabled] . . . school districts to provide special facilities for socially maladjusted and emotionally disturbed children and to receive state reimbursement on the costs where approved programs were conducted. At present such districts are reimbursed $3000 for each qualified professional worker.

Under this legislation there are presently several patterns of programs being carried on.

1. The custodial programs in Chicago for delinquent, truant and incorrigible children at present enrolling approximately 2400 children. This is largely a custodial and corrective program.

2. School social workers are employed in 95 public school districts, and 173 professionally trained persons work with an annual load of 7100 children with serious problems. This is primarily a preventive program with a big majority of the children referred being identified in the early stages of maladjustment. Less than 20% have reached the more serious stages of maladjustment.

3. A few classes have been organized in Illinois for children with perceptual problems, or other symptoms of an organic nature.

4. Experimentation is being carried on for emotionally disturbed children in a few instances with home instruction programs, and with private tutoring, where the problem seems to justify these kinds of approaches. Generally these children cannot yet tolerate a group situation.

170

5. Encouragement is given to the use of school and clinical psychologists in studying, diagnosing and counseling with these children and their parents and teachers, so that there is a better understanding of the problem and a resultant better handling of these children in their classes. This is limited to those school districts employing qualified psychologists.
6. Schools are encouraged to refer children to local mental health clinics when possible, and to encourage parents seeking the help of medical, child and family services available. Many cases annually are referred to the Institute for Juvenile Research and its traveling clinics.
7. Recent legislation providing for special facilities for multi-handicapped children is opening the way for study of and implementation of services to many handicapped children where one of the handicaps may be social maladjustment or emotional disturbance.

References

[1] Office of the Los Angeles County Superintendent of Schools, Division of Research and Guidance. "Preliminary Materials: Guidance Handbook for Elementary Schools." Los Angeles: the Division, 1956. p. 15.

[2] Gillespie, James B. "Juvenile Delinquency: The Physician's Responsibility and Role in Prevention." (Reprint of article in *Illinois Medical Journal* 114, September 1958.)

[3] U.S. Department of Health, Education, and Welfare, Social Security Administration, Children's Bureau. *Health Services and Juvenile Delinquency.* A Report on a Conference on the Role of Health Services in Preventing Dissocial Behavior. Washington, D. C.: Superintendent of Documents, Government Printing Office, 1955. p. 10, 12.

[4] The Board of Education of the City of Detroit, Citizens Advisory Committee on School Needs. *Findings and Recommendations of the Citizens Advisory Committee on School Needs.* Detroit: the Board, 1958. p. 20.

[5] School District of Philadelphia, Division of Special Education. *The Education of the Child with a Handicap.* Philadelphia: the School District, 1958. p. 9.

[6] Pontiac Public Schools, Pupil Personnel Services. "The Counselor's Role in Discipline." Pontiac, Michigan: the Services, 1959.

[7] Office of the Los Angeles County Superintendent of Schools, *op. cit.*, p. 7, 8.

[8] Chwast, Jacob. "Realistic Goal-Setting in Treating Delinquents." *The Apto Journal* (The Journal of the Association for Psychiatric Treatment of Offenders) 2:1; September 1958.

[9] U.S. Department of Health, Education, and Welfare, *op. cit.*, p. 23.

[10] The Superintendent of Public Instruction, State of Illinois. *The Illinois Plan for Special Education of Exceptional Children: The Maladjusted.* Circular Series "F," No. 12. Springfield: the Superintendent (n.d.). p. 12.

[11] Madison Public Schools, Department of Child Study and Service. "Guidance in the Madison Public Schools." Madison, Wisconsin: the Department, 1957. p. 2.

[12] The Board of Education of the City of Detroit, Citizens Advisory Committee on School Needs, *op. cit.*, p. 33.

[13] Madison Public Schools, Department of Child Study and Service, *op. cit.*, p. 4.

[14] Newton Public Schools, Division of Counseling Services. *Meeting Special Needs of Individual Pupils.* Annual Report, Division of Counseling Services, 1957-1958. West Newton, Massachusetts: the Division, 1958. p. 51.

[15] Milwaukee Public Schools, Department of Pupil Personnel. *Annual Report of the Department of Pupil Personnel Milwaukee Public Schools.* Milwaukee: the Department, 1957. **p. 34.**

[16] Des Moines Public Schools, Central Committee on Special Education. "Report from the Committee on the Socially Maladjusted." Des Moines: the Committee, 1957. p. 8.

[17] Madison Public Schools, Department of Child Study and Service, *op. cit.*, p. 5.

[18] Newton Public Schools, Division of Counseling Services, *op. cit.*, p. 44-46.

[19] Hartford Public Schools, Bureau of Guidance and Pupil Adjustment. "Handbook of the Bureau of Guidance and Pupil Adjustment." Hartford: the Bureau, 1957. p. 20.

[20] Newton Public Schools, Division of Counseling Services, *op. cit.*, p. 39-40.

[21] Milwaukee Public Schools, Department of Pupil Personnel, *op. cit.*, p. 36.

[22] New York City Youth Board and the Division of Child Welfare of the Board of Education. *Tri School Study of Three Child Guidance Clinics.* New York City: the Board, p. 13.

[23] Los Angeles City Board of Education, Child Welfare and Attendance Branch. "An Exploration of Emotionally Disturbed Children in Los Angeles." Los Angeles: the Branch, 1959. p. 1-2.

[24] U.S. 86th Congress, 1st Session, Senate Committee on the Judiciary, Subcommittee on Juvenile Delinquency. *Juvenile Delinquency.* Report of the Committee on the Judiciary, United States Senate, Made by Its Subcommittee on Juvenile Delinquency. Washington, D. C.: Superintendent of Documents, Government Printing Office, 1959. p. 33-34.

[25] Taber, Robert C. "A Positive School Program for Unreached Youth." A paper presented at the 85th Annual Forum of the National Conference on Social Welfare at Chicago, May 13, 1958. p. 1.

[26] School District of Philadelphia, Division of Special Education, *op. cit.*, 8-9, 39.

[27] Taber, Robert C., *op. cit.*, p. 2-4.

[28] New Britain Public Schools, Office of the Superintendent. "Regulations: Pupil Conduct." New Britain, Connecticut: the Superintendent, 1958. p. 1-2.

[29] Saint Paul Public Schools, Office of Secondary and Vocational Education. "Intra-School Pupil Problems Advisory Committee, a Handbook of Suggested Practices." Saint Paul: the Office, 1957. p. 2-3.

[30] Saint Paul Secondary Schools, Inter-School Advisory Committee on Pupil Problems. "Suggestion for the Creation and Operation of Intra-School Pupil-Problem Advisory Committees." Saint Paul: the Committee, 1952. p. 3.

[31] U.S. Department of Health, Education, and Welfare, *op. cit.*, p. 33-34.

6 PROVIDING HELP THROUGH SPECIAL CLASSES

basic principle: FOR THE EXTREMELY DISTURBED
OR DISTURBING YOUNGSTER THE SCHOOL PROVIDES
SPECIAL FACILITIES WITH SPECIAL PERSONNEL IN
WHICH REMEDIAL AND REHABILITATIVE SERVICES
ARE AVAILABLE. THE SPECIAL CLASS OR CENTER
SHOULD BE CONCEIVED AS OR ALLOWED TO BECOME
A CUSTODIAL OR A HOSPITAL FACILITY.

In discussing the need to provide an adequate and worthwhile curriculum for all children (Chapter 4), reference was
made to the urgency for recognizing the nature and extent
of individual differences in program planning in the regular
classroom. It is generally acknowledged today that there
is in every population a small number of children who suffer
from extreme mental retardation, physical disability, or sense
impairment as well as those who are highly gifted and that
some special provisions must be made outside the regular
classroom for these youngsters. The same is true of a very
small number of youngsters who show extreme social and/or
emotional problems. The actual number of such existing
cases in smaller communities may be such as to make the
establishment of a special class difficult or economically un-
sound because of the small number of students requiring
this help. For these extreme cases some other procedure
must be worked out involving either part-time attendance
in regular classes or therapeutic tutoring in the youngster's
home.

A very small fraction of norm-violating youngsters, with
or without pathology, cannot be successfully instructed or
helped within the limits of the regular classroom. These
youngsters require special facilities, both for their own benefit

and for the welfare of the majority of students. Such facilities should include special classrooms in the schools as well as special study and treatment centers in the community or in the county for the most severely emotionally disturbed.

A special facility means specially trained teachers, special materials and methods, and smaller classes. Merely to remove a difficult pupil from one classroom and place him in a smaller group with other difficult cases will not do much to improve the youngster's situation. When special facilities are established, care should be taken to set down their specific goals and purposes, to think out guiding principles and procedures for referral and admission, to delineate the special materials and methods, and to draw up techniques for appraisal and evaluation. Without careful planning and organization any special facility can deteriorate into a special dumping ground.

Only a few of the largest urban school systems provide a system of special classes or centers for delinquents. Many persons responsible for the establishment and operation of these special schools and classes have indicated the experimental nature of their programs, and they have stressed the need for careful appraisal of the total effect these centers and classes have not only on the youngsters they serve, but also on those whom they were meant to protect. At the same time there is consensus among school people that those youngsters who have been diagnosed as seriously emotionally disturbed by medical authority—and this includes a very small fraction, perhaps less than 1 percent of the school population—should be placed in a special hospital center with adequately staffed medical and nursing personnel.

Guidelines

* The school administrator is guided by medical opinion (preferably psychiatric) in determining which youngsters cannot be contained within the school without danger to themselves or others. In arriving at this clinical judgment, the medical authorities utilize the observations and thinking of other school personnel, including the teacher.

∗ Students are assigned to the special programs within the school after careful study culminating in a case conference of school administrator, psychologist, counselor, nurse, doctor, and classroom teacher.

∗ In establishing special centers in the school for the most difficult pupils, it is necessary to plan different and separate programs and services for those youngsters who are emotionally disturbed and for those pupils who represent the "socially maladjusted" (culturally determined norm violators) but not emotionally disturbed.

∗ The number of students in each special classroom is kept to a minimum so that it is possible for the teacher to develop an effective interpersonal relationship with each student. In certain special programs this may mean classes of six to eight students, or in other situations the number in attendance may be as high as 13 to 16 students.

∗ To avoid a negative stereotype of the student in the special class or school, the administrator and staff conduct a continuous program of education that interprets the functions and objectives of the special center to regular school staff, parents, and citizens.

∗ A therapeutic environment and a special curriculum are provided to aid in redirecting and rehabilitating disturbed and disturbing norm violators. The ultimate goal is the earliest possible return of the youngster to the regular classroom rather than permanent removal from the regular classroom.

∗ The basis of the teacher's educative and rehabilitative efforts with pupils in the special class is the individual child study and inventory, with data furnished by other school and community workers and by the teacher's own observations and inquiry.

* The teacher searches the background material and the personal value systems of his students for clues in making the academic and social instruction more meaningful to them.

* The special classroom teacher judiciously experiments with instructional techniques, adapting them to changes in group structure and to the changing emotional, psychological, and physical needs of his students.

* The teacher understands that he often plays the role of the male identification figure for many of the boys in these special classes and patterns his behavior accordingly.

* The special teacher handles social and emotional outbursts objectively. Regarding a student's behavior from a causative point of view, he does not take such behavior personally; he neither overidentifies with nor rejects the youngster but attempts to maintain a consistent relationship, despite the testing and abuse he may receive.

* The special class teacher maintains close contact with the youngster's parents and with agencies that are working to help his family.

* Results of recent research on emotionally and socially maladjusted youngsters are made available to the teacher in the special center or class, who, as a consumer of research, acts to implement the findings of valid research efforts.

* In selecting and upgrading teachers for special classes, the administrator considers personal make-up, education, and experience as well as the social-cultural background of the teacher.

* The administrator makes adaptation in the school system's standardized procedures and routines that will aid the achievement of the special goals of the special center.

* Due to the special needs of these students, a larger than average allotment of the time of the integrated service personnel is made available to these classes or schools.

Practices

The development of special schools and classes are of necessity determined by the number of students requiring such centers or able to benefit from them. Naturally, the reports concerning these facilities most frequently come from large school systems. Detroit's school system provided a detailed report which includes the criteria for locating and staffing such special centers.

DETROIT, MICHIGAN: In planning education programs and services for pupils with norm-violating behavior, the first problem to be solved is that of the severity of the behavior. In many instances, the child with the milder problems may be retained in the regular grade structure with assistance from such ancillary services as are available.

If the child's deviant behavior is remediated or remains within acceptable limits (particularly if the behavior does not unduly upset the classroom activities or contaminate the other pupils), the rule-violating youngsters may be retained in the regular classroom.

If, however, the child's behavior is grossly deviant and deep-seated, special education provisions, outside . . . the regular classroom, should be provided. In many communities school authorities have shrugged off their responsibilities for many of these youth by suspending them from school. Most of these youth sooner or later come to the attention of juvenile authorities and are placed in state or county correctional institutions where an attempt is made to provide them with educational opportunities. In many instances, however, these institutions are crowded with long waiting lists so that the value of the education program may be limited.

It appears that increasing numbers of communities are expecting the school agency to serve many of these norm-violating youth. School authorities are beginning to study how best to meet this vexing problem. Following are some ideas that have grown out of one community's attempt to provide suitable educational programs for these youth.

The behavior of the more serious norm violators is so bizarre and nonconforming that they cannot be retained in the regular classrooms. The organization of special classes and special

178

schools apears to be one kind of solution. Although this scheme has certain inherent weaknesses, the values generally overweigh the shortcomings.

Several criteria for the establishment of these classes and schools should be followed: 1. Classes or schools should be located so that the pupils do not need to travel too far from home. 2. Good public transportation should be available or chartered transportation provided. 3. The school principal should be understanding and able to give able direction to the program. 4. The class size should be limited to no more than 15 pupils to a teacher. 5. The physical properties of the classroom should be good. The size of the classroom should be adequate to meet the requirements of the program. Suitable light and ventilation are essential. 6. Well-qualified teachers should be selected.

Undoubtedly, the most important element in the total program is the classroom teacher. Teachers for these children must be carefully selected. Only those who have the proper personality, qualifications, and training should be placed in these classrooms.

[The following factors are considered in the selection and assignment of teachers to special classes in the Detroit schools:]

Education: 1. Must be a fully certified teacher. 2. In general the following courses must be completed: Survey on Education of Exceptional Children, Problems and Methods in Teaching Slow-Learning Children, Problems and Methods in Teaching Behavior-Problem Boys, Practice Teaching with Behavior-Problem Children, Mental Hygiene, Group Dynamics, Abnormal Psychology, Tests and Measurements.

Personality Factors: 1. Must be a well-adjusted person. 2. Must have a sense of humor. 3. Must have complete sympathy and understanding for the child with emotional and social problems. 4. Must have a great amount of tolerance for antisocial activity, particularly when it is directed against authority.

Sum of Academic and Social Experiences: 1. Must have a thorough understanding of grouping for academic instruction. 2. Must have a familiarity with the importance of group dynamics and interrelationships within the classroom group. 3. Must have a full appreciation of the importance of providing success experiences to aid developmental growth. 4. Should be acquainted with all social agencies in the community which can help toward adjustment. 5. Should steer child to healthy leisure-time activities after school hours. 6. Should have the ability to secure the

179

cooperation of parents. 7. Should work toward the acceptance of the ungraded class children by the regular grades staff in the building. 8. Will constantly work toward the objective of sufficient adjustment to permit placement in regular grades or non-behavior problem special classes. 9. Should be aware of the importance of classroom atmosphere as created by decorations, pets, plants, children's own handwork, etc. 10. Should be familiar with each pupil's adjustment with an individual plan for his progress. 11. Must be able to interpret and use the findings of intelligence and personality tests. Must be able to administer standardized achievement tests used in special classes. 12. Must realize the necessity for flexibility of program or schedule to permit individual adjustment as situations arise.[1]

Next to the importance of the teacher is the curriculum which is employed in the educational program for these pupils. In many instances, these youth have little regard for the traditional curriculum. The educational goals that have particular worth to middle-class pupils are frequently lightly regarded by the norm-violating group. Textbooks written around middle-class ideals and with illustrations of conforming children are so antagonistic to the concepts of the nonconforming youth that they reject them as tools of instruction. For these reasons, the teacher is required to develop the instruction around the needs of the group and with materials which have been specially constructed or adapted.

The frequently held idea that these youth are interested only in school subjects of a strictly vocational nature is false. Many of these youngsters are academically retarded and inwardly resent their inability to perform adequately in the areas of reading and arithmetic. Remedial instruction in these fields, when properly conducted, is generally recognized as worthy by these youth.

In addition, they should be provided with instruction in spelling and writing, social studies, science, art, music, health and physical education, dramatics, and vocational subjects.

In the early stages of the Detroit program classes were located in undesirable basement rooms in an obscure part of an elementary school. The teachers were in reality not teachers but retired policemen who were noted for their strength as disciplinarians. This program gradually evolved into one where the delinquents

180

were placed in one building. Here, too, the emphasis was on restraining measures and enforced attendance. Gradually through the years as we learned more and more about motivating factors involving antisocial behavior, we began to modify our programs within the light of this knowledge. Even today we are constantly cognizant of the need for continued study of human behavior as this *sine qua non* for establishing an environment designed to meet the greatest number of needs for the greatest number of delinquents.

Today the program in Detroit is organized in an attempt to meet this somewhat idealistic aim. Four schools of observation for boys 12 years of age and older are located in the wings of modern elementary schools. There is a staff specially trained in handling behavior-problem boys. It consists of a principal, a teacher for each 15 pupils, a psychologist or a psychiatrist, and a full-time visiting teacher. The enrollment in these four schools at present is 504.

The maximum capacity is 600. To further augment this program, our department maintains 19 junior ungraded classes for boys between 7 and 12 years of age. These serve several schools within their circumscribed area. These classes are served by the visiting teacher in the particular elementary schools in which they are placed. The number of boys served in these junior ungraded classes usually averages about 285. We try not to place more than 15 in one particular situation and never more than 17. We have a definite, carefully designed plan for selecting boys who will enter these classes. To initiate the transfer of a boy from the regular grades, the principal concerned requests that a detailed study and evaluation be done by the Detroit Board of Education Psychological Clinic. Then upon their recommendation, the boy can be admitted to an ungraded class. If a recognized agency has been active on the boy's case when the principal requests the services of the Psychological Clinic, the latter will request all data from the agency concerned and will use this information to assist them in making a recommendation.[2]

The New York City report deals not so much with how these classes are set up as with the numbers they involve. Through the years the pattern, as delineated by New York City, seems to be that of a constantly increasing number of

181

such centers. Here the problem is not too few but apparently too many students in need of these facilities.

NEW YORK CITY: In New York City there have been classes established in the elementary schools since 1940 for young boys who have had experience with the courts or have been difficult of containment in the regular classes of the school. These classes are labelled A, B, C, D: A for 9-year olds, B for 10-year olds, C for 11-year olds, D for 12-year olds.

The program is geared for the prevention of delinquency and the early identification of potential delinquent behavior. The curriculum places heavy emphasis on remedial reading and arithmetic, manu-mental activities, minimal citizenship training (social studies), and health teaching.

For the socially maladjusted boy or girl, New York City, in 1947, began the organization of special schools known as "600" schools. These are divided into three categories; namely, 10 institutional schools, 2 remand centers, 10 day schools, and 6 annexes to institutional organizations. There are approximately 3500 children in these schools. They run the gamut of deviate behavior from the "bad" disruptive child through the delinquent and the emotionally disturbed to the psychotic child. Only one of these day schools is for adolescent girls.

These schools are specifically oriented for rehabilitation of the child who has failed to adjust to the regular stream of education and who must be removed from this stream because he is a deterrent to the education of himself and those around him.

The cooperation of all of the special services in the Department of Education is needed to cope with this problem within the Division of Child Welfare (Board of Education), the Bureau of Child Guidance, and Bureau of Attendance. In addition, the Curriculum Bureau, the Children's Courts, Juvenile Aid Bureau of the Police Department, etc., have a hand in the conduct of the program of these schools. The specific responsibility for the operation of the "600" schools lies with the Director of the "600" schools within the Division of Child Welfare of the Board of Education.

The children who are sent to these special schools have been referred either by a local superintendent of schools, a principal, a psychiatrist, or other guidance person. Many of them have been excluded from school after a suspension hearing held by the field superintendent because of a delinquent act. Most of these children have had court experience. The key attempt at rehabilitation in these schools is first, containment, and, second, rehabilitation, to the end that the child may be returned to the normal stream of education or to some other suitable placement—either institution, hospital, or specialized private school environment. Many have gone directly into some form of semiskilled or unskilled labor.

Four junior "600" classes have been established in the elementary schools for the more disturbed and more seriously delinquent boy who cannot be contained in the normal class. These classes are, however, in a regular elementary school set-up. Carefully selected personnel for teaching and guidance are provided. Specialized services of the Bureau of Child Guidance and the Bureau of Educational Guidance are immediately available for these classes, which were opened in the school year of 1958-1959. The curriculum is very similar to that employed in the A, B, C, D classes.

In Washington an experimental Boys' Junior-Senior High School was opened in October 1958. Each teacher in the school is a specialist in a subject field or training area and was selected for his ability to work with this type of pupil. In this special school, an attempt was made to maintain the atmosphere of a regular school; for example, the boys are not assigned to a single classroom, as in many special schools, but move from classroom to classroom for their studies.

The following outline represents the outcome of a six-week planning session by the school's staff consisting of the three administrative personnel and the four members of the instructional staff. Certain parts of the over-all plan, e.g., the job-conditioning program, are yet to be implemented. The proposed plan represents original goals for the establishment of a meaningful and effective rehabilitation program for an assigned enrollment of 30 to 50 boys with emotional and/or behavioral problems.

Washington, District of Columbia:

I. Purpose

    A. To provide a highly specialized educational center for boys who are unable to profit from the regular program of instruction because of emotional or behavioral problems.

183

B. To improve the social adjustment, acceptability, and the instructional skill level of these students to the extent that they will be able to return to a regular school program or to seek employment.

C. To provide a specialized job-conditioning program for boys who have previously withdrawn from school.

II. Definition of School and Its Program

A. A junior and senior high school for boys 14 to 18 years of age, inclusive, having emotional or behavioral problems.

B. Program

  1. Psychological and social adjustment program

    a. Preliminary individual diagnosis and continuing observation, association, and appraisal

    b. Regular staff case conferences with consulting psychiatrist, clinical psychologist, social case worker, and others

    c. Planned program of continuing home-school contact

    d. Family counseling service

    e. Planned program of school-community and welfare agency cooperation; i.e., Advisory Board, Juvenile Court, Health and Welfare Departments, Private Agencies

  2. Introductory period

    a. A three-week period of diagnosis and observation within the Boys' Junior-Senior High School

  3. Specialized counseling services

    a. Continuing individual diagnosis

    b. Individual programs

  4. Specialized health program

    a. Diagnosis

    b. Instruction

    c. Directed physical activity

  5. Instructional program

    a. Remedial instruction in basic subjects

    b. Tutorial instruction aimed at maintaining student's position in regular academic program

    c. Arts and crafts

184

d. Job-conditioning unit for boys who have previously withdrawn from school
6. Placement program
   a. Regular school
   b. Employment
7. Follow-up service
   a. Investigation and observation of adjustment in school or job
   b. Long-range follow-up for the purpose of evaluation

Recommended Criteria for Placement and Procedures
in Boys' Junior-Senior High School

III. Enrollment
A. Criteria
   1. Boys who are unable to profit from the regular school program because of emotional and behavioral problems.
   2. Age—14 to 18. Exceptions to be made in special cases upon recommendation of the Department of Pupil Appraisal.
   3. Physical condition—Pupil's physical condition should be that which is satisfactory for regular school placement.
   4. IQ—A pupil must function at least at a borderline intelligence level and give evidence of a higher potential.
   5. Junior high school experience—Pupils should have some junior high school experience, preferably one year in junior high school.
   6. Social Adjustment Class experience—Before placement in the Boys' Junior-Senior High School, junior high school pupils must have prior tryouts in Social Adjustment Class placement at that level.
B. Procedures
   1. Revised Form 205—Form 205, revised (Confidential Request for Individual Pupil Study) is to be completed and submitted to the Department of Pupil Appraisal accompanied by the following:
      a. Report of school behavior—Anecdotal reports at the time of the referral are to come from all pertinent school personnel, such as social adjustment and other teachers, counselors, assistant principals, and principals.

185

b. Report of prior recommendations—If the pupil has had previous study, on the basis of which psychiatric, medical, or school adjustment recommendations were made, report of the outcome of these is to be included in any request for his transfer to the Boys' Junior-Senior High School.

c. Record of community adjustment—A record of all prior social agency contacts and probation or court involvement is to accompany referral forms sent to the Department of Pupil Appraisal.

d. History of home contact—A history of previous home contacts is to be included with the referral form sent to the Department of Pupil Appraisal.

2. Parental advice—Parents are to be advised by the principal or the counselor of the referring school that their boy is being referred to the Department of Pupil Appraisal for possible placement in Boys' Junior-Senior High School.

3. Clinical evaluation by the Department of Pupil Appraisal—The Boys' Junior-Senior High School is rehabilitative in function. Since this is so, a clinical evaluation by the Department of Pupil Appraisal should indicate the possibility of a successful return to a regular school program or employment.

4. Notification of eligibility—The Department of Pupil Appraisal is to notify the principal of the Boys' Junior-Senior High School that the student is eligible for admission. At the same time a completed case file is to be forwarded from the Department of Pupil Appraisal to the Boys' Junior-Senior High School.

5. Request for records—The Boys' Junior-Senior High School principal is to notify the principal of the referring school of the boy's acceptance and request transfer of the following records:

a. Health history and health record
b. Past academic record
c. Attendance record
d. Test record
e. Current program
f. Cumulative record.

Since the Boys' Junior-Senior High School is required to hold a full staff case conference to determine the new student's schedule prior to his admission, the reporting date for the student will be at least one week after the receipt of these records.

6. Intake interview—The principal of the Boys' Junior-Senior High School will notify the principal of the referring school of the reporting date for the student.

7. Disposition—Upon admission, each student will undergo an intensive observation and diagnostic period for placement purposes.

Students showing marked inability to profit by the program of the school may be referred to the Department of Pupil Appraisal for reevaluation.

Upon the decision of the principal of the Boys' Junior-Senior High School, students may be returned to a regular program or released for employment.

As with most experimental programs, the above has undergone adjustments during the school's first year of operation. For example, a delayed admission program and a controlled admissions rate have developed in place of the orientation period as initially outlined. The school has added special services as rapidly as they could be made available.[3]

The last in this series of general reports is a discussion of the rehabilitative principles utilized in the organization and methods of a special school in Chicago.

CHICAGO, ILLINOIS: The Montefiore and its branch for girls in the Motley are located in separate buildings and are designed to meet the needs of maladjusted and disturbed children who are old enough to travel to these schools. While at first thought it might seem that the behavior problems of maladjusted children would be intensified by transfer to a special school, it has been the experience of these schools that the serious types of misbehavior are diminished. Moreover, segregation as commonly understood is not necessarily true when applied to maladjusted children in a special school, because a problem child often is more cruelly segregated when kept in a regular class which cannot meet his need and where he is often doomed to failure and to frustration in expressing himself than when in a special school which does meet his needs better. This is no doubt due to the fact that the Montefiore School concentrates on remedial measures, gives more attention to physical and mental health, and maintains a competent staff not only of carefully selected teachers but also of psychologists, social workers, and medical and psychiatric consultants. The organization and administration of the whole program of the school, both educationally and clinically, is adapted to the particular needs of the maladjusted individuals, with special emphasis upon activities that prove an effective antidote for maladjustments and emotional disturbances. The school makes it possible for the maladjusted child to enjoy success in school instead of experiencing the accumulation of feelings of failure which often characterizes his work in regular schools where . . . [his] needs cannot be met. Placement in a special school should never be considered a punishment; rather, the decision to place a child in a special school should be based upon the fact that the evidence indicates that such placement will be of material benefit to him.[4]

Some smaller systems have also developed special centers. Here the characteristic form is the special class. The following reports are from cities of approximately 44,000, 88,000, and 185,000 population.

YAKIMA, WASHINGTON (44,000): [We] use what is called the Youth Study Center to offer boys suspended for deviant behavior from high school a so-called "last chance." If boy and parents show positive signs through a series of conferences and psychometrics, the boy is permitted to enroll for not less than one semester or more than one year. At the end of this period, he must return to the "regular" class or be excluded. The approach in the classroom (Youth Study Center's maximum enrollment, 15) is strictly on an individual basis. Group therapy is being considered next year.

NEWTON, MASSACHUSETTS (88,000): Nine children will have an opportunity for very special education starting September 1958. These children have been carefully selected after medical and psychological diagnosis and treatment. They have found it extremely difficult to perform in a regular classroom situation. It is believed that placement in a special class providing supportive help during therapy will enable them to adjust to their problem, and after a period of time they will be returned to the regular school equipped to function adequately.[5]

188

SPOKANE, WASHINGTON (185,000): Spokane Continuation School . . . is really a classroom within a high school that provides remedial and recovery opportunity to deviant [and] otherwise handicapped youths and adults who wish to complete high school. Not more than 10 students in class each hour—student may be enrolled for one to three hours, may be working part time, may be having difficulty in a classroom with a particular teacher. Clearing technique is used to prevent "dumping." School staff appreciates facility which frees the regular classroom teacher to teach. Each student works as able at whatever speed he can achieve. Possible to complete two years in one.

Although juvenile detention institutions inevitably differ in many significant respects from the school's special centers or classes, the following statements on rehabilitative goals and methods of two detention institutions may provide useful insights to school personnel dealing with norm violators.

LOS ANGELES COUNTY, CALIFORNIA: The purpose of the educational program is in agreement with the over-all rehabilitation philosophy as held by Juvenile Hall and Probation Departments. The specific aims are to help pupils to understand self and re-adjust to a proper role in society. The school staff implements this philosophy by focusing on the following objectives:

1. Provide an individualized educational program with emphasis on guidance
2. Provide exploratory experiences leading to vocational and avocational skills
3. Provide a remedial educational program as needed
4. Provide diagnostic information to be used for pupil future adjustment
5. Structure the social situation to develop self-control in a group situation
6. Develop independent, worthwhile, happy citizens.[6]

OTISVILLE, NEW YORK: A clinical team has been assembled, consisting of psychiatrists, psychologist, social workers, and a consultant group therapist. Three part-time psychiatrists enable us to have five days of psychiatric services per week. A full-time clinical psychologist is on our staff.

Diagnosis and treatment are handled by the team approach. There are at present five full-time social workers with an average

189

case load of 55 boys each. A program of group therapy is under way for approximately 15% of the population, under the direction of a part-time consultant group therapist. In addition, and commensurate with the clinic's working with the boys, the social workers, psychologist, and psychiatrists are being involved in the general program of the boys by means of a zone plan. Clinic personnel are assigned so that they may work with a group of cottages. This encourages the team . . . to work with the boys' supervisory staff of a cottage unit both on a formal and informal basis concerning boy treatment and programming. Clinic staff are used as consultants by the lay staff for formal and informal in-service training in behavior dynamics and treatment techniques.[7]

It is interesting to observe that detention systems, like the regular school systems, are finding it increasingly necessary to create special centers for their most deviant youngsters. A full discussion of the nature of this problem and means of overcoming it is presented by the State of California in a comment that places particular emphasis on therapeutic rehabilitation services.

THE STATE OF CALIFORNIA: Following a review of a thousand case files chosen at random from the 1955 cases accepted by the Youth Authority, it was estimated that 17 percent or more of the total population of the Youth Authority's correctional schools are "special problem delinquents," who because of emotional disturbances or psychological disabilities do not fit into, nor benefit greatly from, the regular treatment program. In effect, they occupy a kind of institutional "no man's land." They are not generally thought to belong in regular mental hospitals or existing institutions for the mentally deficient. Many are committed by the courts to the Youth Authority because they are delinquent and there is no place else to send them.

Although their number is limited, their impact is great. They tend to disrupt established training programs and they seriously hamper efforts to rehabilitate other more normal delinquents. They require a greatly disproportionate share of staff time, and most important, as they grow older, they are likely to join the hard core of adult criminals who commit a large share of the most serious crimes, and who constitute the major portion of the continuing population of the State's prisons.

190

Special problem delinquents require psychiatric care and treatment to help them develop socially acceptable conduct and behavior. With such care and treatment, many of them can be expected to fit into and benefit from the regular programs of work, training, and counseling provided at correctional schools. Furthermore, the likelihood that they will lead normal productive lives after release is greatly increased.

For many years, the problem of dealing with these emotionally disturbed teen-age delinquents has confronted California's courts, probation departments, private agencies, the Department of Mental Hygiene, and the Youth Authority. . . .

After staff study, the Youth Authority developed a proposed special treatment program based on the following general principles:

(1) The program is designed to provide for wards that will be sent to the Youth Authority who are in need of psychiatric care and treatment, it being agreed that wards diagnosed as psychotic or defective will still be committed to the Department of Mental Hygiene.

(2) It is proposed to place the necessary staff in already existing Youth Authority institutions as it is not believed feasible or advisable to create special institutions for this type of case. By placing clinical teams in each of the six Youth Authority schools, the segregation of these cases by age and sex would follow the pattern already existing in the Youth Authority treatment program. Outpatient clinical teams located in the two reception centers would make this service available to the parolee, thus providing a completely integrated program between the institutions and parole.

It is anticipated that under this program the Youth Authority will have a continuing population of approximately 800 of these special problem cases and it is estimated they will average about 18 months' stay in the agency's institutions. It is recognized that there are many details in this program still to be worked out. . . .

It shall be the purpose of the Youth Authority in this program to provide the type of treatment for the emotionally disturbed delinquent that will integrate therapeutic practices with strong environmental controls. This should provide an opportunity for the youths so treated to gain stability and at the same time protect society from their misbehavior. The living group and

191

all environmental influences are an integral part of the treatment process. The staff will make maximum use of all the latest scientific methods including group counseling, tranquilizing drugs, interpersonal relationships, and individual counseling and therapy.[8]

This program was launched after authorization by the 1957 Legislature. Special treatment teams, headed by a psychiatrist and including psychologists and social workers, have been developed at the Preston School of Industry and Los Guilucos School for Girls. This treatment is provided for the most disturbed wards. Seventeen percent of the wards fall into this category, yet they are not mentally ill enough for commitment to state hospitals. The department requested funds in the 1959-60 Budget to extend the treatment program to the Paso Robles Youth Authority School for Boys and the Fred C. Nelles School for Boys. It is planned that the program will be established eventually in other schools. About 200 wards were enrolled in the psychiatric treatment program in the two institutions after the first year of operation.[9]

The Essex County Youth House in Newark, New Jersey, which has received a special recommendation from the National Parole and Probation Association, supplied information specifically requested by the NEA Juvenile Delinquency Project. The Project particularly wanted to know size of enrollment, length of stay, line of authority relationships with regular schools, and ratio of students to special service personnel. The answers provided by the Youth House indicate some of the reasons for its success: the high ratio of staff personnel to youngsters, a factor which must be considered by any system planning to set up a special center; the adequate provision of special services, a necessity for the fulfilment of the rehabilitative responsibility; and the close liaison between the center and the regular school; and, finally, a realistic philosophy of the purpose and methods of a special center.

NEWARK, NEW JERSEY:
1. 1,200 boys and 400 girls between the ages of 8 and 18 enroll annually. Average daily population—60 boys and 20 girls.

2. Longest stay is four months. Average length of stay for annual intake is 18 days. However, two-thirds of our average daily population (80) are with us approximately three months for study, psychiatric and psychological examinations or pending possible placement in private or state institutions for the emotionally disturbed youngsters.

3. (a) The teachers at Youth House are employed by the Institution and paid from County funds. (b) When a youngster is remanded to Youth House for study, the school he attended in the community sends us the educational background of the youngster and the results of any psychological or educational tests the youngster has been given. A liaison officer between the schools and Juvenile Court, which is located in the same building as Youth House, is in daily contact with us and most cooperatively obtains for us any other information we might desire to know about the child's school history. We in turn share with the school in the community any progress the youngster has made at Youth House or other information which may be of help in understanding the youngster and in assisting the youngster to adjust in the community. Groups of teachers and guidance counsellors from the various schools in the community visit Youth House to study our program and exchange ideas about how we can work toward the rehabilitation of our youngsters.

4. The type of staff and quality of service rendered to youngsters in detention depends on the philosophy of the institution. The philosophy of Essex County Youth House is: The majority of youngsters committed to our care either cannot or will not set their own limits so that they can conform to the laws of society. It is, therefore, our responsibility as adults to set limits of behavior for them and these limits should conform with standards set by the community since eventually most youngsters will be returned to the community.

The manner in which we set those limits and help youngsters accept them is very important. It may be argued that they must be taught that they cannot be laws unto themselves and that if they do not conform they must be forced into conformity by use of physical force or physical deprivation. The fact remains, however, that most of the youngsters have already been physically abused and deprived many times before coming to us.

One more beating, one more pushing around, one more deprivation to obtain conforming behavior would breed only negative results, deepen their sense of hostility toward adults and society. We believe, therefore, that the youngsters can best be helped to set their own limits of behavior to conform with the laws of society by giving them, while in detention, an opportunity:

1. To experience, perhaps for the first time, a non-hostile, non-punitive environment. By constructive efforts on his part, without undue comparison of those efforts with any standard other than his own ability, a child is helped to gain acceptance and a sense of achievement. In the event of disruptive behavior an effort is made to determine the need such behavior serves so that it may be handled constructively with consideration both for the needs of the child and the welfare of the group.

2. Be observed by professional persons, competent and objective enough to evaluate personality and behavior.

3. Have symptomatic behavior handled in a professional manner.

4. Be provided with and become part of a program commensurate with his needs and abilities.

5. Feel through staff attitudes and program a sense of security while in custody.

6. Develop an understanding of his own behavior pattern underlying his anti-social acts, provided emotional and/or intellectual functioning together with length of stay make it possible.

7. Recognize a need for change and effect a modification of behavior by mobilizing existing strengths and abilities.

To carry out this philosophy, Youth House employs only staff members who are emotionally stable, capable of accepting its philosophy and, most important, capable of working with youngsters in accordance with the philosophy. We have a staff of seventy including a consultant psychiatrist, consultant psychologist, five psychiatric social caseworkers, a social group worker, a physician, two chaplains, five teachers, and thirty-four counsellors. The counsellors are similar to cottage parents and trained recreation leaders. Most of our counsellors are college graduates, and the minimum educational requirements for counsellors are two years of college with continued matriculation.

Fortunately, the Board of Chosen Freeholders and our Board of Trustees are deeply aware of the nature and importance of our work, and therefore, have provided us with a budget to pay

194

our staff members adequate salaries comparable to the best in the country.

Reports on actual teaching methods and techniques used within the special school or classroom were not explicitly discussed in much of the material submitted. Nevertheless, a number of reports did touch on this topic, and from these one can glean some clues to techniques in the special center or classroom. One group of comments dealing with the teacher's relationship to the student particularly stressed the need for understanding and sympathy as the basis for classroom work with these disturbed youngsters.

PHILADELPHIA, PENNSYLVANIA: Children must be guided and encouraged to make the maximum progress of which they are capable. Children's learning is based not on their limitations, but on their abilities.

The teacher is the person in the school who is closest to the child, and he must have specialized training in order to gain state certification for the work with the handicapped. Over and beyond his professional studies, however, he must be a very special kind of person to be successful with handicapped children. He must have knowledge but, even more important, he must have an understanding of how to use this special knowledge in leading children to take next steps. He must have sympathy for the difficulties and frustrations the children encounter, and yet be firm in developing acceptable patterns of behavior. Sensitive to quick changes in emotional responses, he must be ready at all times to provide stimulation or redirection to the children's attention and to their energies.[10]

DETROIT, MICHIGAN: When an outburst of delinquent behavior occurs in the classroom, do not be disturbed; handle it with objectivity and understanding; try to get into the delinquent's world and see things from his point of view. Mistaken handling of the situation might cause further difficulties.

The . . . teacher should be constantly aware that hostility and aggression towards him are not a personal insult. The class disturber is a child in emotional conflict, and needs help to straighten out his thinking. He may be transferring hostilities engendered in his home situation, and anyone in authority would receive the same abuse from him. He may provoke his

195

teacher simply to test the sincerity of the seeming affection and sympathy which may be a new experience which he is not ready to cope with. His aggressiveness with classmates may be an expression of his jealousy of the teacher's attention to others; he may simply be making a bid for much needed attention; he may be demanding punishment for some entirely unrelated "wrong doing" for which he suffers guilt feelings; he may be trying to prove to himself, by provoking the teacher's wrath, that all adults are alike and thereby justifying in his own mind continued aggressions against the adult world and society in general; or he may be motivated by any of a host of other reasons.

Each outburst is an emotional crisis, and here is where the . . . teacher serves his most vital role. The teacher who meets open abuse and obscenity with sympathy and affection will often find a bewildered and tearful youngster just beneath the surface of extreme hostility. Above all, ungraded teachers should never regard these outbursts as a reflection on their teaching abilities. This is behavior to be expected from these highly disturbed boys. The objective is to reduce them in intensity and to achieve a progressively wider span between upheavals. This can be done only through a complete understanding of the child and all his background, and the creation of an atmosphere of acceptance and security with abundant opportunities for success experiences and recognition for socially approved behavior, and if possible by influencing parental handling.[11]

Another group of statements related to teaching techniques deals with such specific practices as play therapy, group counseling, and motivational grouping.

NEW YORK CITY: A program of play groups for disturbed children six and seven years old has been in operation in a number of . . . elementary schools for the past 10 years. These children are not only severely disturbed themselves but interfere with the instruction of the other children in their classes.

Carefully selected teachers or teacher-counselors are given intensive training by a competent group therapist in child development, dynamics of behavior, observation and understanding of children's behavior in groups, and methods of dealing with disturbing behavior. They are then given one group of five or six children for one hour a week in a playroom setting. They keep careful records of the sessions and discuss them with the play-group supervisor who is an experienced group therapist. They do not attempt deep therapy, but rather, function as understanding sympathetic adults in a permissive play setting. In many cases, the children referred to the play groups have had clinical studies made by school psychiatrists, psychologists, and social workers, so that their psychological needs have been clinically determined. Most children are ready for normal functioning in regular classes after about a school year of participation in the play groups one hour a week for that period.

THE STATE OF CALIFORNIA: The latest innovation in the Youth Authority institutional program has been the use of group counseling techniques as a part of the treatment program. One of the major problems of the Youth Authority ward is that he has not learned to work purposefully or behave in a socially acceptable manner within the larger community group. Therefore, it is important that these boys and girls learn how to become constructive and accepted members of a group. It was this concept that led the agency to encourage the individual institutions to experiment in the group counseling field. Preliminary use of this technique has indicated it has very real advantages for many of our wards and a more organized and coordinated program in group counseling is now being planned for use throughout the agency's treatment program.[12]

NEW YORK CITY: The stereotype of the juvenile delinquent is the boy or girl of low intelligence and poor school achievement; he or she is seldom thought of as a gifted individual capable of superior school functioning.

In a study of approximately 5000 gifted tenth-year students . . . about 60 percent were not functioning at capacity in school achievement (90 percent in every major subject); at least 10 percent were reported by school personnel as showing severe personal and social problems; and 1 percent have been known to have had serious delinquent behavior.

Although this project does not concern itself primarily with juvenile delinquency, it has some bearing on it, if only to show that gifted young people are not immune. The methods used in the study to convert under-achievers into achievers have direct bearing on methods of combating delinquency: clinical study, psychotherapy, remedial services, raising of sights, intensified guidance services, motivational groups, parent groups, weekend camping, and stimulation through discussion groups of peers.

197

This study is still in progress, but incomplete results show some trends, particularly with reference to those methods that seem effective in improving school achievement, and those that do not. Tutoring, for example, is one of the least effective. One approach proved almost too effective: in a motivational group of 10 students, nine showed improved grades for the current semester. Some members of the group beat up the lagging member. Thus there was improvement in achievement, accompanied by an increase in delinquent behavior.

Whenever dealing with a special school or class, the administrator should always be ready to adapt the usual school procedures in special ways, using his authority to support the unusual requirements of this complex program. Thus, in a system where the attendance officer is usually notified by the regular school only after a student has been absent three days, the special school would be permitted to request his services at their discretion—after one, two, three, or even more days have passed, depending on the school staff's assessment of the individual case. With an extremely individualized program and a fluctuating school population, the special school, if tied to a standard once-a-year budget estimate and request, may be forced to put an unnecessary limitation on its ability to adapt its program to new students or to profit from new research. The following article makes other suggestions along this line.

NEW YORK CITY: Some attention has been given to the instructional needs of the school by providing additional teaching time to reduce the size of classes. Special classes have been set up for poor readers and slow learners. But there has been no additional staff made available to cope with needs related to the school population. For example, maintaining attendance at the school is difficult, and the amount of clerical work involved in reporting and follow-up is formidable. No special provision has been made in terms of clerical help, and there is no resident attendance officer at the school.

The number of teachers available for patrol and other building assignments is insufficient, and trouble spots such as toilets, corridors, exits and lunchrooms are not as well supervised as they might be.

In planning school buildings attention should be given to the avoidance of blind corridors and stairways. Above all, schools in difficult areas should be given special personnel allotments so that buildings may be properly patrolled.[13]

The most complete reports on actual curriculum structure were submitted by the Special Schools of Los Angeles County, California, which are operated through the County School Board for the Juvenile Detention Authority. These are programs which have been designed specifically for legally designated delinquents. However, they have implications for the regular school in its work with the potential or active delinquent. In fact, two groups of conferees at the interdisciplinary National Invitational Conference, sponsored by the NEA Juvenile Delinquency Project, were of the opinion that the detention school has more than mere implications to offer in the education of delinquents. One discussion group advocated an experimental program that would incorporate the resources of the detention school.

NATIONAL INVITATIONAL CONFERENCE: Perhaps in no other agency is there found the close interdisciplinary approach to the delinquent problems than is found in state and private schools throughout the U.S. The possibility of setting up experimental schools within the training schools should provide for the public school a wealth of knowledge about the delinquent child himself, about his family, and about methods and techniques which are most successful. What better source of material or opportunity for research can be found than in this area of very direct contact with delinquents and their families?

A large portion of the remainder of this chapter will be devoted to the reports submitted by the Special Schools of Los Angeles County, referred to earlier. The first of the detention school reports is that of a reception center, which first receives the boy; like all special schools, it seeks to identify individual needs and to furnish the youngster with an opportunity for achievement.

LOS ANGELES, CALIFORNIA: The reception centers maintain a school program similar to the individual's community school. The primary aims and objectives [see page 189 of this chapter]

199

of the Special Schools are used as the guide in meeting individual needs. Many boys express amazement in their success. "This school is better than the *outs,* I seem to know what I'm doin'." Each boy works in relationship to his achievement. This identification of success is meaningful, since, very likely, the boy's previous attempts to achieve have met with failure. The school experiences must be meaningful and successful before the individual consents to procedures of diagnostic data gathering.

Generally, superficial data are available concerning the individual's educational experience. A transcript of straight failures isn't much help in determining educational acumen; or for that matter, in determining "why" he failed. The process of data gathering is interwoven in the curriculum in such a manner so as not to constitute a threat to the only thing "he" has left, *resistance.*[14]

Reports on two programs of junior camp schools were also contributed by Los Angeles County. The Oak Grove Boys Camp School was a pioneer in this type of probation rehabilitation facility, and its present program uses many of the approaches cited in Chapter 4. Students are assigned to ability groups on the basis of diagnostic testing, and after each youngster is assigned to a group, a very specialized remedial program with a weekly evaluation grade is developed for him.

LOS ANGELES COUNTY, CALIFORNIA: The curriculum at Oak Grove is one that has evolved out of experience dealing with socially and emotionally maladjusted youngsters of junior and senior high school age. It is designed to meet the individual needs of all boys from the non-reader to the superior high school pupil.

Since the majority of the boys in the junior camp schools have a past history of failure and maladjustment in the public schools, an intensive remedial program has been developed. This program is designed to eventually rehabilitate these young people through psychological readjustment and strengthening of their academic potential.

When a boy enters school for the first time he is given an orientation by the principal. Tests administered at the Probation Rehabilitation Center with written observational reports are analyzed, and the boy is assigned to one of four ability groups. Four levels of classes are provided in order to give the individual boy the opportunity to be working in a group with boys of equal or near equal ability. The four class levels are:

"A" Class, Developmental Level, Grades 1-4
"B" Class, Remedial Level, Grades 5-6
"C" Class, Remedial Level, Grades 7-8
"D" Class, High School Level, Grades 9-12.[15]

[As an example of the program variation in the four class levels, the following represents the teaching of language skills.]

"A"	"B"	"C"	"D"
READING	READING	READING	ENGLISH
Alphabet,	Recognition	Comprehension	Grammar
phonics	Comprehension	Reference skills	Literature
Dolch reading	ENGLISH	Organization	Journalism [16]
Basic readers	Punctuation	skills	
SPELLING	Usage	ENGLISH	
Dolch lists	SPELLING	Sentences	
State series	State series	Usage	
		Syntax	
		Penmanship	
		SPELLING	

Once [a youngster is] assigned to a class, the initial test results and diagnostic information . . . [are] forwarded to the teacher of the class in order that a program may be arranged to meet the individual's needs.

Teaching techniques in the developmental and remedial classes are varied and flexible to help meet the individual differences in the learning process. Tape recorders are used for phonics, word recognition, spelling and multiplication tables for boys with good auditory memory. Filmstrips, flash cards and the tachistoscope are used with boys who possess good visual perception. Tracing a word a number of times in the kinesthetic approach helps others. Usually a combination of these three methods is used to insure a measure of success.

An individual program is developed for each boy. Workbooks and State texts are issued to the pupil covering those subject areas in which they are weak academically. An assignment sheet is used which divides the books into daily assignments. The pupils do their assigned work on an individual basis, working at their own rates of speed. If the pupils experience difficulty with their assignments they may call on the teacher for individual instruction. Before they receive credit for their assignments their work must be corrected by the teacher. The date of completion is then marked on a wall chart. The chart enables the pupil to keep a record of his own progress and serves as a form of motivation.

A combined general shop and woodshop along with courses in music, art, arts and crafts and mechanical drawing are also offered in order to provide an opportunity for pre-vocational exploration.

A variety of tests are given periodically in order to provide educational and vocational counseling. These tests are of great importance in determining the pupil's needs.

A technique found most successful as a motivational factor is the establishment of a "weekly expectancy level" for each pupil. Each boy is given a number of assignments called jobs to complete during the week. Factors of intelligence and mental age help determine the number of "jobs" assigned. How each boy measures up to his "expectancy level" is an important factor in determining his weekly grade of evaluation.[17]

The report of the Joe Scott Camp School of Los Angeles County, which gives a very detailed picture of what happens in a specific subject field, describes teaching techniques more fully than any other material submitted to the Project, but it should be noted that a discussion of this topic was not the central purpose of the original report.

LOS ANGELES COUNTY, CALIFORNIA: The boys entering are between the ages of thirteen and fifteen, and their achievement levels vary grossly from the first grade through junior college. Accordingly, the IQ's range proportionately from fifty-nine through one hundred and fifty-nine.

The ninety-five boys enrolled in the school program are grouped into five classes, namely:

"A" Class—Regular and Enrichment—Grades 9-12
"B" Class—Regular High School—Grades 9-10
"C" Class—Remedial and Jr. H.S.—Grades 7-9
"D" Class—Remedial—Grades 5-7
"E" Class—Developmental—Grades 1-5.

Each class has a sponsor. The sponsor is the homeroom teacher, except in the case of "E" Class. Since these boys are "point one" and below, all teachers instruct the class according to their particular educational specialty.

A great flexibility is permitted in advancing from group to group. The Achievement Test results are used as superficial placement criteria. These results, then, are used as points of departure. Generally, boys in Classes "D" and "E" can advance as many as five achievement grade levels within six to eight months.

Information is utilized from the Reception Center with additional information being supplied by community schools. A comprehensive form is prepared on each boy, outlining immediate behavioral characteristics and testing data results. This immediate picture of the boy serves to . . . [provide] the classroom teacher with specific information. Generally, the school staff does not delve deeply into the background of the boys. The pupils are treated in every respect as normal boys. However, when circumstances out of the ordinary occur, the teacher resorts to the extensive files on the boys kept by the Probation Department to determine suitable treatment.

The curriculum is similar to any other school district in Los Angeles County. A continuity program is outlined to meet each individual's needs. This individual program is in conformity to the program offered by the community school. All state requirements are met in accordance with the Education Code.

There will be no attempt to outline course content per se. The special involvement technique will enrich the regular course content materials. Before activating any total involvement activity, the teacher should first consider the following questions:

1. Is the activity in the realm of the individual's active knowledge? Is the activity related to present living experience of the pupil, and is it socially significant?
2. Does the activity give promise of [an] outcome relatively valuable in life today?
3. Is it hard enough to challenge . . . easy enough to insure some degree of success?
4. Will the activity lead to more worthy things?
5. Will the activity foster an inquiring, investigative attitude?
6. Will the activity develop relationships leading to organization of experience by locating information, assimilating, comparing, evaluating, and finally concluding?
7. Is the activity flexible enough to include unforeseen activities that arise, and also to provide for individual differ-

ences in pupils? [Will] each individual . . . feel that the
activity was especially designed for him?
8. Will it stimulate the pupil's interests . . . hold his attention
span?
9. What is the range of ability or degree of maturation for
each pupil?
10. Will there be a correlation and integration with subjects,
home, community, state, nation, world?
11. Will the activity provide learning experiences which will
develop the knowledge, skill, and attitudes that are appropriate to the physical, mental, emotional, and social
maturity of the individual?
12. Are the materials available for the activity?
13. Are the pupils capable of manipulating the materials?
14. Is the environment conducive and wholesome for the
release of free expression and creative activity?

This is by no means an inclusive list, but . . . merely
suggestions and considerations.

The arts and crafts program is so designed as to afford a
progression of successes in various media . . . [and] exploration
with a variety of tools and techniques.

In the beginning the boy is resistant and contends that he cannot draw. The instructor agrees with him. He then informs
the pupil that he also cannot get up from his seat. The boy
becomes incensed and jumps to his feet. "Now I know you can
get up from the seat," informs the instructor. "Now apply this
same attempt to your work."

In the beginning, the boys start out drawing. The medium is
the two-dimensioned surface of the paper, and the tool is a pencil.
The boys are not permitted to trace a piece of work or copy it
outright. To permit this would ultimately condone the reason
why most boys are here . . . taking another person's property
for their own. It is permissible to select several pictures, choose
the most appealing aspects of all, and finally organize a completely new picture. This is analogous to looking up a word in
a dictionary, using it in a sentence, the sentence in a paragraph,
and finally a meaning in total context.

Woodburning is next. The medium is wood, and the tool
changes to a woodburning tool. Block printing helps to understand the printing industry. The boy now is using a carving tool
to incise lines in a semi-resistant media of linoleum. In leather

carving the medium is leather, and the tools are a variety of stamps and swivel knife. Again the boy is cutting into the material; however, now there is an attempt to raise the surface in a bas relief. Copper foil modeling is a more resistant medium, and a new variety of tools are used to model or raise the copper from the back. This project includes the making of a frame around the foil modeling. Power tools are now used. The boy culminates his experiences by finishing a full three-dimensional piece of plaster-of-Paris sculpture. The medium is wire mesh and plaster, and the tools are pliers, rasps, and a knife.

In short, the pupil moves from a two-dimensional surface to a full three-dimensional object. Individual help is afforded each pupil. There is much pride generated from this involvement, and the end products are signs of achievement. Paradoxically, the production of particular works is not the aim, rather the development and control of feelings gained thereby, which, of course, profits the work as well as the worker.

With the accumulation of wholesome experiences and creative preoccupation, the individual's general attitude becomes constructive rather than negative or destructive. In the majority of cases, the individual's creative successes are used as transfer experiences in coping with academic subject matter.

Field trips are quite common at Joe Scott School, and the entire environment is used as the school's classroom.

A short hike to the top of the hill had the boys thirsting for greater exploration. The tape recorder was used to record preliminary discussions on a major project involving the integration of all courses of study in one field trip.

The plan was to make a trip deep into the chaparrals. Five teams were determined, and each team was assigned specialists for gathering rocks, plants, insects, and animals or their evidence. Scouts were chosen and indoctrinated on preliminary excursions into the general area for familiarization of the terrain.

First aid and life saving were discussed, and rules were established for personal conduct. Warning signals were devised by whistle calls. Intensive studies were made by committees on rattlesnakes, scorpions, tarantulas, and other poisonous insects. Live rattlesnakes were brought in to study how they strike and easy methods of capturing them. Water was to be carried by all boys. The mathematics team figured out the amount of water and how much each boy should drink during the predesigned rest periods. Sanitation was also provided for.

Again the mathematics committee figured time of departure, arrival, duration of the exploration, lunch, and return time to the school. Another responsibility of the committee was to determine the size, shape, and description of the cases of the material collected.

The science committees were divided into subcommittees of physical science and biological science. They would also arrange the collection of materials with suitable labels.

The English committee was responsible for the reports before and after. Each participant was also to write his personal experience during the trip.

The industrial arts committee was assigned the task of making the cases for the exhibits.

The social studies committee made reports on the historic significance of this specific area explored, and what part it played in winning the West.

The excursion was a success, and it inaugurated the museum section of the multi-purpose room. Five huge cases house the collections.

The study of the Westward Movement led into the study of many aspects of the American scene. Five huge maps were designed to picture the historical, agricultural, mineral, and industrial wealth of America. The last map was rendered in full topographic effect and small models symbolized the specific activity.

Mathematics and English are correlated with the social-studies projects.

To afford a more stimulating and realistic approach, mathematics is taught on the basis of short-term goals. A good many boys in the lower achievement classes are likely not to finish their high school education. With this in mind, the instructors of mathematics are meeting the needs of realistic problems. Supermarket sales advertising is brought in for each member of the class, and they are instructed to do the purchasing of groceries for an entire week. The Sears catalog is issued to each boy, and he is given a sum of money to furnish an entire room. He must make a cost sheet and show how he will pay for the purchases on a monthly installment plan. Problems on balancing the budget and the checkbook are approached with realistic earnest.

Other projects involve going outside and measuring the school building to determine how much area is glass as opposed to concrete block. . . .

One boy made a full-scale architectural drawing of the entire camp with the aid of a ten-foot metal tape. The cut-off gauge from the circular saw was used to determine the angle of pitch in the roof and to determine the height of buildings.

Creative writing is used as a group projective therapy. Each pupil is instructed to write down on a sheet of paper all those things that would make him happy. On an unlined sheet of paper the pupil is to draw the most appealing form of happiness. In this an attempt is made to bring the individual to a more realistic frame of mind.

Displays are set up on such subjects as the home. Words cut out of magazines are tacked indiscriminately throughout the display. The words are positively inclined. The less astute learns to identify the words, spell them, pronounce them, and relate them to a scene involving the home. This technique is in its exploratory stage as yet; however, it has met with a great deal of enthusiasm and identification.

Group discussions are widely used in all subject areas from sex to murder. Role playing is employed in the classroom as a part of the English program. The boys write their own plays and perform them. Music is used as appreciation and background for unit bulletin board displays. Recently a most inspiring display was executed about "Our Heritage, Our Country, Our Guarantees, Our Obligations." The display interpretation by the committee was culminated with music from the Standard School Broadcast's "Patriot's Song Book."

Even the object lesson learned from a turtle is pointed out. A turtle was captured on one of the many excursions, and he was tied to a stake in front of the school. In a few days the turtle had dug a circular trench around the radius of the stake in its effort to get away. His object was to get free. A force was pulling against him, and he didn't know how to cope with it. Life is very much like the experience of this turtle. Society creates a circle around us. The limits of the circle are the laws of society. We can live with a great deal of freedom, if we can only learn to move about in the circle.

Most boys are in grave doubt about their ambitions upon entering the school. Those who do choose an occupation are highly unrealistic. Many of the boys will terminate their educational experiences upon being discharged and returning home to the community.

A special program is designed for those who will be seeking jobs shortly. A personality and vocational inventory test is administered to each boy, and he is counseled to [be] . . . realistic . . . concerning job opportunities in light of his particular interests, abilities, and potentials. Every effort is made to pull the individual's "wants" and "needs" closer together into a more realistic outlook.

A daily physical education and activities program is offered. The need to satisfy physical expression and create a wholesome avenue for the release of emotional tensions is quite apparent. Competition is possible on a high level of interclass and interpersonal relationships.

To help those who are lacking in physical coordination, a special program is offered in personal physical fitness. The boys are tested on push ups, sit ups, chin ups, running 440 yards, 100-yard dash, kicking the football for distance, throwing the softball for distance, basket shooting for thirty seconds and calisthenics. The gymnasium is also used for tumbling and buck-vaulting.

The rudiments of all major sports are taught, and there are regular interclass competitions in basketball, volleyball, softball, soccer and track. Trophies are presented for class championships, and personal trophies are given to the first and second place winners in all track events.

First aid and life saving are embodied in the physical education program, as well as sportsmanship education and audience participation.

The object of the educational program at Joe Scott Boys Camp School is to teach children techniques rather than theory. Every effort is made to deal with the subject matter in terms of the concrete and practical rather than in terms of the abstract. The curriculum is to suit the individual in accordance to his interest, achievement, and capabilities. . . . Realistic and short-term goals are established to insure success and to insure the building of confidence that is so necessary in restoring the individual to his rightful sense of integrity and dignity of a human being.[18]

The next report is something of a rarity in this volume, for it deals with a special facility for girls. The norm-violating

208

girl is not as frequently in trouble with school authorities as is the norm-violating boy. In fact, after an examination of all the material submitted to the Project as well as the Invitational Conference discussions, it became obvious that norm-violating boys attract the exclusive attention of the community.

Los Angeles County, California: Located near San Fernando, California, El Retiro Girls School is the only girls' school operated by the Los Angeles Division of Special Schools. While the girls at El Retiro come to the attention of the courts because of "delinquent" behavior, they are youngsters between the ages of thirteen through eighteen with emotionally unstable personalities symptomatized by hostile, aggressive, impulsive acting-out behavior. For this reason, the treatment program must be conducted in a "secured custody" setting.

The basic objectives of the educational program are predicated on those outlined as the "Aims and Objectives of the Special Schools." To enable a more positive treatment program, there exists a continuity of total objectives between the Probation Department and the Special Schools. In the classroom, emphasis is placed upon developing constructive and satisfying human relationships through a curriculum designed to meet individual needs. This is easier said than done, for working with this type of girl has led to the discovery that one cannot judge her ability to function in a school setting on the basis of intelligence quotients. Although the girls are of average or superior intellectual abilities, they are poor achievers in an academic environment.

Because the program is therapeutically oriented, it is essential that a . . . clinical study . . . [of] each girl [be completed] before she is accepted into the program. This information has a strong bearing for determining what group a girl will be best suited. Furthermore, transcripts from the community school, principal's interviews and observations, and educational testing data make up the final criteria for determining group assignments.

Limited by a wide variance in age, intelligence, and emotional instability, three classes have been organized to expedite the fulfillment of each girl's needs.

Class Group "A": This group was designed to meet the needs for remedial correction and skill development. The girls function on an achievement level between the fifth and seventh grades. Consequently, the teacher must resort to elementary procedures and techniques to overcome the unconscious fluctuation between infantile behavior and chronological development. Fortunately, the classes are small, numbering fifteen pupils per teacher-station.

Reading, writing, and arithmetic are integrated into a core program to detract from the identification of elementary pursuits and to maintain a higher level of interest. Typing is introduced, since this group is more mechanically inclined. A manipulative skill, such as typing, is very satisfying to the less academically inclined. The concrete experiences of arts and crafts balance their ineptitudes in dealing with abstract problems. The physical education and activities program serves as the tension relief valve.

Class Group "B": Classified as the "anti-school group," this mixture of hostile, aggressive, non-conforming, and acting-out girls is a real management problem. They have short attention spans and are explosive. However, they can function on an achievement level between the eighth and tenth grades. Due to their non-academic inclinations, strong motivational techniques are necessary. Academic activities are introduced in a core approach with the use of the project method. Here again, there is a strong need for the mechanical or object manipulation such as used in arts and crafts and home economics. The music and dance programs provide for the kinesthetic expression of the acting-out girls. The physical activities program serves as a balancing device in satisfying the more predominant need for physical expression through contact activities. This characteristic is also true of the girls in Class Group "A." The need for this physical expression is so great that the girls would rather engage in football than in home economics activities.

Class Group "C": Group "C" can best be classified as the "transition" group. Composed of eleventh and twelfth graders, taking the regular high-school academic curriculum, these girls are making their final transition for returning to the community schools. They have been in the program the longest and have gained some insights into and understanding of their behavior, by experiencing positive and appropriate relationships with adults and peer groups, and internalizing standards and controls which heretofore have been lacking. Individual attention is minimized and greater emphasis is placed on personal responsibilities for homework assignments, research projects, work habits, etc. The reasoning behind this approach is that these girls will return to their community schools where the competition among classes of forty pupils is keen, and there is likely to be less individual attention available than they have become accustomed to.

Curriculum undertaken consists of French, English, Composition, Literature, Algebra, Science, Government, and necessary State requirement toward high school graduation.

Out of necessity, these grouping patterns are very flexible, allowing for growth of the individual. Upon arrival the girls are assigned to "A" group, and as the girls resolve their inner conflicts they may be advanced to the other classes. The minimum entrance IQ is eighty. Concern for this safeguard is realistic when one understands that this form of therapeutic treatment can be successful only when the individuals are equipped with sufficient acumen to participate in the program.

In an effort to utilize our community resources and provide for terminal education and vocational exploration, a work-experience program has been established. At present a test program involves two girls: one girl is employed as a power sewing machine operator in a sportswear manufacturing concern; and, one girl works in a television establishment as a general office worker. The program has met with success and shows promise for expanding the program.[19]

As work-oriented programs called "on-the-job training" have developed in the regular school, so is a work-program emphasis developing in detention schools. California was one of the states pioneering this program.

Los ANGELES COUNTY, CALIFORNIA: The Senior Boys Forestry Camps. Organized on the basis of a tri-autonomously administered institution, the senior camps function under a concerted effort to afford each individual an educational-work-adjustment program. The Probation Department provides for the boys' physical needs and conducts counseling therapy programs. A very comprehensive work-experience program is offered by the Department of Forestry and Fire Warden. It is from this identification that the senior boys camps are designated as work-centered programs. Although sharing a small portion of the total program, the Division of Special Schools serves a specialized need which is divided into two major categories, "terminal education" and "continuation education."

The boys work with the Department of Forestry and Fire Warden for eight hours a day, constructing and maintaining park facilities, building roads, clearing fire breaks, and fighting brush and forest fires. Consequently, by circumstance, the educational program becomes a night school operation. . . .

Limited to three hours of class-content time (from 6:00 p.m. to 9:00 p.m.), the principals face the problem realistically and design their programs to fulfill the two major classifications of boys' needs, terminal education and continuation education. . . .

Using the accumulated educational data forwarded by the reception center school, the principal interviews the boy and together they determine a realistic program to meet his specific educational needs.

[*The Physical Education Program*] . . . is a joint venture between the Probation Department and the Special Schools.
Content:
1. Individual and team participation training.
2. Learn game rudiments and skills of major sports.
3. Learn track and field rudiments and skills.
4. Individual and group competition contests.
5. Incentive motivation program
   a. Trophies
   b. Awards of recognition.
6. Personal physical fitness program.

[*The Remedial Program*] . . . is specifically designed for pupils [who are academically weak]. Individual needs will be met as follows:
1. The learning of developmental skills, grades 1 to 5.
2. Remedial treatment for boys in grades 9 through 12 with achievement levels from grades 5 through 8.
3. Groups limited to small number of boys to insure individual attention.
4. Classes are conducted by qualified persons duly credentialed and who deal with these problems in the community schools.
5. Use of materials which are at the levels of interest offering most understanding and progress—games, puzzles, oral recitation.

212

6. This remedial program involves mathematics, reading, spelling, and writing.

The General Education Curriculum:

1. Content:
    a. The use of all available state texts on all grade levels from . . . [first] through the eighth grade.
    b. All texts on these levels are used in the remedial program.
    c. Occasionally seventh and eighth graders enter on their chronological grade level. Texts used accordingly.
    d. Generally texts used in the community schools are used to fulfill requirements in the ninth grade through twelfth grade.
    e. State requirements are met as needed:
        (1) First Aid and Life Saving—fulfilled in physical education classes, and in the work experience program.
        (2) Driver Education—continuation education needs for graduation fulfillment.
        (3) History and Civics—American History, U. S. Constitution, American Ideals and Institutions, California State and Local Government.
    f. Sciences, General and Biological
        (1) Use of camp environment as a laboratory.
        (2) Rock collections, plant collections, geological studies, etc., through the work experience program offered by Forestry and integrated in the classroom.

2. Procedure:
    a. Individual approach; sub-group approach; panel-discussion type approach; general group discussion approach.
    b. Use of acceptable and practical life adjustment texts where they apply to the problem relative to areas of investigation.
    c. Use of current periodicals and publications, such as the "Life Adjustment Series," etc.
    d. Utilization of community resources to educate in regards to sex, alcoholism, narcotics, law enforcement.
    e. Current Events: (total population exposed) Discussion of what is going on in the world to develop awareness

and necessity for a well-informed citizenry, plus the development of the following skills:

(1) How to read a newspaper.

(2) How to read a magazine.

(3) The aesthetic and practical values of being able to competently read and interpret periodicals.

f. Communication Arts—practical approaches:

(1) Practical letter writing, business and personal.

(2) Filling out necessary forms for job applications, contracts, checking accounts, income tax, etc.

(3) Formal grammar.

(4) English composition and creative writing.

(5) Development and maintenance of school news sheets and orientation handbook.

g. Social Studies:

(1) Racial classifications and ethnic subdivisions are discussed on an interpersonal level to broaden mutual understanding.

(2) Purposes of societal agencies, disciplines, enforcements, and the relation of personal experiences to society.

h. Vocational Education:

(1) Vocation Interest Inventory to be taken and explored with terminal education prospects.

(2) Letter writing correlation with seeking information in regard to job interest or intention (within limits of Probation Department policy).

(3) Invite representatives of business concerns, corporations, State employment agencies, trade unions to discuss realistic job possibilities.

(4) Exploration of apprenticeship training programs.

(5) Exploration of the various armed services.

i. Arts and Crafts Program: Full range of creative expression offered from freehand drawing, appreciation, and expression in resistant and non-resistant materials.

(1) Release of work tension.

(2) Production of a real, practical, and satisfying expression.

j. Audio-Visual Education will be purposefully used where and when this type of education is beneficial in various units of study

(1) Motion picture projector.
(2) Slide and filmstrip projector.
(3) Tape recorder.
(4) Record player and radio.[20]

A very appropriate conclusion to this chapter is provided by the summary of the program of Chicago's special schools for the prevention of juvenile delinquency, for it offers a broad survey of the program's organization, procedures, teacher qualifications, and public relations.

CHICAGO, ILLINOIS: Chicago provides five types of social adjustment schools which help prevent delinquency.

1. The Montefiore and Moseley, special day schools for boys, operating on a 6½-hour day and a 12-month school year.

2. The Motley Branch of Montefiore and the Haven Branch of Moseley, day schools for girls, operating on a 6½-hour day, 12 months a year.

3. The Chicago Home for Girls, a branch of Montefiore, a semi-private residential institution for girls who need to be removed from their own or foster homes, for whom the Board of Education provides a full-time teacher for 10 months of year.

4. The Chicago Parental School, a residential school for boys, operated on the cottage plan, 13 school months a year. For boys placed here the Board of Education provides housing, food, clothing if necessary, and "cottage parents," as well as specially qualified teachers who do not reside in the institution.

5. The schools within the Audy Juvenile Detention Home, the House of Correction and the Cook County Jail, branches of the Montefiore School, for which the Board of Education provides, for 52 weeks a year, specially trained teachers and educational supplies to make it possible for boys and girls detained in these custodial institutions to attend school during their period of residence.

6. Adjustment rooms in 12 selected elementary schools for boys under 12 years of age.

Program of Special Services

The special services offered in schools for social adjustment include a resident dentist and part-time physician, resident psychologists, a part-time psychiatrist, and field adjustment teachers who are qualified social workers and attempt to coordi-

215

nate the efforts of home, school, courts, and community agencies in helping the child to adjust. The school, therefore, has all the facilities of a child guidance clinic.

Since social, economic, and emotional factors in the child's environment contribute to maladjustment and emotional disturbances, these schools must work in active cooperation with the courts, social welfare agencies, health agencies, and recreational and other neighborhood agencies. All cases are cleared through the social service exchange of the Welfare Council of Metropolitan Chicago, and data and reports are exchanged with scores of other agencies.

Boys and girls enrolled in the Montefiore and Moseley Schools and their branches receive a hot noon-day meal and carfare if they live more than a mile away from these schools. In cases of need, extra meals are supplied.

Program of Education

The schools for social adjustment provide a full program of academic work both on the elementary and high school levels, together with a wide range of shop and craft activities and many opportunities for creative expression which have a distinctly therapeutic value. Each child is given instruction in reading and the language arts, in mathematics, the social and the physical sciences. The instruction is, of necessity, largely individual so that every child may be reached on his own achievement level or in small groups of others who have similar difficulties and are in need of help. Remedial work in reading and arithmetic is provided by teachers specially trained in the skill of coaching. All children have library periods, recreational opportunities, music, and art.

The boys have opportunities to work in a variety of shops, electric, wood, metal, auto, and print shops, as well as in mechanical drawing, reed and rug weaving, and crafts laboratories provided both for educational and vocational values.

For the girls, emphasis is placed upon personal appearance, with classes in the arts and techniques of personal grooming. Homemaking and home management are also stressed in the attractive home arts laboratories. Typewriting gives every girl some promise of economic value and holds before her the possibility of a white-collar job in pleasant surroundings.

The Chicago Parental School adds to this program gardening in its spacious open acres, intramural activities the year round,

216

the delight of the outdoor swimming pool through long spring and summer months, and a carefully planned recreational program for each cottage.

Procedures in Transfer of Students to and from Social Adjustment Schools

All action on transfers of children from, or return to, the social adjustment schools and their branches are executed under the authority of the General Superintendent in charge of Special Education.

A. Procedures in Assignment and Transfer from the Chicago Parental School. Boys and girls are assigned to the Chicago Parental School by the Judge of the Family Court of Cook County. When pupils are sent to the Chicago Parental School from other Chicago schools, the sending schools will be responsible for transferring, as promptly as possible, cumulative folders, record cards, child study reports, and other pertinent materials, by mail, attendance officer, or other school personnel.

The Superintendent of the Chicago Parental School, with the approval of the Assistant Superintendent in charge of Special Education, is authorized to transfer a boy from his school to any school within the Chicago Public School System which, within his judgment, will most nearly meet the needs of the child.

The receiving principals or directors are requested to enter these children, regardless of membership or of time of year, and to use every facility of the school and the community to help the child.

When a child is transferred back to a regular school, he remains under the jurisdiction of the Superintendent of the Chicago Parental School for a period of one year. If, during that time, he fails to make a satisfactory adjustment, he may, on the approval of the Assistant Superintendent in charge of Special Education, be returned to the Chicago Parental School at the request of the principal of the school to which he has been paroled.

B. Procedures in Assignment to and Transfer from Montefiore and Moseley Schools and their branches. Children are transferred to the Montefiore and the Moseley Schools and their branches by order of the General Superintendent through the

217

office of the Assistant Superintendent in charge of Special Education.

Application for transfer is made on the School Problem Report accompanied by the Attendance Officer's Report, both in triplicate. The Attendance Officer's Report should be made even when truancy is not the major issue, since its information may be helpful in understanding the case. In every instance, however, a letter from the principal, in triplicate, should furnish an over-all survey of the case. The School Problem Report, with the Attendance Officer's Report and the principal's letter, is sent by the principal to the office of the District Superintendent who investigates the situation. If the transfer proves to be the necessary next step on behalf of the pupil's welfare, the District Superintendent marks it "Approved" and forwards it to the office of the Assistant Superintendent.

The Assistant Superintendent in charge of Special Education is authorized to transfer a boy or girl from the school in which the pupil is enrolled to any school within the Chicago Public School System which, within his judgment, will most nearly meet the needs of the child.

The transfer will authorize the principal or director of a Chicago public school to accept the child in question.

The principal of the social adjustment school will notify the principal or director of the receiving school and furnish necessary data on the pupil's needs.

The receiving principal or director is requested to enter these children regardless of membership or the time of year and to use every facility of the school and the community to help the child.

Qualifications of Teachers in Social Adjustment Schools

Since the State of Illinois provides a partial reimbursement for the excess of educating socially maladjusted children in special schools, all teachers in these schools for social adjustment must meet both the requirements of the Board of Examiners of the Chicago Public Schools and the qualifications established by the Office of the Superintendent of Public Instruction of the State of Illinois.

Requirements of the Board of Examiners. The teacher must hold a valid Chicago Teachers Certificate and must meet the following requirements of the State Department of Public Instruction:

The teacher must add a minimum of 24 semester hours of special training in an accredited college or teacher training institution as follows: 1. Introductory course in the education of exceptional children; 2. Mental hygiene (with special reference to the problems of childhood); 3. Psychology of the exceptional child (including clinical psychology); 4. Psychology of the adolescent; 5. Testing and measuring; 6. Recreation: crafts, hobbies, leisure-time activities; 7. Casework procedures and practice; 8. Social problems course.

Public Relations

Social adjustment schools, in order to perform their function effectively, require the sympathetic understanding and cooperation of the whole city. This relation is fostered by: 1. Field adjustment teachers who interpret the purpose and place of the school in education and in the life of Chicago; 2. Welfare and social service agencies which supplement and fortify the services of the school; 3. Professional groups who give guidance and advice to the work; 4. Men's and women's service groups who give both moral and material support to the efforts of these schools; 5. The "foster" parent-teacher association made up of members of other parent-teacher associations, of civic-minded citizens, and of people interested in the social welfare of children. These associations sponsor "open house programs," training schools, and benefit performances.[21]

References

[1] Detroit Public Schools, Department of Special Education. "Ungraded Classes for the Socially Maladjusted." Detroit: the Department, 1958. p. 3-4.

[2] *Ibid.*, p. 1, 2.

[3] Public Schools of the District of Columbia, Office of the Assistant Superintendent. "Boys' Junior-Senior High School." Washington, D. C.: the Office, 1958. p. 1-5 *passim.*

[4] Chicago Public Schools, Montefiore School. *Montefiore School: Twenty-Ninth Annual Report, 1957-1958.* Chicago: the Public Schools, 1958. p. 3-4.

[5] Newton Public Schools, Division of Counseling Services. *Meeting Special Needs of Individual Pupils: Annual Report, Division of Counseling Services, 1957-1958.* West Newton, Massachusetts: the Division, 1958. p. 76.

[6] Office of the Los Angeles County Superintendent of Schools, Division of Special Schools. "General Statement of Special Schools." Los Angeles: the Division, 1958. p. 1-2.

[7] The New York State Department of Social Welfare. "Otisville State Training School for Boys, Otisville, New York." Otisville: the Department, 1959. p. 4-5.

[8] State of California, Department of the Youth Authority. *California Youth Authority, Biennial Report 1955-56: Delinquency Prevention, Diagnosis, Treatment and Rehabilitation.* Sacramento: the Department, 1957. p. 8-9.

[9] State of California, Department of the Youth Authority. *Department of the Youth Authority, 1957-58 Biennial Report.* Sacramento: the Department, 1959. p. 8.

[10] School District of Philadelphia, Division of Special Education. *The Education of the Child with a Handicap.* Philadelphia: the School District, 1958. p. 8.

[11] Detroit Public Schools, Department of Special Education. *Ungraded Classes for the Socially Maladjusted.* Detroit: the Department, 1953. p. 20-21.

[12] State of California, Department of the Youth Authority. *California Youth Authority, Biennial Report 1955-56: Delinquency Prevention, Diagnosis, Treatment and Rehabilitation.* Sacramento: the Department, 1957. p. 7.

[13] Board of Education of the City of New York, Curriculum Council and the Division of Curriculum Development. "Ways in Which Schools Aid in Juvenile Delinquency Prevention." *Curriculum and Materials* 11:5; November-December 1956.

[14] Los Angeles County Special Schools. "A Report: The Role and the Program of the Los Angeles County Special Schools." Los Angeles: the Schools, 1959. p. 11-12.

[15] *Ibid.,* p. 24.

[16] Los Angeles County Special Schools. "Oak Grove Boys' Camp School: Program and Curriculum." Los Angeles: the Schools, 1959. p. 1.

[17] Los Angeles County Special Schools. "A Report: The Role and the Program of the Los Angeles County Special Schools." Los Angeles: the Schools, 1959. p. 25.

[18] *Ibid.,* p. 28-35.

[19] *Ibid.,* p. 35-38.

[20] *Ibid.,* p. 15-20.

[21] "Types of Social Adjustment Schools in Chicago," a report submitted to the Project by Edward H. Stullken, principal, Montefiore Special School.

chapter 7 **WORKING WITH THE FAMILY**

basic principle: THE SCHOOL RECOGNIZES AND AC-
CEPTS THE FACT THAT THE FAMILY IS ONE OF THE
MOST IMPORTANT INFLUENCES IN THE LIFE OF AN
INDIVIDUAL, THAT FEW PARENTS ARE WILLFULLY
NEGLIGENT OR HAVE ANY WISH TO RAISE A DELIN-
QUENT YOUNGSTER, AND THAT PARENTS ARE IN A
STRATEGIC POSITION TO UNDERSTAND AND EVALU-
ATE THE GROWTH AND DEVELOPMENT OF THEIR
OWN CHILDREN. THE SCHOOL, HAVING RECOG-
NIZED AND ACCEPTED THE RESPONSIBILITIES OF
IDENTIFYING POTENTIAL OR ACTUAL DELINQUENT
BEHAVIOR IN THE SCHOOL SITUATION, WORKS WITH
THE FAMILY IN A COMMON ENDEAVOR TO ACHIEVE
WHAT IS BEST FOR THE YOUNGSTER.

The contemporary partnership of home and school in the
mutual enterprise of child rearing and nurture is generally
recognized and accepted, particularly in the middle-class
milieu, though this relationship is not so evident in the lower-
class homes, which are less often represented at PTA functions. The parent-teacher conferences with lower-class parents are less easily scheduled and frequently assume a very
different tone from conferences with middle-class parents.

Gaining the understanding and the cooperation of the
parent or parents of the norm violator is never a simple or
easy task, but it is always a crucial point on which treatment
and help are frequently postulated. In those instances when
the school cannot establish a working relationship with the
parent either because of the parent's lack of interest or sheer
neglect of the youngster or the physical absence of any effective parent, the school must face the problem of working
virtually *in loco parentis,* and it must enlist the cooperation
of some family service agency to aid the youngster.

221

Techniques which schools can use in reaching "hard-to-reach" parents still need to be worked out. The negative and even hostile attitudes that are so often the rule in many difficult cases tend to discourage even the most willing and conscientious school worker, but so long as the youngster is enrolled in school, his case can never be "closed," nor can his family be "abandoned" as hopeless. As long as someone in the school and/or the community is intelligently concerned and is prepared to act on the best evidence and knowledge available, there is hope for the youngster and his family.

As Document 1 of this series pointed out, in working with the lower-class parent the school will need to keep constantly in mind the differences in values and focal concerns between the middle class and the lower class. It is all too easy for middle-class youth workers to dismiss the lower-class parent with negative judgments as to his way of life and the quality of his relationships with his children. Many of these parents themselves need, more than anything else, some feeling of understanding and acceptance on the part of the school and the community. The following guidelines present some clues for working with parents.

Guidelines

* The school makes it possible for all parents to participate in the study and evaluation of the total school program; through this cooperative effort the school develops the community understanding and support—moral and monetary —necessary to maximum effectiveness for all youngsters, including the norm violating.

* Parents of youngsters needing help, regardless of their status, are included in the school's rehabilitation program; a special effort is made to include lower-class parents in small interest groups concerned with such problems as difficulties in reading, arithmetic, and speech as well as such problems as mental retardation and norm-violating behavior, thus enabling parents to understand, accept, and assist youngsters with their problems.

222

* In recommending and in interpreting special services—psychological, psychiatric, casework—the school staff is aware of and is prepared to encounter negative and hostile attitudes of some parents toward such help.

* In relating to parents, the staff member is sensitive to his own status and tries to neutralize the factors of language and culture that frequently act as barriers to effective communication.

* The school staff, in working with parents, keeps constantly in mind the differences in values, levels of aspirations, and focal concerns that characterize the homes and neighborhoods in different milieus.

* In discussing the youngster's problems with the parents, the staff members should take care not to alienate the parent or to be themselves alienated through differences in background; such conferences should be scheduled for reasonable and convenient times.

* Special programming is planned to bring in parents who do not participate in the parent-school activities. This is particularly relevant to lower-class parents.

* The school works closely with the parent-teacher organization and emphasizes programming for child welfare and better family living.

* In difficult home situations, the school uses its special service personnel who have liaison functions in building and maintaining cooperative parent-school relationships.

* The school is cognizant of the nature of the youngster's household; special attention is given to those youngsters who live in a female-based household without a positive and adequate father figure.

* When the school fails through no fault of its own to effect and maintain parent contact, it must then make an extra effort to assist the youngster in his social and emotional adjustment.

* When parents are either nonexistent or completely incompetent, the school should designate a staff member such as the counselor, athletic coach, principal, or teacher to act as a parent-substitute figure.

* The school meets its responsibility for identifying and referring the hard-core or multiproblem family. After referral is made, the school cooperates with the agency directing the family casework.

Practices

In discussing the problem of reaching the "unreached youth" the New Jersey Youth Study Commission pointed out:

The role of the family as the primary social institution responsible for raising children has been many times described. Family members are in a position to be the very first, psychologically as well as chronologically, to reach the child. If the child is raised "properly" the family has succeeded in communicating the basic values and standards of society—in such a way that the child takes over these values and standards and incorporates them into his daily attitudes and behavior. He becomes an integrated member of the community, sharing the expectations which society has of him and seeing himself as someone who counts, with a definite role to play—now and in the future.

It is clear that families sometimes fail to give their children the love, knowledge, and guidance necessary for safe passage through childhood and adolescence. The reasons for failure may lie within the parents themselves or they may lie outside in the community. Let us look first at the parents themselves.

Our findings indicate that inadequacy within the family may show itself in two basic ways. The first way shows itself in parents who actually do not have the knowledge or the appropriate attitudes and values to transmit to their children. They may be immigrants unfamilar with American culture, or they may be fifth-generation Americans who rigidly adhere to outmoded traditional standards of behavior which are entirely inappropriate for growing up successfully under present-day conditions.

Parents, in other words, may not know what to teach their children in order to help them to become integrated members of

224

the larger community. Most commonly, perhaps, this deficiency stems from their own lack of education, their restricted interests and aspirations, and their indifference to acceptable means of self-improvement through schooling and hard work.

The second basic form of family inadequacy is the incapacity of parents to effectively transmit the appropriate cultural traditions which they do, in fact, possess. The content of the teachings may be excellent but the manner of their presentation is ineffectual. Here the parents' own problems typically prevent the development of the warm and understanding relationship between parent and child which is necessary for effective communication to take place and to stick.

This most commonly occurs where the mother or father or both are emotionally immature or mentally disturbed. The situation is sometimes aggravated further by the absence of one parent from the family life.

What can we do about these inadequate parents—of whatever type? Here the Commission strongly advises caution. We must be particularly wary of using the "delinquent" parent as a handy scapegoat. And we must see through the flimsy promises of panaceas such as "punish the parent and all will be well."

To blame the inadequate parent is useless. To punish the parent is worse—for it can be dangerous for both the parent and child, as well as for the community. Many authorities have described the harm that can result to already strained relations between parent and child when a parent is punished for a delinquent act committed by an offspring. How to help the inadequate parent—that is the problem.[1]

This chapter will deal not only with practices of schools in regard to the less adequate type of parent but will also present those practices designed to help the school in working with more able and cooperative parents. The parent-school, or more precisely the parent-teacher, relationship is one key to any youngster's school adjustment. When school and family work closely together, a promising result is likely, but when school and family are in opposition, an entirely different climax may be in the offing.

Parent-teacher conferences will do much to bring about greater understanding between these persons so important in the youngster's life. The potential or active norm-violating youngster can be assisted much more through a face-to-face parent-teacher conversation than by impersonal marks on a report card. The parent-teacher relationship can be a hurdle cooperatively overcome or the stumbling block in the youngster's path to better adjustment. Any step taken to reach better understanding between family and school is a giant step forward in helping the child help himself. Many school systems now require periodic parent-teacher conferences or make school time available for them.

PINELLAS COUNTY, FLORIDA: Thirty minutes each day for conferences with parents [is] required of all teachers (except on Fridays and the days preceding vacations (holidays).

EAST WHITTIER, CALIFORNIA: Regular conferences for reporting pupil progress in lieu of or addition to report cards. Conference days are established by the Board of Education where pupils are released so all teachers are free for continuous conferences. Teachers are scheduled for late afternoon and evening parent conferences.

The factor of time is an important one in the scheduling of parent conferences. Many parents who are working during the school day must accept a loss of pay in order to visit the school. Other parents may not wish to tell their employer that they desire time off to answer a school's request for a conference about a son or daughter in difficulty. Every school system should have a school staff member who is especially trained to work with parents and who can adjust his working hours to visit homes for conferences with parents during their off hours. School personnel whose time for these conferences is limited to school hours will find that some parents can never come to school at the suggested hours for visits. Very often these same parents are cooperative when a school staff member visits them. Whenever possible, an appointment should be made in advance of the visit.

NEW YORK CITY: A special research study was made of those parents who could not be seen by the counselors at school. These "hard-to-reach" parents consisted of (a) parents who said they could not come to school and (b) parents who did not respond

226

at all to the counselors' repeated attempts to see them. Twenty-five of these parents were visited by a research assistant.

These "hard-to-reach" parents were not hard to reach in terms of being inaccessible or resistive. When arrangements were made to visit them at home at hours convenient to them (generally, in the evening), all were responsive and cooperative.

The parents who were visited varied in background, aspirations and expectations. Generally, those who had replied that they could not come to school were prevented by practical limitations while those who had not replied at all were further deterred by attitudes, feeling that if the child is not in trouble there is no need to go to school, or feeling hesitant about going to school because of inability to speak English. The first group was generally from a higher occupational and educational background, had higher aspirations for their children, more frequently expected their children to attain these goals and were more aware of educational and career opportunities than the second group.

This study demonstrated the value of having a person with a flexible time schedule to see parents for whom special appointments had to be arranged.[2]

Every member of a school staff should acquaint himself with the families and the neighborhood from which a school draws its pupils. To accomplish this, the entire staff at one school in Michigan, under the leadership of the principal, acted as "surveyors" of certain information during the summer months. By visiting with families in their homes, the teachers' understanding and feeling for children with whom they came in contact were improved.

The parent-school relationship is of special importance to the norm-violating youngster who has been assigned to a special class. The following directive is taken from a handbook on classes for socially maladjusted students.

DETROIT, MICHIGAN: It is of first importance that the ungraded teacher should do everything possible to promote good feelings between the school and the parents, thus making . . . possible . . . harmonious work for the welfare of the child. Teachers should impress upon the parents that everything possible is being done for the child and make them feel welcome to visit the school whenever they wish.

Home visits are essential for the thorough understanding of the child and for the establishment of rapport between the home and the school. A teacher should formulate a definite plan of interview before calling, and the needs of the child should be central in the discussion with the parents. Through such close contact the teacher will have a good idea of the help the parents can offer in the boy's rehabilitation.

Parents should be notified promptly of the absence or tardiness of the boys. Notes should not be entrusted to other boys to deliver, but all such letters or notices should be mailed to the home in plain envelopes.

Check carefully the type of discipline used in the home; home attitudes as reflected at times by parental nationality; age at first serious misbehavior; quality of moral training; and, particularly, the types of school misconduct. In many cases, antisocial behavior follows a definite pattern of deterioration.[3]

As suggested earlier, it is advisable to designate a particular person to serve as the school contact with the parents of a particular norm-violating youngster. This person may be chosen because of a special relationship with the student, because of a special knowledge of the parent or previous contact with the parent, or because, as in the following suggestion, he possesses special skills.

Los Angeles County, California: Many counselors expressed a definite need for a psychiatric-social caseworker or a specially trained person who could work effectively as the school contact person with parents. Most classroom teachers, and even certain counselors, have been shown not to have the special training in social service, in professional attitude, in family relations, in sex-instruction, and in adult education to be able to give adequate parental service as the school contact person, in attempting to secure cooperation with parents who are too dominant, neglectful, or ineffective. In fact, classroom teachers often fear such contacts, as most of their training has been in regard to children and adolescents, with no relation to adults. This psychiatric-social service, then, must require special training and experience.

In one or two schools having a large majority of Negro and Non-Anglo enrollment, an effective contact person has been chosen . . . [from] the same social, cultural, and nationality

228

background, capable of being accepted in the homes and able to speak in their own tongue. Such specially trained and understanding persons have, in one or two instances, proved very effective in securing parental cooperation to bring about correction of delinquency where all other techniques had failed.[4]

Sometimes a teacher's ability to work with parents arises from a special language skill or special understanding of the parent's culture and background. Thus, in New York City school social workers with a knowledge of Spanish were hired to aid in the work with Spanish-speaking parents.

Perhaps in no other area are more anecdotes reported than in the area of parent-teacher misunderstanding. Consider the conflict in the mind of the pupil whose immigrant parents from a malaria area force him to sleep in a room with closed windows to keep the "bad" night air out, while his teacher tells him he must sleep with windows open to let the "good" night air in. A knowledge of the culture and background of the parents would have eased this problem. However, misunderstanding due to cultural differences may not exist solely between teacher and parent. The following comment from a United Nations report describes how cultural difference and conflict may arise between parents and children.

UNITED NATIONS: According to some opinions it is claimed that juveniles assimilate certain aspects of new culture patterns at a faster rate than adults. The problem of culture conflict which results in the delinquency of juveniles in families having immigrant parents and native born children in the American society is well known. A similar conflict situation may also occur in the less developed countries during the transition period from an agricultural to an industrialized economy. Culture patterns in the cities are different from those of the rural areas, and children who immigrate with their parents into the urban centres may absorb local culture patterns quicker than their parents and cause a conflict situation within the home. In such circumstances, the school could pay particular attention to avoiding maladjustment in juveniles by the provision of appropriate educational measures for children as well as assisting in the education of parents by establishing cooperative relationships with them in order to ease the conflict situation.[5]

A necessary forerunner to success in parent-teacher relations is that the teacher or any caseworker recognizes that the parent has his own opinions, has his own cultural background, has a language which may or may not have class or ethnic implications. A teacher and parent cannot reach a decision about a youngster until they have come to an understanding of each other's values. This lack of understanding and a tendency to take "sides" always add to the difficulty of conferences.

CHICAGO, ILLINOIS: The caseworker often had to cope with his feelings toward a parent who had for whatever reason been unhelpful to his child. But the caseworker's identification with children against "bad" parents was usually held in check by the realization that today's bad parents are the product of a similar set of parents, just as today's young delinquent without change will also become an inadequate parent. This is obvious, but it is remarkable how often the parent took steps to cooperate only after the worker took stock of himself and realized the parent was reacting to the worker's unconscious side-taking against him.[6]

If parent-school conferences are to realize their greatest potential, staff inservice education in the methods of effectual communication with parents and in conference reporting is an ongoing requirement. Whenever contacts are made with a home, records similiar to the following should be kept for the future use of other professional workers who may be called in if the youngster's problems become more demanding.

PONTIAC, MICHIGAN:

Record of Home Visits[7]

Name of student_____ Address_____ Telephone_____
Date_____ Home visit made by_____
Father_____ Health_____ Education_____ Occupation_____ Interests_____
Mother_____ Health_____ Education_____ Occupation_____ Interests_____
Brothers_____ Ages_____ Significant facts regarding them_____

Sisters_____ Ages_____ Significant facts regarding them_____

Purpose of the visit_____ Appointment for visit_____

230

Record of Home Visits (continued)

The home is located in a residential___ industrial___ rural___ section.
It is comfortably___ adequately___ inadequately___ equipped.
The pupil studies in his own room___ in a family room but alone___
in the presence of others___.
It appears to be a home where parents exercise complete control___
where parents and children cooperate___ where there is not control___.
This child contributes to the life of the family by_____
Parents' ambitions for the child_____
Problems to be faced in realizing these_____
Parents' attitude toward school is_____
Ways the school can serve this home_____
Ways this home can contribute to the school_____
Remarks:

If the basic level of family-school cooperation is the parent-teacher conference, perhaps the second level is the parent group. In many schools this group has been formalized into a parent-teacher association. Such organizations are still largely untried in terms of the roles they might play in preventing and controlling norm-violating behavior. For example, one such group took direct action in the field of setting standards for student behavior.

HAMMOND, INDIANA: To fight the influences which make delinquents out of juveniles, the Morton School Parent-Teachers Association has noted a set of ten recommendations to protect youth.

The proposals evolved after the juvenile protection committee conducted research on the problem, discussed the reports, and took aim at the sources of delinquency.

The suggestions, to be mailed to members in September with the annual membership letter, urge encouragement of youth by example; cooperation between adults and police in enforcing the curfew law; church-going; firm discipline; cooperation between school, court, and police in guiding youth's entertainment; setting up a parent-student code and qualified psychologists for the school system.

In tackling the juvenile protection problem. . . . [the association] attempted to pinpoint the causes of delinquency. It collected opinions of local, regional, and national officials.[8]

In some localities school people have led in the formation of committees to study local needs and make recommendations. A conference composed of officials of 30 state-wide

231

organizations was sponsored in June 1958 by the New York State Elementary and Secondary School Principals Associations in cooperation with the state education department. The recommendations below, excerpted from the report of this conference, particularly concern parents.

THE STATE OF NEW YORK: *Representatives of Laymen's Groups and Civic Groups proposed that*: Each school have a strong parent-teacher association. Increased cooperation of mass communications media be gained to reach and inform more parents—with stress on achievements rather than delinquency.

Representatives of Religious Groups proposed that: Educational programs, supplementing those of the public schools, be provided by religious institutions for young people, including such extracurricular activities as music, dramatics, and discussion circles for gifted teen-agers. Parent education seminars be held on child development and parent-child relations, utilizing community specialists.

Representatives of Labor Groups proposed that: Parents who are wives of labor leaders be more active in school-parent groups.

Representatives of Government Groups proposed that: The name of each child born and names and addresses of parents be recorded in the State Department of Health so that parents can receive booklets on the home and parent-child relations.[9]

On the West Coast a Governor's Conference on Youth Participation in Community Affairs discussed the expectations and the desires of both youngsters and parents.

THE STATE OF CALIFORNIA: Youth participants joined adults enthusiastically in the 14 sections which considered the family. It was agreed that the family was the basic social institution where the needs of each individual might be met and the foundation for love and mutual respect built. The example parents set was found to be important. Families are responsible for developing strong persons able to cope with existing pressures.

Participants agreed that young people expect parents to show love and respect and to set the example for the kind of behavior they expect. The importance of consistency was stressed. Parents should provide supervision, give a sense of security, and help build the core values. Youth expect parents to provide guidance and discipline and to give reasons that youth can comprehend.

Appropriate punishment was to be expected along with discipline. Young people wish parents to show trust and to accept them in the family as persons. Family discussion was hoped for in contrast to "arguments."

Discussion in the groups showed that parents would like to know the truth in matters affecting young people. They would like to know where their children are. They expect respect and understanding. They wish young people to accept responsibility. Parents would like to be accepted as persons, too. They would like youth to have trust in their wisdom and would like them to discuss their problems with them. . . .

Group members urged the importance of family life education, suggesting possible expansion of present senior problems classes. Parent and child counseling might start with full-time counselors in the early grades. Family councils were stressed. Families need to plan together for hobbies, trips, and entertainment. They need time spent together and also "time apart." Parents should include children in their world of enjoyment and responsibility. Programs involving all age groups are needed. Some urged half-day work only [for] mothers; others said, "no work for Mom while kids are young." Working families should strive for at least one evening a week together. Families must set the pattern for religious training. Parents need to realize [that] maturity comes at different paces with different children. All family members need to learn to listen. "You can't communicate with closed ears."

Parents are responsible for moral and spiritual values; they set the example in church attendance. Families should discuss together such matters as conformity, "the haircut," driving and the family car, cliques, and how to develop a "team" spirit in the family. The quality of family time together was thought to be more important than quantity. "Respect for parents increases respect for authority."

Care needs to be given to guard against overprotection as against neglect; TV stations should be urged to build up culturally beneficial programs.

Homes were likened to service stations where "we fill up and drive on." The family should try to give every type of service needed.

Parent conferences: Close cooperation between the home and the school was favored by all groups discussing this problem.

It was pointed out, however, that high-school students are at an age when they are becoming more self-reliant, and parent-school cooperation should take an appropriate form. Planned student-home-school conferences at the eighth- or ninth-grade levels were suggested as a desirable means for agreeing upon a long-term school program.[10]

However, only the very exceptional parent-teacher organization or parent-youth committee will ever reach all the parents of a given school. There are always parents "too busy," "too tired," or "too overworked" to respond to the usual school motivations for cooperation. But such parents can be reached.

NATIONAL HEALTH CONFERENCE: In certain urban areas of economic deterioration, where parents are so beset by bread-and-butter problems that they cannot readily focus their attention on problems of child rearing, groups of parents may be brought together around some common problem other than, but related to, child rearing. A child welfare worker in Iowa, for example, reports that she has been conducting a discussion group composed of mothers who are recipients of aid to dependent children grants. The initial focus of this group was on the problems of living within the public assistance budget, but they eventually came to discuss the problems of child rearing. . . .

To reach the unreached in parent education it is necessary that the content of the discussion and reading materials be geared to the educational level of the parents. While it is true that mothers with advanced schooling have shown a great increase in fertility in recent years, less well-educated mothers continue to produce a large share of the children. In 1950, with a total of nearly 16 million children under 5 years of age in the country, the mothers of nearly 5 million had no more than grammar school education. The mothers of about 9 million had completed 1 to 4 years of high school and the mothers of 2 million had gone to college. While educational attainment may be only a rough measure of ability to comprehend and learn, it seems obvious that if the parent education effort is to be extended, it must in part be geared to mothers who have enjoyed few educational advantages.[11]

The parent with a special problem sometimes comes seeking help. In Pontiac, Michigan, the school offers an evening

234

course on family living, which the parents of "children in trouble" with court or school are especially invited to attend.

Always the school must keep in mind its responsibility for aiding the family in any way that it can. Usually this aid consists of seeing that the family gets information on what special help is available and where it may be found.

MADISON, WISCONSIN: The parents of emotionally disturbed children are apprised of the various appropriate services of help available to them in the community. If a parent indicates a willingness to avail himself of such help, . . . a copy of our report is forwarded to the agency [with the parent's consent], with a covering letter prior to the parent's making an initial contact. On occasions telephone or personal contacts are made with agencies involved.

An effort is made to educate . . . [the parents] to the general functions and procedures of the agency to which they are being referred. Special emphasis is placed upon:
1. The fact that treatment is usually time consuming and results are often slow to appear.
2. The obligation they have to the agency of asking them for any information they wish, expressing their desires and their dissatisfactions.[12]

The Family Service Association of America states that teachers are an important source of referrals of families needing help.

Our almost 300 agencies have an interest in the teachers as an intelligent source of referral of families whose members need the kind of help that can be given by our agencies. Thus, in published material which goes to teachers a list of Family Service Agencies and the kind of referrals they can accept from teachers which relate to delinquency prevention might be valuable in many localities.

Many of our agencies are becoming increasingly interested in mental health education, preventive activities, or family life education and have speakers and discussion leaders well trained in family counseling who are now using their knowledge and skills in working with groups in various kinds of family life education programs. Many of our agencies accept such assignments with Parent-Teacher Associations, etc. One result has

235

been that troubled parents who attended such group discussions often applied for family counseling at a much earlier date than otherwise and thus tragedy sometimes [was] averted.

Occasionally the attempt to help the family is less direct and the school tries to improve the pattern of family living through its work with the children.

HOUSTON, TEXAS: The Visiting Teacher Service is presently cooperating with a community project known as the Hawthorne Project, name being taken from the school in the area. The initial purpose was to see that every child in the neighborhood who is eligible attends nursery school or kindergarten. Neighborhood Centers and Exchange Club provide nursery school facility.

The intent was to improve the pattern of family living as well as to help the children in this Latin-American area. There is much academic retardation and poor school attendance. It is felt that the language factor was a contributing element, and it was hoped that through the nursery and kindergarten education of children in this area they would have an improved facility for using the school program.

Suggesting available service and seeing that a family accepts such suggestions are two very different things. Although the school cannot require that a family seek a certain type of help, an increasing number of systems are requiring a willingness to accept a referral as a condition of readmission of a suspended or expelled youngster. And if the referral is carried through, research indicates that even the hard-core problem family can help itself.

NEW YORK CITY: Although the detection of children with problems was found to be relatively simple, referral of them and their families for help with their difficulties proved to be much more complex. These were families who did not ordinarily avail themselves of agency services, usually did not want help, and often did not see the need for it. Yet they were the families who caused concern in the community because of their propensity for getting into trouble. . . . The children were often unhappy and neglected—"problems" at home, at school, and in the neighborhood; the parents were beset with difficulties—marital, economic, physical, and emotional. Consequently, these families required an inordinate amount of time on the part of the referral

236

unit workers in relation to the results that could be achieved. This interfered with the major functions of the referral units (detection, diagnosis, and referral, not treatment) and yet the existent social pathology was so gross that it could not be ignored. . . .

. . . in 46 percent of the cases the parents denied the existence of a problem in the child or simply refused appointments with the community agency to which they had been referred for help. In 35 percent of the cases the family problems were so serious or numerous, or there were so many children in the home, the parents seemed unable to take action on behalf of a specific child. Such problems included grave marital conflict, alcoholism of the mother or father, and poor environmental conditions . . . [such as] extremely bad housing. Another fairly large group (13 percent) was comprised of families in which the mother was deceased or chronically ill to such a degree that she could not fully assume her duties, and the remaining 6 percent of the families were either seriously neglectful of the children or required further study.

In view of the above, it is not unexpected to find that the majority (59 percent) of the parents included in the study had little awareness of their part in the child's difficulties. If they admitted the existence of his problem (and 15 percent of them did not), they blamed it on an external agent such as the neighborhood, his associates, or the school; and in 18 percent of the cases, the parents blamed each other for being too lax or too severe in their management of the children. Occasionally they attributed the difficulty to extreme sibling rivalry, but on the whole the tendency was to minimize, disregard, or justify the child's problem. . . .

In an unofficial experiment . . . when the most difficult and unpromising families were assigned to the supervisor and her two most seasoned caseworkers, it was found that good results could be obtained, provided that help could be sustained for an extended period, that the family diagnosis admitted some possibility of improvement, and that the goals to be reached were not too high. With many regressions and periodic crises, progress still ensued if the workers were consistently realistic, helpful, and unpunitive, and if they were both skillful in mobilizing community resources and willing to assume the major responsibility for unification of effort on behalf of specific families.[13]

237

In the city of Portland, Oregon, in cooperation with Multnomah County, a committee was formed as a result of a meeting called by several interested community groups after an outbreak of juvenile offenses received wide publicity. This committee recommended and discussed a possible contribution the school might make to the community's effort to aid the delinquent youngster's family.

PORTLAND-MULTNOMAH COUNTY, OREGON: [Recommendation:] *In addition to the coordination of agency program activities that the Community Council carries on, there is a need for specific case planning among the agencies concerned about a particular child and his family where delinquency is either a potential or actual problem.*

[Discussion:] The best way to carry out this responsibility is still unknown, but experience in our own community, as well as in others, indicates that the following points need to be considered:

a. A small percentage of the families in a community account for the major work load of agencies involved with juvenile delinquency—in several cities approximately six percent of the families account for 55 to 70 percent of the caseloads.

b. Family patterns tend to be repeated from generation to generation. It is extremely important to find successful ways of helping children in these families to change the basic family pattern as they marry and have children of their own.

c. Too often, one agency after another has worked with one or more members of these families without really succeeding in helping the family to become socially rehabilitated and strong enough to avoid succeeding breakdowns and difficulties.

d. Recently, experience in St. Paul, New York City and other cities indicates that greater success may be achieved with these "hard core" families if central case planning, reporting and treatment efforts go on steadily among the agencies involved with a particular family.

e. More specifically, this means that with each case one agency should be primarily responsible for coordinating the case planning and for seeing that all agencies interested in this family coordinate and clear their activities with each other. This also means that no agency endeavoring to help the family would drop or discontinue its efforts, except as the central case planning indi-

238

cated some other approach should be tried. The Community Council should call together the appropriate agencies to determine what system should be developed for the efficient exchange of information on cases. We should not lose track of unsolved problems.

f. Centralizing responsibility for case planning is difficult. Presumably a different agency might carry the primary responsibility in different case situations. Over all, however, it seems advisable to have one organization or agency responsible, either for carrying central case planning, or for seeing to it that another agency has accepted such a responsibility. It is suggested that in our community the logical place to lodge the over-all responsibility so far as school children are concerned is with the School Social Work program, providing it can be greatly expanded. The school is the one organization in the community that deals with most of the children and is in contact with them daily. It is in the best position to know of the headway or improvement the child is making. It does not lose track of the child, and it must of necessity be concerned with the child's development from six to eighteen years of age.

g. It should be emphasized again that the community should know that not all families can be helped with present knowledge and social work skills. More needs to be learned before any system can assure results in every case, and the public should be aware of that. Social agencies should strive to use their contacts with families or children as a way of developing sufficient relationship so that help can be given and used constructively.

h. It is recognized, too, that prevention work is needed often before children are of school age and with adults before they have children. This means, of course, that the prevention program should not be left entirely to any one institution such as the schools, but that every agency should be backed up with public encouragement in its efforts at prevention and at "hanging on" to families where it may be of constructive help.[14]

A pilot project combining group counseling for adolescents and education for their parents is operated jointly by the North Shore Child Guidance Center, a voluntary, nonprofit group, and the school systems of Great Neck, Manhasset, Port Washington, Roslyn, and East Williston, New York.

Long Island, New York: The plan focuses on a particular group of adolescents—those who, because of mental health problems, make it difficult for their teachers to teach and their classmates to learn, or who stand in the way of their own ability to make use of the school experience; and who would not be likely through their own or their parents' efforts to come to either a private or voluntary mental health service. . . .

No adolescent will be excluded because of his parents' unwillingness or inability to pay a fee or because of their refusal to attend the parents' discussion classes. From the Center's point of view, the only criteria for *not* including an adolescent would be (a) that the nature of his difficulty called for some other form of treatment, or (b) that his parents explicity forbade his participation. . . .

Referral: Each school superintendent has appointed a liaison representative to join with three members of the Center's professional staff (the parent-education director, group counselor, and administrator) to form a working committee which will administer the project. The school liaison representative in each district represents the project in his individual school system; receives potential referrals from teachers, guidance counselors, and psychologists; makes the initial contact with the parents and the adolescents; and arranges an interview for the parents with the parent-education director of the Center. Periodic meetings of the working committee are held in order to perfect methods of procedure and to deal with the difficulties that inevitably arise in the establishment of a new service.

The parent-education director is, in this phase of the project, responsible for acquainting the parents with the nature of the service, for establishing an equitable fee (or for waiving the fee if such action is indicated), and for arranging with the parents to take responsibility for getting the adolescent to the first group meeting which is held at the Center after school hours (probably from 3:30 to 5). . . .

The group counseling is conducted by a psychiatric social worker who has had training and supervised experience in this field as well as in working with adolescents. He is supervised by the administrator and is in frequent consultation with the psychiatric director. He will be available to the adolescents for individual interviews on an "as needed" basis, and the Center will also undertake to provide psychiatric examination and treat-

240

ment for any of the adolescents, if in the course of the group's progress it appears indicated.

The parents' classes are led by a professional parent-educator with previous experience in this highly specialized field and with qualifications as a parent-education specialist according to the standards of the Child Study Association of America. An effort will be made to see each pair of parents before the start of the parents' class. The parent-education director will also be available for individual consultation with parents who may need or desire it.

Conferences between the group counselor and the parent-education director will take place at least once a week in order to provide for maximum integration in the Center's work with each family. Detailed case records will be kept for both the counseling groups and the parent-education classes for use in supervision and research.[15]

There is another group which is becoming increasingly significant as the courts intensify work in the areas of delinquency and child neglect and as the institution of the orphanage slowly disappears. This is the foster parent. As the final report of this chapter, the State Committee on Children and Public Welfare of the State Charities Aid Association of New York briefly delineates the problems facing foster parents and the steps that may be taken to help them.

THE STATE OF NEW YORK: In the course of any one year in New York State some 25,000 children are cared for in foster homes. These are children who have had to be removed from their own families and homes because of such serious and compelling reasons as mental or physical illness of the parents, death in the family, or other factors resulting in a broken home. Most of these children have lived under serious deprivations prior to placement in foster homes.

In modern child welfare work every effort is made to keep the family together and to prevent the break-up of the home. Foster care is used only after every other effort to keep the child with his own family has failed. An increasing proportion of the children who do need foster care are "difficult," in that they present more than the ordinary emotional and physical problems.

During the past decade a great deal of attention has been given to the problems of the children who are to be placed in foster homes, but relatively little to the particular problems which face foster parents. The foster family has the delicate and difficult task of serving as a bridge for the child between his removal from and eventual return to his own family. Foster parents must also span the gap between one foster home and another if it becomes necessary for the child to live in a series of foster homes over an extended period of time.

The foster parents who care for dependent children, assigned to them by the public and private child caring agencies, are providing a service that is essential and . . . exceedingly difficult.

In October 1951 the State Charities Aid Association, through its State Committee on Children and Public Welfare, established a program of discussion meetings for foster parents. This gave the foster parents an opportunity to get together to talk over their common problems. The meetings also served to bring the attention of the community at large to the importance of the contribution made by foster parents.

The program has been carried out in close collaboration with child welfare leaders. From the outset this relatively simple plan has been received enthusiastically by the foster parents, child welfare workers in the local communities, and by community leaders who have followed the progress of the meetings. . . . Foster parents are, of course, essential to a well-rounded child care program. But, except for the services of the caseworker, relatively little has been accomplished in helping them with their somewhat special problems. Yet they welcome every opportunity to learn how to do a better job with the children under their care.

If there is an interest in your community in establishing such a series of meetings, the simplest approach is to organize a small committee, including representatives of interested agencies and citizen leaders who can bring in the necessary voluntary help to handle certain aspects of the program. It should be stressed at the outset that this series of meetings cannot be successfully undertaken without the interest and cooperation of the agencies working with foster parents. Representatives of the agencies should be included in every step of the plan.[16]

Schools cannot accomplish their mission unless school programs and procedures are supported by parents and by community leaders. The school's continuing effort to increase and deepen its contacts with parents is both necessary and rewarding.

References

[1] New Jersey Youth Study Commission. *New Ways to Reach Unreached Youth: A Challenge to New Jersey.* Third Annual Report and Recommendations of the State of New Jersey Youth Study Commission. Trenton: the Commission, June 1958. p. 46-48.

[2] Board of Education of the City of New York, Demonstration Guidance Project. "Progress Report 1957-1958." New York City: the Project, 1958. p. 10.

[3] Detroit Public Schools, Department of Special Education. "Ungraded Classes for the Socially Maladjusted." Detroit: the Department, 1958. p. 22.

[4] Office of the Los Angeles County Superintendent of Schools, Division of Research and Guidance. *School Factors Related to Delinquency.* Los Angeles: the Division, 1951. p. 31, 32.

[5] United Nations. *International Review of Criminal Policy.* A Report Prepared by the Secretariat for the First United Nations Congress on the Prevention of Crime and the Treatment of Offenders. Geneva: the United Nations, 1955. p. 41.

[6] Juvenile Protective Association of Chicago and Chicago Police Department. *Report on the Englewood Project.* Chicago: the Association, 1958. p. 22.

[7] Pontiac Public Schools, Pupil Personnel Division. "Record of Home Visits." Pontiac, Michigan: the Division, 1958.

[8] Hammond Times. "PTA Takes Aim at Delinquency." Hammond (Indiana) *Times*, April 6, 1958.

[9] University of the State of New York; Elementary and Secondary School Principals Associations; and New York State Education Department. "Conference on Juvenile Delinquency." Minutes of the Conference. Albany: the Associations, 1958. p. 5-8.

[10] State of California, Governor's Advisory Committee on Children and Youth, Department of the Youth Authority. "Governor's Conference on Youth Participation in Community Affairs." Sacramento: the Department, 1958. p. 16-18, 23.

[11] U.S. Department of Health, Education, and Welfare, Social Security Administration, Children's Bureau. *Health Services and Juvenile Delinquency.* A Report on a Conference on the Role of Health Services in Preventing Dissocial Behavior. Washington, D. C.: Superintendent of Documents, Government Printing Office, 1955. p. 16-17.

[12] Madison Public Schools, Department of Child Study and Service. "Guidance in the Madison Public Schools." Madison, Wisconsin: the Department, 1957. p. 7.

[13] New York City Youth Board. *Reaching the Unreached Family.* Youth Board Monograph No. 5. New York City: the Board, 1958. p. 3-4, 17-18.

[14] County of Multnomah and City of Portland, Oregon, Citizens Committee on Juvenile Delinquency. "Report of Citizens Committee on Juvenile Delinquency." Portland: the Committee, 1958. p. 17-19.

[15] North Shore Child Guidance Center. "A Proposal for a Special Group Counseling Project for Troubled Adolescents." Manhasset, New York: the Center, 1959. p. 2-6.

[16] State Charities Aid Association, State Committee on Children and Public Welfare. *Step by Step: A Guide for a Program to Help the Foster Parents in Your Community.* New York City: the Association, 1952. p. 1-3.

243

WORKING WITH LAW-ENFORCEMENT
chapter 8 AND COURT PERSONNEL

basic principle: THE SCHOOL, LAW-ENFORCEMENT
AND COURT PERSONNEL DEVELOP A COORDINATED
AND COOPERATIVE PROGRAM IN ALL COMMON
AREAS RELATED TO JUVENILE NORM-VIOLATING
BEHAVIOR.

The police, courts, and state or local youth authorities
and commissions all play a vital role in working with the
norm violators who come within the purview of legal authority. Most of these boys and girls are also the concern of the
school. When the norm violator comes to the attention of
the police, probation, or parole worker, a routine conference
with some delegated school official is in order. By sharing
information through joint study and planning, personnel
from school, legal agencies, and court can do much for a
youngster's present and future welfare.

In many communities the organization of juvenile police
bureaus with specially trained officers in the police department has established a strong bridge linking the law-enforcement agencies with the school and other community resources. Similar functions that serve to coordinate efforts
and improve communication with other agencies can also be
cited in the operation of the probation and parole workers.
The school should open its doors to these officials who are
legally concerned with those norm-violating youngsters either
in school or soon to be returned to the classroom. These officials, like teachers, guidance counselors, and principals, are
important members of the professional team whose objective
it is to help the youngster and his family to more effective
personal and social adjustment.

Unfortunately, most, if not all, communities attach a
stigma to police contact and to juvenile court appearances.

244

Thus, when some minor or even major violation is uncovered, home and school sometimes join forces in "protecting" the child from police and court. If school and home err, it is often on the side of overprotection from legal agencies that aim to help rather than to hurt. The decision "to refer or not to refer" a norm-violating youngster to the police and the courts is never a simple or easy decision to make. Sometimes decisions are made not to refer the youngster to police or to the court because of the nature and quality of the operation of the juvenile court, which is often a juvenile court in name only. Although much needs to be done to improve the police and court operation with respect to handling and helping juveniles, school officials who note minor or major norm-violating behavior but who are uncertain about the referral action that should be taken might well confer with police and court officials in order to route the action in the direction that promises the most constructive results.

The Illinois Youth Commission has pointed out that there are many graduated stages or steps in the "delinquency-making" process, each one of which leads the norm violator to become more deeply confirmed as a delinquent and, ultimately, as a criminal.[1] These stages involve: being arrested rather than "let off" with a reprimand or warning; being seen in juvenile court rather than released to parents without official hearing; being placed on probation by the judge rather than discharged; being sent to a state training school rather than placed on probation; being committed to a reformatory rather than receiving a suspended sentence. Each step alienates the norm violator from the dominant authority and fixes more firmly upon the young person his identification by the official community as "a delinquent." Thus identified, the norm violator may come to know, feel, and play this as his role in life.

The school that operates in isolation and shows little interest or first-hand knowledge of the pupil's contacts with police, probationer, or parole worker will fail in its opportunity and obligation to both the youngster in trouble and the professional workers who are legally charged with the heavy respon-

245

sibility to the delinquent. The following guidelines provide a number of action-principles which are aimed to maximize the combined school-police-court operation on behalf of the pupil who is, or should be, in the hands of legally constituted agencies.

Guidelines

* In order to understand the nature and extent of the local delinquency problem, the school, court, and police collate and share their information.

* The school and/or court appoints or designates a court-school liaison person who works on a year-round basis.

* The school thoroughly investigates and uses the appropriate alternatives for action offered by compulsory education laws to aid the norm-violating youngster.

* The norm-violating student is suspended from school only after a careful study is made of the youngster and his home background. When he is separated from school, provisions are made for appropriate agency contact and plans are outlined for his ultimate return to school.

* The school maintains a close contact with every youngster who is suspended from the school; when the youngster passes the age for compulsory school attendance, he is referred to the appropriate community agency that may best serve him.

* The norm-violating youngster is excluded from the school only when the violation or conduct is so extreme that expulsion is warranted for the good of the school and/or the student. The school recognizes that exclusion is not a solution to the student's problem and, therefore, in advance of exclusion, attempts to insure employment or supervision of this youngster by other agencies of the community.

* The school, court, and police recognize truancy as a significant clue to potential delinquency, analyze local records,

and develop a procedure for detection and follow-up as part of a long-range program for combatting delinquency.

* The school cooperates with other agencies, particularly police and court, in developing educational programs for the prevention and control of delinquency and for citizenship training.

* The school and the court work out programs and procedures for the norm-violating youngster awaiting trial, on probation, under detention, or released from probation or detention.

Practices

Since identities of juvenile offenders must be protected by law, police and court personnel are reluctant, and justly so, to release information other than on the basis of professional exchange. However, a constant sharing of information in full confidence should be encouraged and authorized by the administration of both the schools and the probation department—the only limitation in this exchange is that the information shared be relevant to the service or program provided by the agency seeking the information.

In recognition of the confidential nature of case information, it is mandatory that only authorized adult persons participate in the exchange. The data or information received from other agencies is released only to those who are involved in the rehabilitative program, and members of either agency should feel free to question the reason for any breaches of confidence. Therefore, a definite channel is established for the proper exchange of information.

Commonly designated for information exchange roles are such school administrative personnel as principal, assistant principal, or dean; such school counseling or social work personnel as guidance counselor, visiting teacher, school social worker, attendance officer; and such police or court personnel as juvenile police worker and probation officer.

There are many possible ways of financing the position of the school-court liaison worker. Sometimes the school provides the funds, sometimes the court, and sometimes these and other agencies in the community contribute to the support of this position. In Kansas City, Missouri, for example, this position is financed entirely by the school.

KANSAS CITY, MISSOURI: Our connections with other interested community agencies are much strengthened. We now have, for example, a regularly assigned school person working directly within the framework of the Jackson County Juvenile Court. She has earned the confidence of the Judge and his staff and has proved . . . to be an asset to the Court itself. We have found our relationships easier and our communications much more direct. Also . . . within the framework of Juvenile Court, we have assigned a teacher to work with those pupils who are detained by Court action in the Jackson County Detention Home.

In Ventura County, California, however, financial support of the school-court worker is derived solely from the court.

VENTURA COUNTY, CALIFORNIA: A deputy probation officer is assigned on a full-time basis to the schools of the county in an effort to adjust and resolve serious behavior situations within the school in order that the problem may not develop to the stage where exclusion or referral to the juvenile court becomes necessary. . . .

This officer has the following assignments:
1. Works with school representatives, students, and parents in regard to school attendance problems and behavior problems of a serious nature.
2. Serves in a liaison capacity between schools and the probation department in order to keep school representatives advised of students in detention, releases from detention, and returns to schools from juvenile court and placement situations.
3. Serves as field supervising probation officer in selected cases of students who have been returned to school under informal supervisor or as wards of the juvenile court wherein it is indicated that frequent and regular follow-up contacts are required.

248

This officer has a regular school visitation schedule and calls on the larger schools on a weekly basis and visits the smaller schools bimonthly. The schedule is closely followed, and school authorities arrange for conferences with students and parents in advance. . . .

It is clearly understood that the schools will continue to dispose of ordinary problems through normal school channels and processes, and only those serious cases which the school has been unable to resolve are referred to our officer. In addition to handling some of the more serious "headache" cases for the schools, the program has been the solution to the breakdown in the lines of communication between the school and our department regarding movement of youngsters to and from school to court, detentions, and juvenile court dispositions, etc. For instance, our officer calls each school every morning from which youngsters have been detained in juvenile hall during the past 24 hours and advises the school of this fact and the circumstances of the detention.

An Oregon community completes the pattern with its example of mutual financing that involves city, court, and city and county school units.

HOOD RIVER, OREGON: About five years ago our school district, along with the County Unit school district, the County Court and the City of Hood River jointly financed a juvenile officer for the County of Hood River. This officer was responsible to all four agencies. Juvenile cases are turned over to him and he works with the school authorities and the courts. We have found this has been extremely satisfactory. We spend a great deal of time through guidance and counseling in all our schools.

A natural outgrowth of the concern for youngsters with problems which is shared by court, police, and school is a cooperative endeavor to set up programs for prevention and control of delinquency. One such program offers an example of the diffusion of ideas. It was originated by a judge in a six-county area in West Texas; a California police chief, who submitted the next report, read about the program and sought the help of the judge in developing a similar program in his own county.

DEL NORTE COUNTY, CALIFORNIA: The students are taught not only that crime does not pay; they are *shown* that crime does not pay. . . .

It is not, right now, enough to teach our youth the ways and means of government and to allow them to draw their own conclusions about lawlessness. They must be shown, even to the extent of shocking them into the reality, that criminal practices are stupid and unprofitable. This is brought about by a series of programs presented to the entire student body . . . [with] speakers from the field of law enforcement, judiciary, probation, welfare, penitentiary authorities, and even paroled prisoners . . . [who] are considered far enough along the road to rehabilitation that their criminal history, as told by themselves, will be a constructive influence. This phase must, of course, be carefully prepared in order for such a person to be presented in a proper light and all chances of hero worship avoided.

A mayor's youth council, which meets once a month and is composed of representatives of the school, county health unit, county juvenile office, county probate judge, Idaho Department of Public Assistance, Idaho Employment Service, and other interested persons, furnishes the next example of a cooperative program.

COEUR D'ALENE, IDAHO: We had some trouble with juvenile driving, so the youth group working with the police (city, county, and state) put on some pick-up drives; this hasn't cured all the problem but has reduced the problem a great deal.

A number of juveniles were purchasing beer, etc.; so school people and law enforcement officers, prepared a list of all students in the county, grades 7-12, giving names, ages, birthdates, and address of each pupil; these lists were then placed in the hands of all operators of cafes, beer taverns, and dispensers of alcoholic beverages. Since the students know of the list, the attempted purchase of such beverages is greatly reduced.

Juvenile violation of traffic rules is a troublesome problem for the law-enforcement officers and courts in almost any community. One high-school principal, who discerned a marked correlation between student use of automobiles and low academic achievement, established, with the support of the board of trustees, a system of student driving permits.

250

Rexburg, Idaho: No straight "A" student had the use of a car. Only 15% of the "B" students drove a car to school. Car use jumps with the next group to 41% with a "C" average. Car use takes another big jump in the "D" group and in the group of students who failed or quit school, 83% used cars to drive to school and had them available for use during school hours. . . .

. . . rules and regulations intending to improve the educational atmosphere of the Madison Junior and Senior High Schools . . . [were] adopted:

1. Junior and Senior High School students who drive cars to school must make written application to the School Board showing the reason or need to drive their car to school. Those granted permission will receive student permits.

2. Students driving cars to school on the student permits must park them in designated areas.

3. Students failing to comply with established rules and regulations concerning the use of cars will have their student permits revoked. If the student persists in non-compliance to established rules and regulations, he will be subject to expulsion from school by action of the School Board.

4. The use of tobacco, alcohol, or narcotics by any student will not be tolerated. Students failing to comply with this rule will be cited to the faculty for committee action. If necessary, the student will be referred to the School Board for final disposition of his case.

5. Regular attendance shall be expected from every student. Excessive absences without a doctor's permit will be just cause for dismissal from school.

6. Students are expected to register on the designated days. Students registering late will, no doubt, find many classes they had hoped to take, filled.

The only cost of the program thus far has been for printing and mass distribution of the information above. This cost has been shared equally by the city and the school.

The problem of laws or rules concerning smoking has attracted considerable attention. Violation of school smoking laws is a common complaint about the delinquent or predelinquent student. Groups in both Los Angeles and Portland have commented upon this problem.

Los Angeles County, California: It is recommended that Boards of Education and local district administrators, through their state-wide organizations, re-study Section 16073 of the Education Code, so that a *realistic approach* may be taken toward the cigarette and smoking problem in our senior and four-year high schools, because *the present situation leaves educators in an untenable position.*[2]

Portland, Oregon: [*Recommendation:*] The city ordinance which prohibits use of tobacco by those under 21 should be repealed. This would leave in uniform effect the state law which prohibits use of tobacco by minors under 18.

[*Discussion:*] However, repealing the city ordinance alone will not solve the problem. Law enforcement officials are practically unanimous in declaring that this is a most difficult law to enforce. Many high school and college students are regularly smoking in public as well as in private.

Complete disregard of the law of the land in one regard leads very easily to disregard of other laws. The juvenile who is easily swayed and emotionally disturbed may thus learn disrespect for all law. Many parents smoke. Movie, television and sports idols make daily appearances in advertising media to tell others to smoke the brand they have smoked for many years. Try then to tell a teen-ager that only the cheap and the dissipated smoke! A realistic approach must take into consideration the question of lowering of ages under all laws. Any lowering of age should take into consideration health and safety education.[3]

In the course of commenting on youth problems to his board of supervisors, a superintendent of schools pointed out some of the responsibilities accepted by the law-enforcement agency in working with schools.

San Francisco, California: The Police are most helpful in providing outside controls for such functions as the "Annual Football Pageant," which is city-wide in scope. Assistance is also provided for school dances and evening graduation ceremonies. The schools themselves exercise excellent controls in these events; the potential troublemakers are the non-school juveniles and the undesirable fringe. High schools always face

252

the problem of the out-of-school unemployed youth returning at noontime as a potential disturber.

Juvenile Bureau officers are assigned by districts to cover certain schools. This makes possible a better contact with the schools as the officers and school administrators get to know each other personally. The officer visits the school (in plain clothes) at least twice a month, even when there is nothing under investigation at the time. Juvenile Bureau officers are also readily available to talk to groups of students at the school's request. . . .

Since the schools are in the business of training the students to drive automobiles, it is important that the Police and the Juvenile Court coordinate their activities with the schools. This is accomplished by the assignment of a Traffic Education Officer, who operates a "traffic school" for persistent offenders. All moving traffic citations are handled at the Youth Guidance Center, at a regular traffic court twice a week. The Traffic Education Officer acts as bailiff during these hearings.[4]

The examples cited thus far have been supplied by a police chief, a mayor's council, a principal, and a superintendent of schools. The next, however, comes from a superior court judge, juvenile division, who reports on how the division played a coordinating and organizing role in its community.

PHOENIX, ARIZONA: In attempting to cope with the delinquency situation, interested persons and agencies cooperated with us in setting up, in sequence, such bureaus as the Family Aid Bureau, Juvenile Aid Bureau, Driving Schools for Traffic Offenders, and later on our Neighborhood Council Program. . . . Strangely enough most of the demand for the Neighborhood Council Program came from the schools within the district areas. Local leadership talent, previously untapped, was enlisted and utilized, and professional agents, at the suggestion of the neighborhood group, have given increased supervision in the needed areas.

We participate in the school-community discipline programs at the high school level; this commonly is made up of school counsellors, deans, assistant principals, peace officers and functions most effectively in an interchange of ideas and information concerning the children. . . .

We introduced and helped activate in Arizona in 1955, the Delinquency Control Institute, as originated in the University of Southern California. It is given each year at Arizona State University at Tempe, with the instruction nucleus from the University of Southern California faculty.

In conjunction with the Sociology Department of Arizona State University, we have activated training programs for college students interested in our field, in both part-time work projects and observation courses.

In order to coordinate interest and channel all pertinent information to the public, we organized the Arizona Conference on Crime and Delinquency Prevention and Control with unrestricted membership so that any person with an interest in this area could belong and participate. This is the successor to the Arizona Probation and Parole Association. This organization holds annual meetings and sponsors programs to help gain recognition for the problems of law enforcement, probation, parole, education, welfare, and the "frequency" problem as well as the "multiple" problem family that concerns the community, the entire state and nation. In the juvenile probation process we have used private institutions and treatment in foster homes for children who have responded to that type of program. These cases are selected on a screening basis for individualized treatment of each child's problems, based on a combined evaluation of clinical and school reports and all the social background that can be amassed.

Another program operating under court sponsorship is directed toward the family of the potential or active norm-violating youngster.

OAKLAND COUNTY, MICHIGAN: The Child and Family Protection and Youth Assistance Program for Oakland County is a program of the Juvenile Court established by court rule for every area in Oakland County. . . . [Its] purpose is to assist socially unadjusted families, children, and youth at the local community level as a recognized community responsibility. The program is begun by local citizens organizing and assuming community responsibilities for the problem families and children. . . .

The Court's objective is to aid local groups and committees in their local efforts to prevent neglect and delinquency. Staff

254

members of the Court will be assigned to advise and assist local committees whenever requested by the community. The major concern of the Juvenile Court is the adequate emotional, social adjustment of the child in his family and school and neighborhood. The Juvenile Court hopes to avoid an official court action or court record on the family or child. The ages of the children dealt with will comply with the Probate Court-Juvenile Division; namely, any child under 17 years of age. Local Committees can extend this if they decide a service is locally needed.

The initial impetus may develop from a private citizen, police officer or from the PTA or service groups. Thereafter, assistance of the Juvenile Court Protective Service staff may be obtained. The organization of committees then follows. A local resolution or ordinance then is sought and a caseworker is assigned from the Protective Service staff to work with the particular area. . . . local activities and responsibilities . . . [should] be handled by the Protection Committee. Generally, two committees—General Citizens Committee and Casework Committee—are suggested.

The General Citizens Committee formulates plans, interprets programs, gains support for children's needs and aids in conditions and facilities for child welfare. It provides and maintains an up-to-date inventory of all available community resources for child, youth and family care; provides parental and youth codes; induces youth participation in helpful religious and recreational activities; plans in the community for family and child welfare.

The Casework-Executive Committee composed of people involved and skilled in the child welfare services assists the caseworker with casework planning for children and families. The committee members may be nominated by the City Commission, School Board of the district, or a sponsoring organization, such as PTA, or service clubs. The Juvenile Court confirms the nominations. The members serve as volunteers without compensation.

The sources of referrals are parents, schools, police, community individuals, Juvenile Court and social welfare agencies. The committee attempts to enlist the cooperation and support of the parents and child in planning steps towards an adequate community adjustment. When a program is considered failing by the committee, the support of the Juvenile Court may be

255

sought. The [case] material is for the use of the Casework-Executive Committee only—strictly secret and confidential. Treatment plans are based on the individual needs of the child and family. The case may be assigned to the caseworker for further treatment; it may be referred to a private or public social agency or to a minister of the proper religious faith; or to a medical, educational, psychological, or psychiatric specialist. Termination of contact with individual child or parents occurs when satisfactory improvement is noted by the caseworker and affirmed by the casework committee.

The Oakland County Government provides the operating expense for the caseworkers. A special grant of the McGregor Fund provides salary and expenses for a director and his secretary.[5]

[A resolution adopted by the Pontiac, Michigan, City Commission in April 1959 serves as a sample for such a program.]

Section 1. There is hereby established a Youth Assistance Program of the City of Pontiac, in pursuance of the Rule of the Oakland County Juvenile Court.

Section 2. This resolution embodies and shall be known as the Youth Assistance Program of the City of Pontiac, in cooperation with the plan adopted by the School District of the City of Pontiac. Its purpose is to protect, safeguard and improve the physical, mental, emotional and moral welfare of all of the youth of the City by strengthening and improving home and family and community living conditions. This program is also designed to assist in the prevention of delinquency and neglect.

Section 3. An Executive Committee and a Citizens' General Committee shall be appointed jointly by this Commission and the School Board of the School District of the City of Pontiac.

Any citizen or person of good repute in this City may call the needs of an individual child, youth or family to the attention of these committees by written communication signed and bearing the sender's address and phone number. Such communication shall be deemed a private communication as against all persons other than Executive Committee members. Upon receipt of such information, said Executive Committee shall investigate the facts through a trained social worker. He may furnish necessary casework assistance or may refer the matter to the committee. In their discretion, the committee may request the child and his parents or guardian or other custodian to appear

256

before them in a private hearing at a time and place to be designated by them to discuss the welfare of said child and family and to plan how said parents and the community may meet the child's personal, physical, mental, moral, emotional, social or behavior problems.

Section 4. Records of the proceedings before said committee shall be kept confidential and the secretary of the said committee shall keep the same as secret files and destroy the same when the case is closed.

Section 5. The social worker or the Executive Committee may request the parents of said child to do anything deemed necessary for the welfare of said child or family, may request the child and the parents to have any medical or hospital care or needs attended to, may outline a course of reasonable parental supervision and request the parents to abide thereby, may ask any community organization either public or private to render its assistance to said child, and may have further hearings at later dates to ascertain whether the referral program for said child has been effectively carried out.

Section 6. The program of said committee shall be conducted without publicity or notoriety concerning any given child or family, and the attendance before said committee and the complying with the directions of said committee shall be voluntary on the part of the child and the parents; provided, however, that it shall be the duty of said committee to report any failure to comply with such program together with any emotional, social or behavior problems of said child to the Juvenile Court of Oakland County if and when it shall appear that said child or said parents, guardian or custodian of said child are unwilling to or have failed to comply with such programs specified by said committee for the welfare of said child.

Section 7. The members of said committee shall serve as voluntary citizens without compensation; provided, however, the reasonable cost of miscellaneous office supplies, clerical help and office space may be supplied by the City of Pontiac and/or the School District of the City of Pontiac as, in their discretion, first appropriated and provided for by specific authorization and resolution of the governing body of said City and/or School District.

Sometimes a community does not have the requisite probation and court services, and its citizens act to provide these services. For example, in Hampton, Iowa, a town of less than 5000 population, five local citizens serve on a juvenile committee formed to help with juvenile court work. The committee members receive no compensation for the time and effort that they contribute. The committee has four main functions: (a) It investigates the background of the case and makes unofficial recommendations to the court. (b) It polices the case after sentence has been passed. (c) It helps the court find probation officers for norm violators going before the court. (d) Its members study and explore measures that can be taken on the county level to prevent juvenile delinquency. Likewise, in a much larger community, citizens took action to secure these needed services.

LINCOLN, NEBRASKA (100,000 population): [The Lincoln Youth Project] has actually been a citizens' action program. However, it has also had a professional fact finding staff. It has been a program consisting of the activities of citizens' action committees in each of the areas in which there are particular needs integrated with the work of the staff members who have engaged temporarily in case finding and reaching-out casework. This was not done to provide a community service, as such, but as a demonstration and to determine needs and inadequacies of services through actual experiences in handling cases and the obtaining of examples. Possibly a survey of the adequacy of casework services by the performance of casework has not been performed before.

The Youth Project was not preceded by a survey. The Youth Project is the survey. It was not preceded by the preparation of a detailed plan of procedure and the working out of agreements with the various agencies. . . . Detailed reports have been published by the Youth Project regarding needs and requirements for development of an effective and comprehensive program. . . .

In the report, "Need For an Adequate Juvenile Court in Lancaster County," information from the previous report, "Police Contacts With Juveniles in Lincoln Between October 1, 1956 and September 30, 1957" was summarized as follows:

During this one year period 1101 juveniles residing in Lancaster County who were under the age of eighteen were contacted by the police. . . .

Of the 374 juveniles who were not released by the police and whose cases were referred to other city or county officials:

1. Ninety-six, or 25.7 percent, were taken before the Juvenile Court.
2. One hundred forty-seven, or 39.3 percent, were released without action by the Juvenile Probation Office. Their arrests were for:

Armed gang	4	Sex offenses	14
Burglary	17	Shooting of B.B. gun	1
Car prowling	4	Trespassing	3
Car theft and joyriding	16	Weapon possession	1
Larceny and		Obtaining merchandise	
shoplifting	39	or money under	
Liquor laws	10	false pretense	1
Pool hall violation	1	Possession of stolen	
Property damage and		property	3
vandalism	14	Miscellaneous	9
Runaway or missing			
person	10		

3. Forty-two, or 11.2 percent, were placed on unofficial or "office supervision."

Of the 101 sixteen and seventeen-year-olds (included in the larger group listed above) who were taken before one of the Courts:
1. Nineteen, or 18.8 percent, were taken before the Juvenile Court.
2. Eighty-two, or 81.2 percent, were tried as adults in Municipal, County or District Court.

It was also pointed out in the report, "Need For an Adequate Juvenile Court in Lancaster County," that:
1. The four district court judges rotate the assignment for the handling of delinquency and neglect cases each year and have joint jurisdiction over the juvenile probation staff. There is no single judge who specializes in work with juveniles and who is responsible for the probation program.
2. Under the present law when it appears that a juvenile has committed a felony, the county attorney determines whether he should be tried as an adult or handled as a juvenile.
3. The juvenile probation staff members have not had special training in the recognition and treatment of behavior disorders.[6]

There are three trends in the development of juvenile courts. In some metropolitan areas the functions of the juvenile courts are expanded to family or domestic relations courts. In addition to the usual delinquency and child protection cases the court handles divorce and other cases involving children. A second trend is in the development of diagnostic and casework services. Clinical methods are used in varying degrees in diagnosis and treatment. As an example, the Minnesota law provides that a complete diagnostic and clinical report be made on a juvenile before he appears at a court hearing.

The third trend is toward state-wide juvenile court systems which are now found in three states, Connecticut, Rhode Island and Utah. A state with a state-wide juvenile court system is divided into districts, each of which has its judge, district probation office staff and district detention facilities. The judge may hold his hearings in various parts of the district. If there is an adequate and competent probation staff in the district, good probation services can be provided in the whole rural area.[7]

The Lincoln Youth Project is strongly in favor of the development of a more effective juvenile court program. We feel that a juvenile probation staff should be trained and qualified in the recognition and treatment of behavior disorders and juvenile maladjustment. They should concentrate on preventive work and endeavor to help juveniles as soon as problems come to their attention. We feel that many . . . of the cases, who were released by the juvenile probation staff, were in need of supervision and assistance to prevent a repetition of the misconduct or the development of more serious delinquency. We also feel that most of the . . . sixteen and seventeen-year-olds who were tried as adults in Municipal, County or District Court should have been handled as juveniles and efforts made to prevent a continuation or repetition of their unacceptable behavior.

The police also have a very important function in the handling of delinquents. Lincoln has a Juvenile Bureau staffed by a Lieutenant and a police officer. Both have completed training courses at the Delinquency Control Institute of the University of Southern California. The Juvenile Bureau is a part of the Detective Bureau and is not directly under the Chief of Police. The caliber and the training of the officers of the Juvenile Bureau appear to be good. However, there is a particular need for more specially selected officers with similar training to perform police work with juveniles and with child protection cases. The Juvenile Bureau should be made a separate division within the Police Department. . . .

In November, 1958, the Nebraska Constitution was amended to permit the establishment of juvenile courts separate from the district courts and with such jurisdictions and powers as the Legislature might provide. Approval of a majority of the electors of a district is necessary to establish a court. The Nebraska Committee for the Juvenile Court Enabling Act, made up of a large number of prominent citizens in the State, conducted a campaign to pass the Constitutional Amendment. The Youth Project provided the Committee with considerable typing, mimeographing, mailing and other assistance. More than sixty local clubs were contacted by telephone by the Youth Project staff and arrangements were made for approximately fifteen speeches by members of the Committee. The Youth Project staff also organized distribution at the polls of reminders to vote for the amendment. Volunteers to work at the polls were recruited from among the students of Union College and Nebraska Wesleyan University and the members of the Parent-Teacher Association. Approximately 90 of the 104 polls in the city were covered during the last four hours that they were open on election day by the volunteers.

In January, 1959, a juvenile court bill was introduced in the Legislature and immediately there was a storm of opposition to it. The "Lancaster County Committee For a Juvenile Court," made up of prominent members of various citizens' organizations, was then formed to work for adoption of a suitable bill. The Youth Project provided mailing and mimeographing services for the Committee and also helped to make arrangements for meetings. The report, "Need For an Adequate Juvenile Court in Lancaster County," was published to provide factual information. In June, 1959, a substitute juvenile court bill was passed unanimously. It permits by a vote of the electors the establishment of juvenile courts in counties of over 50,000 population.

One of the Youth Project committees met with the Chairman of the Mayor's Juvenile Crime Prevention Committee and with the Chief of Police and other members of the Police Department. At that time a Lieutenant was the only officer assigned to the Juvenile Bureau. Subsequently another officer was assigned. Financial assistance was provided by a local foundation and in

March, 1959, he was sent for a three month course at the Delinquency Control Institute of the University of Southern California. The Youth Project has recommended that a third officer be transferred to the Bureau and that he also be sent away for training.[8]

In some instances school and court and/or the community law-enforcement agency have organized a single unit to help youngsters with problems. Thus, in New Jersey a Children's Bureau is a joint project of the Board of Education and the Department of Public Safety. The functions of the Bureau are to provide prevention, early detection, and protective service and to work through a team approach in solving the youngsters' problems in relation to the school program, to other individuals, and to their environment.

PASSAIC, NEW JERSEY: The Passaic Children's Bureau was organized in 1937 in the interest of finding a way to meet the ever-growing problems of children and adolescents. The Bureau was established through the interest of the then mayor, who was serving as a member of the State Juvenile Delinquency Commission. . . .

The emphasis from the beginning has been more upon prevention-protection and readjustment than upon correction and punishment.

The Children's Bureau as a whole is composed of several units bound closely together through the integrated approach to problem solving. The Police Unit is composed of three plain clothes detectives and one police woman. . . . These four people belong to and are paid by the Department of Public Safety. They were selected by the Board of Education from a number of candidates from the police roster. There is an agreement between the Board of Education and the Department of Public Safety that no one of these persons shall be removed, nor shall any assignment be made to the Bureau without the consent of the Board of Education. This agreement has been adhered to throughout the 20 years of Board of Education Sponsorship.

The police personnel work under the immediate direction of the Bureau Director. Any police officer who apprehends a juvenile must immediately turn such offender over to the Children's Bureau, where he is assigned to one of the investigators.

Through their close cooperation with the schools, the Bureau Police become acquainted with boys and girls in the school situation. They are well acquainted with places throughout the city where there are active groups of boys and girls. Our police spend much time in the Bureau automobile observing boys and girls in their home environment and in recreational activity. Boys and girls respect them as representatives of the law as well as friendly advisors.

The Police Unit Personnel takes the responsibility for presenting to the County Courts those cases which, because of their seriousness or persistency, need to be heard by the Judge of the Juvenile Court.

The police personnel have prepared for their important function by attending courses in child development, and human relations and by inservice training at group meetings of the Staff of the Bureau and the Guidance Counsellors of the schools.

A secretary maintains complete records of all contacts made with the child, his parents, or any other person or agency by whom he may be known. These records are strictly confidential and are kept in locked files. These case folders include the results of psychological and medical examinations, reports from schools, case histories for psychiatric referrals, letters, notes and items from the press referring to the child or the incident in which he was involved.

Another important unit of the Bureau is the Census and Attendance Department. We learned early in the functioning of the Bureau that truancy was frequently the beginning of more serious delinquent tendencies. Its ramifications are very apparent. This department is also responsible for issuing working papers and reporting labor law violations to the State Department of Labor. The two secretaries in the unit maintain a complete, accurate census file of every child in the city. This includes a record of every child from day of birth, if born in our city and all other children in families moving into Passaic, when there are other children of school age.

There are three Attendance Officers—two men and a woman. They are not truant officers—they do not chase after children to return them to school, but rather, confer with parents regarding absences, so as to determine the cause and attempt to correct any basic fault.

The Attendance Officers visit the schools daily. Service is available to the parochial schools as well as to the public schools. We do not wait for children to be absent several days before checking the absence, but make an investigation for a half day's absence if there is any indication that it is not a legal one.

The Attendance Officers refer cases of need and neglect to the proper Bureau office and work closely with the Police Unit. One of our Attendance Officers is a college graduate with teacher certification, they are linguists with eight or nine central European languages at their command. One has been in social type work with boys and girls for many years. During the past year the Attendance Officers made 2724 home visits. This, along with 1811 visits of the police personnel, totals 4535 home contacts. This is over and beyond the many parents counselled by others in the Bureau. The Attendance Officer is usually the first representative of the Board of Education to contact parents in the home. This initial contact is important in developing attitudes toward the educational program and the services offered them through the Children's Bureau.

Every boy or girl applying for working papers visits the school guidance counsellor first, and every paper is checked carefully by the Director of the Bureau in an attempt to correct poor adjustment of the individual to his job and to check too frequent turnover.

The Children's Bureau has the services of two full-time psychologists. We want every boy or girl reported for a violation of a law to have an individual psychological test with counselling by the psychologist. Parents are asked to accompany their youngster so that they, too, may be conferred with. The Children's Bureau is not mainly for delinquents. If it were, our job of prevention would be a very limited one. We are interested in *children* with *problems*, school problems, home problems, and community problems. We are interested in the gifted as well as the slow learner, the boy who is under privileged and rejected, as well as the boy whose parents are over protective.

The psychologist visits the schools to observe children in the classroom situation. We realize that the schoolroom and the psychologist's office are two very different situations. The psychologist is responsible for making recommendations for placement in special classes, recommendations for skipping a grade, for adjustment in the school program and for the psychological testing relative to referrals to clinics, etc. He is a part of the team, and his opinions are given careful consideration when we look at the whole child. Parent education is a definite part of his

264

program, he counsels with parents after testing children. He is a group leader in Adult Education classes for discussion of good Mental Health procedures and conducts a psychology club activity for selected seniors in the high school.

It is the responsibility of the social worker to visit homes and to be concerned about the child's environment—his recreational activities, his place in the home environment, his church affiliation, camp placement—and to follow through when children are referred to clinics or agencies offering services outside the realm of the Bureau itself. She, too, works closely with civic groups and PTA. She knows that early referrals are valuable in rehabilitation. The social worker therefore maintains contact with the community nursery schools. Since there is no family agency in Passaic, much of the social work connected with family service is carried on through the Bureau social worker. She is in frequent contact with the Welfare Department, Red Cross, State Board of Child Welfare and all agencies concerned with recreation, welfare, financial aid and medical assistance. Her work is coordinated with that of the Medical Department of the schools. She is a member of the team serving as liaison between home, school and community resources. She frequently consults with and serves as resource person for local, county, state and national associations. . . .

The Director of the Bureau completes the team. He is also Assistant Superintendent of Schools and Coordinator of Special Services. He is responsible for placing physically and mentally handicapped children in an adjusted class or program. His interests cover the training and opportunity classes and the program of guidance in the schools.

Using the services of the professional staff and of the many agencies devoted to child care and child welfare, we have what is generally referred to as the "team" approach. We see the child from every viewpoint including that of the child himself and base recommendations on the results of our study of the child in all of his associations.

Referrals come to the Children's Bureau from the police, the schools, citizens, parents, and sometimes children themselves come to the Bureau with their problems. When the Bureau was first organized the large percentage of referrals came from the police—now this is reversed and the larger percentage come from other sources.

We believe we use the scientific approach to meeting the needs of children. We are interested in their physical condition. Their health and physical development, or lack of it, is frequently the cause for much more serious behavior patterns developing. Our files report many interesting but serious situations in which children have found themselves because of poor physical well-being, sometimes through no fault of their own.

Our second approach is that of the child's emotional condition, and we look into the psychological phase of his life. Here we find the school misfits, problems of failure, personality clashes and very often just everyday "growing up" through adolescence.

Our third step in the scientific approach is that of the environment. Parents need to understand that "doing for" and "giving to" are not the answers. Children need love—security—affection and acceptance. The spiritual needs of the child's life are . . . [taken into consideration]. We are interested in the adjustment to home, to the club or gang and in helping the boy or girl find his place in his community.

When boys and girls come to us we provide them with continuing supervision if that seems to be the answer to their problem. We demand restitution if they have destroyed or stolen what belongs to others. Some are dismissed . . . [if] the first offense has been trivial and some whom we cannot reach after every effort, must be referred for court action. . . .

The fact that 56.4% of our delinquents have had only an initial referral and 18.6% have repeated only once and the fact that only 5.2% of adult offenders last year were known to the Bureau as juvenile offenders, is some proof of the success of this approach.[9]

The incidence of juvenile arson, like many other forms of delinquency, is increasing to such an extent that schools and fire departments now recognize the need to initiate or extend cooperative efforts for preventive and educative action, and in some cities positions for juvenile officers on arson bureaus have been established.

COLUMBUS, OHIO: [This city has assigned one member of the arson bureau as Juvenile Arson Investigator.] He handles nothing but fires involving juveniles and teenagers. . . . Many cities are in accord with Columbus and have recommended that juvenile arson investigators be added to their present arson squad or bureau. Detroit, for one, has requested that two juvenile officers be added to the Fire and Police Arson Squad. [One official] was prompted in this move by a tremendous increase in juvenile fires and related offenses during the past year. In other cities new arson squads are being formed.

The report of the Committee on Juvenile and Teen-Age Fire Setters of the International Association of Arson Investigators states:

It is our most unpleasant duty to inform the membership of this organization that the juvenile and teen-age fire setting problem has again shown a marked increase in the past year. Just to keep the record straight and to eliminate any misunderstandings, we are referring to "set fires" and not fires caused by "children playing with matches." Juvenile fires have reached such proportions in some parts of the country it is now the number two cause of all fires. This is not a figment of one's imagination, but cold facts that can be substantiated by statistics and records. . . .

Ninety-eight percent of the agencies answering our inquiry report a definite upward trend in the number of juvenile fires. The other two percent remain at about the same level as in 1957, at which time they reported an increase. One of our larger cities reports that ninety-five percent of the "set fires" investigated involved juveniles. Our records show that 1958 was the first year in which a great number of juvenile female fire setters appeared in the picture. The percentage of females is small, but relates a large increase over the past years. The national average will show that from forty-five to sixty percent of all set fires involve juveniles, both male and female, between the ages of twelve and eighteen years. These figures have been quoted from records where the fire causes have been determined either "Incendiary" or "Juvenile Arson." There is no telling how many juveniles are involved in the thousands of fires that are carried as "unknown" and "undetermined." The national average would probably increase another ten to fifteen percent if these fire causes could be determined.

The motives we have encountered are varied, but, in most incidents, parallel those of the adult fire setters. The number one motive is malicious mischief or vandalism. The other motives in order are: thrill and excitement, spite or revenge, to cover up other crimes, mentally ill and fraud. The fraud motive only appeared in automobile fires. There is one incident on record where a juvenile female tried to commit suicide by means of fire. Many cases of arson to cover up the crime of breaking and entering by juvenile gangs have been reported by the larger cities. A mid-western city reports membership in a juvenile gang could only be attained after the applicant had successfully set a fire of note.

Property damaged by fire varies from small brush fires and barns in the rural sections to schools, churches, lumberyards, public buildings and dwellings in the urban and metropolitan areas. Schools and churches seem to be the prime targets for juvenile fires. The school fires are prompted by motives of spite or revenge and thrill and excitement. The church fires can be attributed to the mentally ill, malicious mischief and vandalism. . . .

We believe the only solution to this problem can be through education of the younger children after their first experience in fire setting or playing with matches. Here is where we must draw our battle line. At this time the adult as well as the child must undergo a complete education in fire prevention. They must be impressed by the seriousness of their acts and deeds. This educational program must be a community project where one hundred percent cooperation is required in the home, school, church, police and fire departments, juvenile case workers and the juvenile court. Everyone involved must be made to understand that juvenile and teen-age fire settings is a grave moral problem, as well as a great . . . waste of private and public funds.

Whenever a problem of truancy arises, the school, by reason of its legal responsibility, is brought into direct contact with court and law-enforcement agencies. Because truancy is generally the area in which these agencies work most closely, it offers a natural starting point for cooperative research and planning. A study of truancy and drop-out records would be advisable as an initial step in this cooperative effort. A New York City study of 1500 unlawful absences from school revealed that a high frequency of truancies among girls was due to the fact that they were being kept at home to help with the household; in this same study it was noted that a large percentage of habitual truants suffered from problems of physical health.[10] A study of case records of drop-outs, conducted by Tacoma-Pierce County, Washington, indicated that the youngster who dropped out of school had a marked tendency toward frequent school absences in the primary grades.[11]

Such studies, in defining the areas in which truancy problems arise, suggest possible solutions. For example, in order to remedy family situations which compel girls under 16 years to become truants, out-of-school girls beyond the compulsory attendance age might act as baby-sitters or household helpers through a school-arranged and -supervised schoolwork program. The other data suggest the importance of providing use of school health services in the first stages of truancy; finally, the data suggest that the establishment of remedial programs for primary-school absentees or, alternatively, the use of home instruction for absentees in the primary grades may cut down on retardations and, ultimately, on truancy and early school drop-out.

In Nashville two kinds of special service personnel—the attendance worker and visiting teacher—operate within the same division of the schools. This leads to a closely coordinated program of truancy detection and control which has been evaluated by the director of this division in the following statement.

NASHVILLE, TENNESSEE: Our program . . . is set up as the Visiting Teacher and Attendance Division of the Nashville City Schools. . . . We look upon the function of the two services as follows: The attendance worker carries out the requirements of the Tennessee Compulsory Education Law, employing casework techniques in so doing. There is, of course, underlying this function the authoritarian controls that may be used, if necessary. The visiting teacher's function is three-fold, as we see it: (a) To give casework service to individual children, who for some reason or other are emotionally or socially unable to take full advantage of the school program; (b) to help teachers to understand the meaning of children's behavior and to help them in identifying the children who need help; and (c) to bring to the attention of the school administration [those] factors in the school program that may hamper a child's full utilization of the school program or lacks in the program that need to be met.

We recognize that truancy may be the first sign of dissatisfaction with school, and often the attendance worker will refer to the visiting teacher a child whose problem is deep seated and needs the skill of a trained case worker. . . . While we do not look upon the visiting teacher service as solely a program to prevent juvenile delinquency, we feel that it does undoubtedly serve to meet the needs of children who are hostile to society and who are not having parental interest and support that will guide them to good citizenship. . . .

We cannot say with assurance how far exactly our program has been effective in the prevention of so-called delinquency. We do know that in the 20 years that we have been serving the Nashville schools there has been no increase in truancy on a percentage basis.

Another evaluation of a sound truancy prevention program is provided by the chief probation officer of Ouachita Parish, Louisiana.

MONROE, LOUISIANA: Our program works in this manner. A teacher may observe certain symptoms of behavior in her class. . . . [and a child manifesting these symptoms] is referred to the principal. This is the situation where the child is becoming a chronic disciplinary problem or is a repeated truant, and the principal calls the visiting teacher and myself [the chief probation officer] on the case. Let me stress that we are not truant officers. But we have found that a child who is repeatedly truant or who is a disciplinary problem usually has problems at home. We counsel with this child and with his family. In a few cases it is the teacher who is partially at fault. We ask the teachers' cooperation in helping with these cases, and in extreme cases the child may be transferred. In the beginning a number of teachers wanted to refer all their problems to us [in the probation office]. By having the teachers refer the problems through the principal and visiting teacher, more responsibility was placed upon the teacher in the classroom. We found that the idea of social promotions was being very much abused. Some teachers were promoting a boy who was a disciplinary problem even though he wasn't eligible for promotion. By the time a boy reached high school, having been socially promoted, he had difficulty in reading an assignment. This created more of a problem than ever. By working with the schools and bringing attention to the fact that many of our disciplinary problems and repeated truants were caused by promoting a boy before he was ready, we have helped to eliminate abuse.

One technique for preventing the establishment of a pattern of truancy is that employed in Carlsbad City, New Mexico, where the names of truants are identified in a daily school bulletin; thus all teachers are alerted to the existence of the problem and may help determine the nature of the trouble and, if possible, suggest a more promising approach to normal school adjustment.

The next, and final, truancy report is fully detailed. It includes a series of form letters utilized by one school system in a carefully planned effort designed to help the greatest possible number of truants without resorting to an official court hearing.

SAN MATEO COUNTY, CALIFORNIA: As a county-wide committee, we set up truancy procedures, and as a result of these, when necessary, a truancy hearing prior to court disposition is held. At this time, all possible means of adjustment are investigated and a program set up whereby the pupil and his parents have an opportunity to try to adjust to the rules and regulations of the school as well as the needs of the pupil involved. In this area, we have been very successful. . . . For instance, in one high-school district, according to last year's report, we had some 800 truancy referrals. By the time we had gone through the first, second, and third step, there were only 80 hearings of the original 800. Of these 80 truancy hearings, it was necessary to refer only 18 to the Juvenile Probation Department for legal procedures. This indicates that a great deal of guidance adjustment and thought went into the preventive program.

TRUANCY PROCEDURES

The local school district has the responsibility of exhausting all its resources in an attempt to adjust the child to school. Then, when all possible steps for adjustment have been taken, and when the school, at its discretion, deems it advisable and necessary, the matter of truancy may be submitted to the proper authorities for assistance. Active court wards should be returned to the agency or institution responsible for them.

Step No. 1—The child must be a truant as defined by law. . . .

    a. The parents must have been notified by the school via registered mail with return receipt requested.

    b. All data, letters, and evidence regarding the case must accompany the request for action. This request shall go to the County Superintendent of Schools for action. A complete documented report is necessary.

[Such a documented report might include some or all of the following suggested letters.]

Suggested letter to parents: #1. Our records show that your child, _____, has been absent without excuse, and we are taking this opportunity to inform you of these absences. They are for the following days or periods, and represent a considerable loss in attendance: (list dates and periods)

Under Education Code Section #16601 and Section #17001, it is our responsibility to enforce the Compulsory School Attendance laws. Therefore, we must arrange a meeting with you to determine what can be done to eliminate these absences. May we ask you to meet with (name of officer) at _____ School on _____, 19____, at _____ o'clock, to consider this problem. Our (name of officer) has visited your home on (date or dates) but has not been able to contact you. Please arrange to keep the appointment indicated above.

Suggested letter to parents: #2. Under the provisions of Education Code Section #16834, 17001 and 17003, your child, _____, is now classified as a truant. It therefore becomes advisable for you, as his parents (or guardian), to meet with us to discuss this matter. Your child has been absent without valid excuse (number or dates). May we request that you meet with (name of officer) in the office of the _____ School on _____, 19____, at _____ o'clock to endeavor to adjust this problem. Our staff has had occasion to counsel with your child several times, and the last such meeting was held on _____ in this office. We have made many attempts to correct this bad attendance, and now it becomes necessary for us to meet with you so that we may attempt a solution without further delay. Court action may result in filing of a petition and juvenile court action.

272

Suggested letter to parents: #3. Since our meeting on ....,
19...., your child has been absent again for .... days without
the necessary excuse, and he has failed to live up to the program
which was developed for him. It may be that other problems
have developed since our last meeting, so we would appreciate
it if you would meet with (name of officer) at the ....
School on ...., 19...., at .... o'clock. Since this
constitutes a second notice of truancy, we feel that the situation
is rapidly becoming serious; therefore we would appreciate this
meeting with you, ...'s parents, for the purpose of
making a final adjustment before habitual truancy results, and
we are forced to take legal action to enforce the Compulsory
School Law (Education Code Sections #16831-16870 and Sections #17110-17118).

Please cooperate in the adjustment of this matter so that further difficulty may be avoided.

Suggested letter to parents: #4. Your child, ...,
has continued to be truant from school and is now classified as
an habitual truant, as defined by Education Code Sections
#16836, #17001, and #17003. We are forced to present a
request to the County Superintendent of Schools to proceed as
is required by law. If we do not hear from you regarding this
matter by (date), it will be turned over to the office of the
County Superintendent of Schools for legal action.

Suggested letter to parents: #5. We have received no reply
to our letter of ...., 19....., regarding the habitual
truancy of your child, ... Therefore, we are today
requesting that the office of the County Superintendent of Schools
proceed against you and your child as is set forth in the Education Code, Section #16838, and Sections #17110-17118, and the
Welfare and Institutions Code #700.

[After the documented history has been received by the
county superintendent, Steps 2 through 4 are followed when
necessary.]

Step No. 2—The County Superintendent of Schools' office will
take the following action:

a. Review the case carefully.
b. Notify the parents by registered mail, with return receipt
   requested, directing the parents or guardian of the child

273

to appear with the child for a hearing of the case at a designated time and place.

Step No. 3—A summary of the Hearing Board regarding the disposition of the case shall be sent to the forwarding school and all parties concerned:

a. The Hearing Board shall be composed of a representative of the school involved, the referee from the Probation Department, a representative of the office of the County Superintendent of Schools, and, when necessary, a representative of the District Attorney's office.

b. The facts of the case shall be carefully considered.

c. The parents or guardian shall be informed of the action to be taken.

Step No. 4—When legal action is necssary:

a. If, in behalf of the student, a petition shall be filed by the office of the County Superintendent of Schools with the Probation Department for habitual truancy under Welfare and Institutions Code Section #700.

b. In the case of action against the parents or guardian under Education Code Section #16838 or Section 17112, the County Superintendent of Schools shall file the complaint in the Superior Court.

c. Disposition of the cases shall be the responsibility of the department through which the case is developed.

d. In cases involving parental omission or commission, the office of the District Attorney shall be notified.[12]

After the procedures for preventing truancy have been developed and put into effect, the school must still expect a certain number of persistent truants. Therefore, it is necessary that school and law-enforcement agencies work out a definite procedure for sharing of information about the youngster apprehended by the police, whether or not he is brought to trial.

MILWAUKEE, WISCONSIN: All juveniles apprehended for violating the school truancy law shall be taken directly to the nearest district station. The commanding officer shall notify the parents or guardian to call for their child at the station, and they shall inform the parent that they are expected to report to the school with the child for a conference with the principal

274

the following morning or afternoon, as the case may be. The commanding officer will immediately notify the Department of Pupil Personnel . . . and report the name, address, birth date, school, and time and place of apprehension.

Officers who have occasion to take such truancy action will in every case make out a referral card for transmission to the Youth Aid Bureau. . . .[13]

The police have notified the school that a youngster has been apprehended—what happens next? The following report describes the actions of one school official after receiving information from the police.

LOUISVILLE, KENTUCKY: Through a close working arrangement with the Juvenile Court, every child who comes before the courts for any reason whatsoever is referred to the office of the director of instructional administrative problems, before . . . being returned to school. A counseling conference with parents and child follows in this office. Prior to this conference, the nature of the charges before the courts and pending or final disposition of the case are fully understood through cooperation with court authorities. When time permits, . . . the director tries to sit in on the actual trial or court conference. The parents and the child are made fully aware in the office conference of the close working nature between the school and the court. No child is returned to school without an admission slip from this office, requisite for which is the parent conference.

During this conference a conscientious effort is made to assist the deviate:

1. To understand himself and his opportunities
2. To make appropriate adjustment and decisions in the light of this understanding
3. To accept responsibility for this choice
4. To follow a course of action in harmony with his choice.

After this child's return to school the local authorities endeavor to maintain rapport and counsel in the light of previous happenings.

A very different approach is found in the next report; here a school representative is always on the delinquency control team which apprehends the youngster.

LONG BEACH, CALIFORNIA: A unique and very effective part of the truancy control program has to do with the cooperation of the city Juvenile Bureau and our Attendance Department. The Juvenile Bureau furnishes four patrol cars and a juvenile officer for each car. The school system staffs each car with an attendance investigator. These cars cruise around the city all day long. When incidents of delinquency occur in any part of the city, . . . members of the community can, and do, phone the Juvenile Bureau or the Attendance Department. Contact can be made immediately with the patrol cars via radio so that the juvenile officer and the attendance investigator can soon be in control of the situation.

Any youngster of school age who is not attending school must carry a pass. If the cruising personnel see a youngster of school age on the street, they investigate; and if the youngster does not have his pass, he is taken back to school. Incidentally, these men are in plain clothes, and the patrol car does not look like a police car.

Whenever possible, school and court should have a working arrangement through which the school can make referrals when a youngster, not necessarily a truant, needs court help.

DES MOINES, IOWA: If the Department of Pupil Adjustment is unable to bring about the desired changes in behavior, as a last resort the child may be referred to Juvenile Court for further action. In some cases the immediate removal of the child from his home is desired and he is taken to the Juvenile Home until plans can be completed for working with him. The final result may allow returning him to his home on probation, removal to a foster home, commitment to the State Juvenile Home or the Training School. Such a commitment may be "withheld during good behavior." In such a case the child may be required to make regular trips to the Juvenile Court for conferences with his probation officer. Again the visiting teacher acts as the liaison person between the Courts and the public schools in working out a remedial program for the maladjusted child.[14]

The usual procedure following apprehension of a juvenile by police is a study of the youngster, his home, and his background. Then, perhaps, a court hearing is necessary to establish innocence or to recommend probation or commitment. Here again, the school needs to be informed of the action taken.

SAN MATEO COUNTY, CALIFORNIA: The school district will be advised by the court each school day of any youngsters referred to the Probation Department or detained in Juvenile Hall.

1. This notification will consist of:
   a. The name of the child
   b. Birthdate
   c. The last school attended
   d. The date of detention or referral
   e. The name of the probation officer.
2. Upon receiving this call, the [school-court liaison person] . . . is to mail a summary of youngster's school adjustment and curriculum record to the probation officer.

When a child has been detained in Juvenile Hall and is to be released pending the Court Hearing, the probation officer is to advise the child and the parent that they are to report to school the following day.

The school is to be advised of the return of the youngster to the school *prior* to re-admittance.

The probation officer is to notify the school of any youngsters placed on informal probation. A call by phone should be made as soon as the decision is reached, and information is to be provided which is relevant to the child's school adjustment.

Following the court hearing, the school will be advised by the probation officer of any factors developed during the investigation which may immediately affect the youngster's re-admission or continued attendance in school.

1. These factors may include:
   a. Conditions of probation
   b. Recommendations as to school programming
   c. Any specific problems which may affect the child's program.
2. This information may be confined to that which is immediately necessary to the school. The probation officer will be available to discuss the situation in greater detail within a reasonable time following the court hearing.
3. The information to be submitted to the school following the court hearing may be transmitted by phone, but it

277

must be done prior to the re-admission conference with parents.

4. The parents are to be requested to accompany the child to the school for re-admittance following the court hearing and be advised to appear at the school after the probation officer has contacted the [receiving] school.[15]

If detention facilities are overcrowded or unavailable, the regular school and law-enforcement agencies must work together to minimize the possibly harmful results of retaining the juvenile offender in school or placing him in a jail. An important statement about this problem was made by the U. S. Senate Subcommittee on Juvenile Delinquency.

In New York, as elsewhere in the country, delinquency rates are rising, and new, additional treatment facilities have not kept up with this increase. On the other hand, legal and public opinion is against expelling children from school because they are problem students. As occurred here in Washington, D. C., with no other alternative, the schools are forced to take care of them. When the inevitable happens, when these children begin to wreak havoc with classroom procedure, upsetting the more law-abiding students, threatening and actually engaging in violence, all sorts of theories begin to arise as to the reasons for the situation. Depending on any person's or group's predilections, they have at different times blamed the race problem, progressive education, and a number of other so-called causes that the subcommittee found, while somewhat related, to be far from the actual cause of the trouble.

The situation becomes further aggravated by the fact that, because of the institution shortage, disciplinary actions taken by officials are often ineffective, especially when dealing with the very maladjusted or extremely troublesome pupil. If the child's action required court proceedings, he was many times returned to the school system on probation because of the lack of enough custodial facilities. At the time the subcommittee was in New York, the Children's Court of New York City and the New York City Board of Education admitted that there were 356 children in the school system on probation who should have been in custodial care. When a child is returned to school under these conditions, he is treated as a hero and becomes an example for other students, attesting to the ease with which a mere student can overcome the severest disciplinary measure of the city authorities—adjudication by the juvenile court.[16]

The regular school should play a more important role in maintaining contact with the youngster under detention, but too often there is little or no exchange of information between the regular school and the detention school. Communication between these schools is particularly urgent when the youngster enters the detention school and when he re-enters the regular school.

A recommended procedure to be followed when the youngster returns to the regular school is that a school-court liaison person or a designated counselor assist the returnee in his adjustment to and acceptance by the school. This opportunity cannot be neglected if the youngster's reinvolvement with the law is to be avoided. At this time it is also necessary that the returning institution aid the receiving school by providing the information needed for the youngster's readmission. Not all schools can designate a school person to visit the detention institutions in order to familiarize himself with the programs offered by each of these centers as well as with a particular norm violator's progress. But every school system has criteria for admission and criteria for establishing grade placement; if the receiving school supplies a list of required information, the detention institution may be able to provide the facts needed by the school to help insure a successful adjustment for the returnee at his new school.

In the material submitted to the Project, the point was made repeatedly that many teachers are unwilling to accept returnees from institutions into their classes or that the teachers are often cold and hostile to the returning student. To get at this problem, the New York City schools have established a special officer to help facilitate adjustment of the youngster and his acceptance by school workers.

NEW YORK CITY: The placement of children returning from custodial institutions is the responsibility of one counselor assigned to the High School Placement Unit. This counselor visits the institutions regularly, interviews children and their parents, and serves as liaison between the institutions and the schools. Considerable progress has been made in modifying the attitude of the school people toward these children.[17]

In Macomb County, Michigan, a vocational training program, PREP (Pioneer Readiness Employment Program), has been instituted to aid probationers or returned detainees; PREP operates special classes in the local high school during six summer weeks for young men on probation. A similar program, reported in great detail, comes from a private agency in the Boston area. The organizing force in this program has been the juvenile court.

BOSTON, MASSACHUSETTS: We have been told over and over again that delinquency, like crime, is primarily a local responsibility. It is the local citizens themselves who must act to prevent and control it.

In 1936 Judge Perkins, then Presiding Justice of the Boston Juvenile Court, with the assistance of many noted and dedicated citizens of Boston, founded the Citizenship Training Group, Inc. Judge Perkins believed that the community should work with all youth-serving agencies in this serious problem of human wastage. He felt the program of retraining delinquent boys should be based on a two-pronged attack. First, the neighborhood and community must be alerted to the factors that breed and nurture the criminal. Second, the delinquent himself must be subjected to correction and training that will return him to a useful and decent life.

For the past twenty-three years the Citizenship Training Group has been a valuable adjunct to the court and has proved that this approach to the delinquency problem is a positive one and a sound investment for the future. . . .

Since its inception in 1936 the training program has been located about a mile from the court . . . at the Boston Young Men's Christian Union. . . . The Union provides the quarters, consisting of six rooms, gymnasium, shower and dressing room and a large hall. It also provides complete maintenance. . . .

The purpose of the Citizenship Training Group is threefold:
1. To create in the probationer a more constructive attitude toward his personal relationships at home, in school, and in the community by helping him to understand and appreciate his opportunities and obligations.

2. To appraise the probationer's physical, mental and social assets by observation and study of his background, personality and behavior.
3. To educate the public as to the problem of delinquency in general and as to the purposes and functions of the program.

The general plan of the Citizenship Training Group is that boys between the ages of twelve and seventeen placed on probation by the Boston Juvenile Court are required, as a condition of their probation, to attend the Citizenship Training Program immediately following their appearance in court. This attendance is for twelve weeks, five days a week from 3:30-5:30 p.m.

The boys on probation to the district courts of Greater Boston are admitted at the request of the Justice of the Juvenile Session of such courts.

The program was founded on the realization and acceptance of the fact that no one skill has pre-eminence in the treatment of delinquency. Insights from the fields of education, psychology, sociology, medicine and religion all must be used judiciously in an adequate treatment program.

Group work is one of the many skills utilized in the training program. When we speak about the value of group activity we do not mean mass activity. The group is small enough to insure individual care and to make important individual relationships within the group effective and revealing.

An essential goal of our work is, therefore, to help the boys develop a capacity for taking responsibility. This assists them in achieving a social maturity which will help them to be successful, happy members of their homes, schools, and communities. In order to develop this ability for community living, the training program utilizes the group activity approach under the supervision of skilled leadership. Group activity as a treatment aid in probation depends upon an alliance with all disciplines.

All children want to learn to read; however, due to physical or emotional difficulties noted in some children who have been attending the training program, it was discovered that 69 per cent of them had a marked reading disability.

For the past ten years the majority of boys with serious reading problems have been given special attention through individual expert counseling. The remedial reading teacher is a person who is first an expert in her field and second a person whose patience, understanding and devotion have aided many boys in overcoming this embarrassing problem. . . .

The Citizenship Training Group firmly believes that working with a delinquent boy demands individual, personalized attention and treatment. To stimulate and strengthen wholesome mental attitudes within the boy, every effort is made to utilize the information conveyed by multiple sources.

Combining the knowledge obtained from physical and mental examination, craft, gym and discussion observations with his own personal investigation of the home, school, church and community agencies, the worker attempts to determine the actual cause of the boy's delinquent act.

Searching interviews with the boy, regular contact with members of his family, his teachers, religious leaders and social workers provide an accurate, detailed account of the boy's past patterns of behavior. This includes his family setting, his attitudes, values, strengths, weaknesses, his educational achievements and reversals, his spiritual concepts and neighborhood interests, activities and companions. While compiling this information the worker attempts to intensify the all-important working relationship with the boy in order to put into practice a wise, positive and practical plan to insure the desired goal of readjustment.

The boy, exposed to and influenced by the daily cooperative spirit of the Citizenship Training Group, is stimulated and encouraged to exert his own effort on the principle that he can thereby learn how to help himself when faced with a decision-making situation.

Conscious of the boy's needs and problems, the worker stands ready to guide, advise and, when necessary, assist as the boy proceeds in acquiring self-confidence and assurance.

Frequently the boy's delinquency may be his way of handling a deep-rooted inner emotional problem. Incapable of properly working out the problem on his own, the boy may become so troubled and disturbed that his behavior is negatively influenced, and he encounters further problems. The worker must seek out these causal factors by completely understanding and appreciating the boy.

Regular, intense counseling and guidance sessions help to provide the boy with deeper insights and fuller understanding of the nature of his problems and the necessary equipment to cope with the forces which initially caused his disturbance. Armed with these essentials to satisfactory living, the boy is assisted in assuming his rightful place within society as a responsible and reliable citizen. . . .

Standard test and measurements are administered to each boy to determine his intelligence, aptitude and social and emotional capabilities. Information from all of these sources is correlated, and a plan for the boy's adjustment is put into effect designed to assist in changing anti-social attitudes and behavior.

. . . The Judge Baker Guidance Center continues to provide personnel to administer projective type tests. . . . [and] assigned . . . a consultant psychiatrist to the Citizenship Training Group. . . . Under his supervision a highly skilled diagnostic team has been organized consisting of a psychiatric social worker, a clinical psychologist and a psychiatrist.

All cases that are to be staffed at the weekly case conferences are evaluated by this team in the light of modern knowledge of the various disciplines. All casework information and other data presented by the psychometrist, probation officer, group workers, teachers and others is carefully evaluated and summarized by the consultant psychiatrist. From this conference come the recommendations that are later presented to the court for further disposition of the boy's case. . . .

The medical program continues to be one of the most valuable services of the training program. All boys receive a complete and thorough medical examination at the Preventive Clinic of the Boston Dispensary. . . . The staff continues to find numerous medical defects that are corrected immediately by the various clinics of the Boston Dispensary.

Although it is compulsory for a boy on probation to attend the training program, it is satisfying and rewarding to note the large number of boys who return to the program on a voluntary basis once they have completed their period of training. Records continue to show nine out of every ten boys come back voluntarily to visit the Citizenship Training Groups. . . .

The Citizenship Training Group continues to provide colleges and universities an excellent opportunity for graduate training in the fields of education, guidance and counseling, probation, social case work and social group work. . . .

. . . the research section continues to assemble important data on all cases appearing before the Boston Juvenile Court. This information has been carefully tabulated and evaluated and made available to public and private agencies and others who requested this service.

Although the Boston Juvenile Court contributes the services of the Executive Director, the Citizenship Training Group does not receive financial assistance from the city, state or United Fund. Support for this program during the year has come from private . . . sources. . . .

Statistics continue to show that more than 1900 seriously delinquent boys have passed through the Citizenship Training Group program. About 1300 of these boys have been restored to decent and useful citizenship. A 70 per cent rate of success with criminally prone boys is an extraordinary record.[18]

References

[1] Illinois Youth Commission, Division of Community Services. *Handbook: Delinquency Prevention Through Community Organization.* Springfield: the Commission, 1956. p. 71.

[2] Los Angeles County Schools, County-Wide Committee Dealing with Problems of Delinquent Behavior. "Report of the County-Wide Committee Dealing with Problems of Delinquent Behavior." Los Angeles: the Committee, 1957. p. 4.

[3] County of Multnomah and City of Portland, Oregon. Citizens Committee on Juvenile Delinquency. "Report of Citizens Committee on Juvenile Delinquency." Portland: the Committee, 1958. p. 15-17.

[4] San Francisco Board of Education. "Spears's Comments on Youth Problems to Board of Supervisors of San Francisco." Report to Board of Supervisors on Youth Problems, Part III. *San Francisco Public Schools Bulletin* 30: 3; February 23, 1959.

[5] Oakland County, Michigan, Child and Family Protection and Youth Assistance Program of the Juvenile Court of Oakland County. "Twenty-Two Questions About Child and Family Protection and Youth Assistance Program." Oakland County: the Court, 1959.

[6] Lincoln Youth Project, Nebraska. *Community Organization Through Citizens' Action in Lincoln, Nebraska.* Lincoln: the Project, 1959. p. 1-2, 8-10.

[7] Lincoln Youth Project, Nebraska. *Requirements for a Comprehensive System of Specialized Community Services To Prevent or Correct Delinquency and Other Juvenile Maladjustment.* Lincoln: the Project, 1959. p. 16.

[8] Lincoln Youth Project, Nebraska. *Community Organization Through Citizens' Action in Lincoln, Nebraska.* Lincoln: the Project, 1959. p. 10, 14-15.

[9] Passaic Public Schools, Children's Bureau. "What One Community Has Done for Its Children." Passaic, New Jersey: the Bureau, 1958. p. 1-6 *passim.*

[10] Lazare, Daniel. *These Left Before Graduation.* Tacoma: Tacoma-Pierce County Study of Education for Exceptional Children, 1958. p. 7.

[11] *Ibid.,* p. 18.

[12] Office of the San Mateo County Superintendent of Schools, "Truancy Procedures." Redwood City, California: Office of the Superintendent, 1955. p. 1-4 *passim.*

[13] Milwaukee Public Schools, Department of Pupil Personnel. "Rules and Regulations Concerning the Attendance and Exclusion of Pupils from the Milwaukee Public Schools." Milwaukee: the Department, 1958. p. 8.

[14] Des Moines Public Schools, Central Committee on Special Education. "Report from the Committee on the Socially Maladjusted." Des Moines: the Committee, 1957. p. 7.

[15] San Mateo County Schools, Intercommunication Committee. "Probation and School Intercom." San Mateo County, California: the Committee, 1959.

[16] U.S. 86th Congress, 1st Session, Senate Committee on the Judiciary, Subcommittee on Juvenile Delinquency. *Juvenile Delinquency.* Report of the Committee on the Judiciary, United States Senate, Made by Its Subcommittee on Juvenile Delinquency. Washington, D. C.: Superintendent of Documents, Government Printing Office, 1959. p. 14-15.

[17] Board of Education of the City of New York, Bureau of Education and Vocational Guidance. "Bureau of Educational and Vocational Guidance Annual Report, 1957-1958." New York City: the Bureau, 1958. p. 44, 46.

[18] Citizenship Training Group, Boston, Massachusetts. *Annual Report 1958.* Boston: the Group, 1958, p. 6-24 *passim.*

chapter 9 WORKING WITH COMMUNITY AGENCIES

basic principle: THE SCHOOL RECOGNIZES THAT
DELINQUENCY PREVENTION AND CONTROL IS A
COMMUNITY PROBLEM AND REQUIRES ACTION ON
THE PART OF ALL CITIZENS. THE SCHOOL STUDIES,
EVALUATES, UNDERSTANDS, AND MAKES USE OF
THE PEER, ETHNIC, RACIAL, AND RELIGIOUS SYS-
TEMS AT WORK IN ITS COMMUNITY. UTILIZING
AND WORKING WITH THE RESOURCES OF ALL AVAIL-
ABLE AGENCIES AND INSTITUTIONS, THE SCHOOL
HAS A LEADERSHIP ROLE IN THE FORMATION AND
CONTINUATION OF A COMMUNITY-WIDE EFFORT
FOR THE PREVENTION AND CONTROL OF NORM-
VIOLATING BEHAVIOR.

Juvenile delinquency is everybody's business. All citizens—
the general public and lay and professional workers—must
get in the act. But some agencies have a more specific man-
date than others to identify, to prevent, to study and diagnose,
to treat the norm violator and his family, or to try to ameliorate those forces that operate to produce delinquent behavior.
The school is only one of these agencies. It cannot go it
alone.

The first United Nations Congress on the Prevention and
Treatment of Offenders, convened in Geneva, Switzerland,
in 1955, discussed the involvement of all institutions in the
community in shaping the child's behavior and personality
and the need for organizing the community resources in
such a way that their influence will be beneficial.

The Congress recognizes that the community, considered in its
local, regional and national aspects, provides the environment in
which social institutions mould the child's behavior patterns and
personality. The neighborhood in which young people live and

form their most important associations is perhaps the most decisive phase of community influence, though it reflects too the broader influences of the society and culture. The factors which shape character derive very largely from these community influences as they operate through the family, the school, the church and other social institutions. Community action to prevent juvenile delinquency is to a great extent a matter of organizing the variety of community resources so as to provide, on the one hand, an environment in which children may develop without abnormalities of character and in which . . . those who are in danger of becoming delinquent may be discovered and guided toward conformity to normal standards.[1]

The point made above that all agencies and organizations which work with youth and families have a direct or indirect effect on delinquency prevention and control is indeed well taken. Here the school, with its large army of trained youth workers, occupies a central position, for it has all the children of all the people, receives them early, and works with them for a long period of time. But, to repeat, it is only one agency, and its efforts are limited by budgetary restrictions as well as its highly specialized functions.

In recent years much research has been carried out in regard to the individual delinquent, with heavy stress on the one-to-one patient-therapist or counseling relationship. However, very little research effort has been directed toward an examination of the nature and quality of the relationship between agencies (or youth workers within a given organization) that deal with the norm-violating youngster or his family. Such research is sorely needed, for, in spite of the often-stated principle of "coordination of community resources involving all agencies and organizations," there is still far too much inter-agency strife and duplication of effort and far too many gaps in needed services. Of course, the school is not immune to this criticism. It is hardly necessary to say that the lack of coordination among community agencies is a grave disservice to the youngster with emotional or social problems.

The school must join with the other agencies of the community in a cooperative and coordinated effort to establish a community-wide program to help the delinquent or any other youngster who needs assistance and understanding. In communities which lack any over-all coordinating plan or organization the school may have to take the initiative in creating this plan; it may have to take the lead in developing better community planning and organization that will insure an effective program of child study, referral, treatment, and neighborhood improvement, particularly for those youngsters in the lower-class community. Once the predelinquent or delinquent youngster has been identified, the child-study and diagnostic-treatment services should be so poised and equipped as to enable systematic, scientific, and individualized (or group) programs that will help, support, and treat the youngster at the earliest moment of need. This chapter delineates some ways in which the school can work with other agencies in a well-planned and coordinated attack on the aspects of community life and individual behavior that are directly or indirectly the cause of delinquency.

Guidelines

* The school cooperates in collecting, interpreting, and using data related to delinquency for purposes of prevention and programming, and it cooperates in efforts of federal, state, or local private or public agencies serving the community.

* The school prepares and makes available to school personnel a list of community agencies, if such a list is not already in existence; it should include the services offered children and families and the procedures of referral.

* The school and other community agencies concern themselves with the development of a "teen-age" image that will make for positive change in the youngster's behavior and in the attitudes of adults.

* The school, through its program, shares with the home and the church a measure of responsibility for the community's moral and spiritual development, each making a contribution within its natural province.

* The school helps to develop programs that will aid youth in finding a place in the economic and industrial life of the community and will make a special effort to aid the "hard-to-place" youth.

* The school participates in planning and carrying out programs of recreation. Whenever feasible, use should be made of school facilities.

* The school encourages a consciousness of neighborhood responsibility and locates, endorses, and supports local leadership in self-organized community projects.

* The school encourages and cooperates with community groups and/or initiates programs designed to improve parental understanding of normal child growth and development as well as awareness of certain factors tending to result in delinquent behavior.

* The school originates, aids, or supports with its prestige worthwhile activities of community groups.

* The school interprets its role in delinquency prevention and control to both the board of education and the community.

* The school cooperates in evaluating community effort in the prevention and control of delinquency.

* The school agency gains insight into the social forces operating within the school and on the school by utilizing the full- or part-time services of a qualified social analyst who brings to both school and community the professional understanding of the sociologist and/or cultural anthropologist.

* The school actively seeks to include other agencies and individuals in its work of delinquency prevention and control; it participates in community committees concerned with the problems of youngsters; and it takes full advantage of the special opportunities offered by agencies legally empowered to act in the area of juvenile delinquency.

Only as a last resort in the face of total community apathy does the school work independently in its efforts to help the norm-violating youngster.

Practices

At one of the 11 workshops conducted by the Project, Edward P. Hooper, supervising sociologist, Illinois Youth Commission, stated:

Learning . . . is a process which one undergoes, not only at the mother's knee or in the school room, but also in the alleys, on the street corners, in the candy and do-nut shops in between. It is here that we propose a program of change, a program dedicated to the proposition that positive interest on the part of significant neighbors can work a change in the social atmosphere of a community and a behavioral change in the lives of all concerned. This, then, is an invitation for the school and the neighbors to join hands in becoming social contractors. The advantages which are offered are those of being able to work from a blueprint (somewhat hazy—to be sure) but a blueprint nevertheless, rather than to allow accidental growth and change to be the rule. Edward Lindeman has said, ". . . there is no escape from the conclusion that crime is a social situation and hence no remedial program which is not at bottom a social movement, can promise success."

I should like to confine my remarks to one rather broad notion . . . there are many roles for the school and school personnel to play. . . . Well known to us all and implicit in nearly all of the literature is the immeasurable importance of the social milieu of the boys and girls who are regularly referred to such agencies as I represent.

The Illinois Youth Commission long ago recognized the fact that it was necessary for us to deal with a "second best" program. It is obvious that, on the surface, the time-worn clichés regarding "no delinquent children—only delinquent parents" have only enough of the truth in them to be bothersome and to get in the way, and not enough of it to provide the basis for any sound, far-reaching program of attack.

Hereafter I should like to have you put quotation marks around the words "good," "bad," "proper," and "improper," as I use them in the rest of this paper.

290

In the Illinois program we have chosen to concentrate primarily on attempting to change the social climate in devalued neighborhoods. We have chosen the neighborhood as the basic area of operation because it is easy to recognize in this approach the possibility of the use of many normally unused strengths and potentials. One thing which seems to us to be sold short time after time in program after program is the leadership existing in these devalued neighborhoods. Through the development of this potential we have in many cases seen a rapid change in social atmosphere. While on the surface it may seem to be minor and not even newsworthy, any social change in such a neighborhood is to us profound and dramatic. Such change as this does not seem possible through the use of any other device now known to us.

As we have searched out and interested local leadership in the problems of their neighborhood, we have seen this leadership develop substantial social programs, instilling a spirit of hopefulness and a desire toward progress where before only apathy or outright antagonism had met outwardly conceived programs.

Using the notion that status seeking is one of the great drives for all persons, we have helped local leadership develop programs in which neighbors get social credit for participation, and on the other hand, lose credit for nonparticipation. This, it seems, is only possible if one is careful not to cross over class lines in the organizing of such a group.

If this group succeeds and begins to grow, it will be because of three things: (1) The selection of leadership was properly made. (2) The leadership selected realistic, obtainable, and positive goals. (3) The leadership provided the proper ideas for implementing the program to attain the goals. With the selection of the goals and the implementation of them, at least one segment of society is starting on the road toward the reacceptance of certain values which are by way of being "good" controls.

Perhaps it would be better said that it is the acceptance of values rather than the values themselves which is the important factor. It is vital that children grow up seeing their parents and their neighbors as instrumental in positive social change. This is true in any area because children can grow up to be savages on the Gold Coast of Chicago just as well as on the Gold Coast of Africa.

Thus, it can be said that where children are unable to find parental or neighborhood interest in any form of social action—where the pattern of life is social ennui or anomie or rootlessness, there are not likely to be many controls either "good" or "bad." For such children (especially for those from homes where controls of any kind are minimal) rule- or norm-violating behavior is most likely to be prevalent. This not only accounts for the child who runs away from home and holds up the filling station but also for the one who runs away from home and goes to college. Both, when we consider a neighborhood whose hallmark is anomie, are incidents of norm-violating behavior. However, since the path of least resistance and toward status satisfaction runs closer to filling stations than to campuses, it is here that we will find most of our norm violators.

The other face of this coin . . . [is] something like this:

If we can find some device to first activate and then implement a desire to make social changes, if we can create a social program in which parents and/or neighbors can invest something of themselves, if we can show children a social interest and activity on the part of adults significant to them (that is, important at their own social level), we will have made a difference in the social atmosphere. In such a case where social apathy has been at least somewhat replaced by social interest and social activity, the first step will have been taken toward the establishment of more adequate social controls. If through the influence of the organizer on the local leadership, this interest and activity is in the "proper" direction, we will be witnessing the establishment of certain value systems which will act in lieu of the middle-class value controls. These controls, which in the past have been the measuring stick of law enforcement and social acceptability, are the essential ingredient which neighborhood consciousness can restore. While it is possible that at some future time we will discover more adequate controls, for the time being it is axiomatic that if we are to combat social problems (including delinquency) on any far-reaching scale, these controls are vital.

We are not manufacturing or synthesizing morals. It is not necessary to form a committee and reproduce the Ten Commandments. However, it is alarming to see great segments of society in which these "core morals" seem to be disappearing.

The hope of the future generations lies in the seemingly innate ability of youth to make use at a future time of those things which they have been allowed only to glimpse.

The dissipation and moral deterioration of the parents of the early twenties did not, for example, deter their children from having the moral fibre and stamina to fight and win World War II, although it probably did contribute to the necessity of their having to fight it.

Thus, we feel that there is adequate justification in this program to hold up for view certain of these useable and needed values so that our children can build upon them a future not nearly so bleak as what we might otherwise envision.

Now, it is obvious that the implementation of such programs as these must be something which will be of interest to the residents of each neighborhood. Constructive use of leisure time in some form as opposed to commercial amusements must be among the tools which such a group will use. Here is one of the first places in which the schools can figure. Meeting places which will allow for neighborhood-centered programs will be needed; play areas, to replace the necessity of trips downtown, will be vital; instruction in sports, drama, handicrafts, and the like will be essential. In Cook County, Illinois, the Chicago "Lighted School House" program is made use of by many such committees as I have described. The function of the school as an institution of the neighborhood should, it seems to me, be that of an interested neighbor. The questions which should be asked by school administrators might be: "How can we, as a social institution of this neighborhood, be most helpful in assisting the residents of this area in *their* program?" "What devices can we use to show that we measure up as 'good neighbors'?" "What assistance can we render to prove to the children that we are as interested in what they learn in the alleys on the way to school as in what they learn in the classrooms?"

The school must first study its community. As one step in such a study the school must identify all other agencies in the community which are concerned with youngsters; it must establish working relations with these agencies for the professional exchange of information and service. If no listing of such agencies exists, the school should prepare one for circulation to its personnel. As suggested in the guidelines to this chapter, a useful addition to such a list as the one given below is a third column, to be updated annually, giving the name of the person to contact and the procedure for referral.

DES MOINES, IOWA

Agency	Type of referral
Child Guidance Center	Supplementary diagnosis and long-term therapy.
Family Service, Catholic Charities, Lutheran Welfare, Polk County Social Welfare	Family and personal maladjustments, arising outside of school, where the problem appears to be one which would necessitate family counseling.
Cooperative Thrift Shop	Needy children are provided with free clothing.
YWCA, YMCA, Boy Scouts	Recreational needs are met.
State Department of Social Welfare, Polk County Welfare	Tuition and residence investigations.
Juvenile Court, Municipal Court, Juvenile Bureau, Board of Control, Polk County Sheriff	Legal action.
State Welfare (Social Welfare), Polk County Child Welfare, Aid to Dependent Children, Iowa Children's Home, Des Moines Children's Home, Soldiers' Relief	Aid to children is given in the form of protection, financial assistance, and over-all child welfare.
Broadlawns Hospital (Mental Health Clinic and Health Clinic), Health Center	Health needs are met and, if necessary, free medical service is given.
Booth Memorial Hospital, Junior League Convalescent Home	Hospitalization is arranged for unwed mothers.
Vocational Rehabilitation	Help in finding employment for the handicapped and aid in equipping them for the job.[2]

Once the school has established working relations with other agencies, it can start making plans to improve the way of life in its community.

NEW HAVEN, CONNECTICUT: The Council of Social Agencies in New Haven is conducting a project known as NIP. This stands for Neighborhood Improvement Project. One of our worse neighborhoods has been selected for this project. A grant has been received from the New Haven Foundation for the appointment of a coordinator and a full-time social worker. Besides this, every agency in town, including the schools, is giving some time to the project: [the Department of Education] is giving them one and a half days of school social work per week for a period of three years.

294

Before any permanent improvement is possible, a development of neighborhood feeling and leadership is necessary. The following statement concisely summarizes the principles essential to a successful neighborhood effort.

ᐟThe State of New Jersey: Certain cardinal principles of organization have emerged as essential. First, neighborhood committees must consist of and be run by the residents themselves. Secondly, organizers must be skilled in selecting the real leaders of the neighborhood to organize a representative committee. Lastly, the sponsoring organization should continue on as a consultant to the committee.[3]

The statement quoted above merits additional consideration, for its principles are significant in terms of the programs to be cited next. It indicates, first, that an organizing leadership must be called into being and that this leadership, in turn, inspires and enables neighborhood or local leadership to engage in the program. At this point, the organizing leadership is changed into a consulting partner. This pattern of development appears distinctly in the following reports from two different programs.

In Chicago a group of four principals functioned as the original organizing leadership. Once this group of school personnel set the idea in motion, the leaders of the various interest groups in the community joined in, assumed leadership, and developed activities in four areas of concern to the neighborhood—beautification, recreation, administration, and student behavior; the result was well-coordinated teamwork. In Hialeah, Florida, on the other hand, the original organizing leadership came from teen-age students. The leaders sparked into action by the organizing group were the teachers. In the program that eventually emerged, the students continued as an active force.

Chicago, Illinois: [Sparked by four school principals, Chicago's School District 7—5.5 miles of the city's teeming West Side—organized itself into an anti-vandalism project.] At a project meeting, four ways of "getting to work" were outlined by community people:
The president of the block club association described possi-

295

bilities for a school-community beautification project, aimed at building a neighborhood pride, through the improvement of homes, yards and streets.

Representatives from social and recreational agencies proposed a study of unmet recreation needs in the area, as a basis for expanding or changing their own programs.

A police officer and a public librarian presented the idea of a speakers' bureau which would bring professional workers trained in combating delinquency to school and parent groups for talks and discussions.

Plans for developing a student code of conduct for leisure time and organizing an all-school youth convention for District 7 were presented by two high-school students. . . .

As well as creating a more attractive community, the beautification project developed adult leadership. Parents became interested in doing more for their children; several volunteered to help with new Scout troops and Cub packs. . . .

Basically, the beautification project accomplished three things: It developed leadership; it helped community people to articulate their needs; it made clear the need for everyone to give his services for a better place to live. . . .

All the schools were encouraged to publicize the recreation programs and to permit program representatives to describe their activities to the children.

Perhaps most significant . . . was a new awareness on the part of recreation people themselves of how they created the vandal or delinquent child. Said one participant, "We ought to look at our own agencies and see what is really being done there. Perhaps we try to get rid of vandals instead of helping them." . . .

Representatives from each of the schools—seventh graders through high schoolers—met regularly . . . to draft a code and plan for the convention. The code was concerned solely with out-of-school behavior, since it was to be adopted by a number of different schools. It is perhaps unique in having been adopted jointly by public and parochial schools.

In the process of formulating the code, the student representatives discussed it with their own student councils and school administrations. In its final form, the code was distributed to all homeroom teachers so that it could be discussed with pupils. . . .

No member of the team was "boss" . . . the responsibilities

were divided and shared on an equal basis. In order to work this way, common interests and understanding among the team members are essential. Each one of us had to be willing to place real confidence in the others, because each of us represented the team in all that we did.

Problems encountered by any member had to be brought to the team and threshed out, if the team was to work effectively. . . . We all became very much aware of interpersonal relationships, which are so important in any kind of administrative work. It was essential to the group process that there be no recriminations but rather a true acceptance of group responsibility.[4]

HIALEAH, FLORIDA: It all started in a ninth-grade civics class which was discussing juvenile delinquency. One of the students asked the teacher why the public and the newspapers were always playing up the "bad things" which teen-agers do and so very seldom give publicity to the "good things" which they accomplish. In other words, why can't adults take a positive approach rather than a negative attitude about juvenile problems?. . . . As a result of the discussion it was decided to hold a contest to select and give publicity to students who are good citizens and who do perform acts of citizenry which are above and beyond the ordinary. . . . Each of the principals of the 20 schools [of Hialeah and Miami Springs] was contacted and the idea was presented to them. . . . The principals appointed a representative from each of their faculties to attend our first group meeting. Out of this first meeting was born the Junior Citizen Award Committee, made up entirely of school teachers.

In subsequent meetings, through various committees, we set up a plan by which any student could nominate another student as the outstanding junior citizen of our communities. This was done in the form of an essay listing the reasons why the nominated student should be considered for this distinction. We were emphatic in insisting that the winners would not be selected on the basis of the prose and syntax of the essay, but rather be selected only on the merits of the accomplishments of the nominated students.

In our first year we were able to offer only paper certificates as awards, as we were unable to raise sufficient funds for more suitable prizes. This year we have three civic organizations who have volunteered to supply us with worthwhile awards on the elementary, junior high, and senior high levels.

In Boston a similar program designed to give public recognition to students practicing good citizenship is a much-needed contrast to the many references to norm violators which abound in the pages of city newspapers.

BOSTON, MASSACHUSETTS: The Citizenship Committee of the Massachusetts Secondary School Principals Association invites its membership to participate in its "Citizenship in Action" program. Specifically, this program will provide for the periodic recognition of those voluntary acts by high-school students in the school and in the community which show that service to others has a prime place in the life of that school.

Member high schools are invited to report significant acts of service to others by their students. . . . At regular intervals the Citizenship Committee of the MSSPA will evaluate these reports and accord public recognition to those schools whose voluntary student actions are regarded as meritorious.

Periodically, members of the Citizenship Committee will visit the high school so recognized and, with the school's permission, present at an assembly a citation to the deserving pupil or pupils whose actions inspired the award. This citation will be made to the pupil or pupils as part of a *total* school recognition, not merely as individuals, and will become the property of the school.[5]

To be most effective, a program must directly involve the people who are to benefit from it; thus, a program to improve the behavior of young people should insure their participation in both planning and work activities. In California this principle has been realized in the Youth Councils, which are organized on a community basis. In Ohio a health program involves cooperation of the State Medical Association, and in Michigan needs of communities are being met by the activity of all citizens—young and old.

LOS ANGELES COUNTY, CALIFORNIA: The youth, for whom a great deal of the planning is done, have ideas of their own on what is needed. A community which recognizes the contributions its young people have to offer has already taken a long step toward creating an atmosphere of mutual trust between young people and adults.

The Youth Coordinating Council provides a way in which this can be done. In 26 communities last year, youth councils were sponsored by their adult counterparts. Young people from youth organizations, both in and out of school, were given a real voice in community affairs. Consultants from the department helped them organize and met with their adult advisors to help them develop worthwhile programs.

Nine of these Youth Coordinating Councils developed or continued Youth Employment programs last year. The Youth Council members volunteered their time, in most of these programs, to help other young people obtain part-time or summer employment. Other projects included helping youth clubs find sponsors, obtaining favorable publicity for youth, sponsoring benefit dances, working to obtain youth centers, assisting in a "Teens Against Polio" campaign, initiating a youth banking and loan system, promoting a car rodeo, keeping a master calendar of social and service events.[6]

THE STATE OF OHIO: In Ohio, and probably in many other states, every county medical association, as a component of the State Medical Association, has established a committee to cooperate with schools in developing health programs. This brings the community's physicians into cooperative relationships which help the school toward more complete understanding and wise planning for the norm-violating pupils.

THE STATE OF MICHIGAN: . . . individual school people began sharing problems (needs of a lower-class community) "with outside of community" individuals. Activities snow-balled. "Outside of community," groups were contacted by these "outside of community individuals." For example, a "Thrift Shop" was set up. Good used clothing was gathered and made available at nominal or no cost. Any incoming monies were used in cases where agency funds were not available. Further steps followed. To date school personnel, service clubs and social agencies have organized to avoid duplication of services or lack of aid. In the offing is a specific "survey of needs" and possible extension of other types of aid seeking to help the community help itself.

In the review of all the materials contributed to the Project, one fact appeared to be particularly prominent and significant: Nearly all special programs were developed in reaction to a specific situation—often a crisis—that crystalized community feelings into a demand that something be done. In Philadelphia and Boston it was murder, while in Hialeah it was criticism of teen-agers in the newspapers that led an interested group to take action. The school administrator or classroom teacher should always be alert for the development of a demand that "something be done" and should be ready to capitalize upon this demand. On the other hand, school-community leadership should try to anticipate and prevent the need for crash programming by coordinated efforts in community fact-gathering, planning, and implementation.

In Seattle a demand that "something be done about Halloween vandalism" led the schools to form a student group to consider the problem. Now, 25 years later, the Inter-High Council which developed from that original student group has received international attention.

SEATTLE, WASHINGTON: Seattle Public Schools have been actively engaged since 1934 in a city-wide program to cut down juvenile delinquency. In that year the first all-city conference of students representing all Seattle public schools was called to consider the vicious problems of Halloween vandalism which had reached alarming proportions. The result of this conference was a student-directed campaign in all schools for a safe and sane Halloween.

The project has been repeated annually, and now involves much more than the prevention of Halloween vandalism alone. The theme in recent years has been responsible citizenship all year round. In fact, Halloween vandalism has been reduced so much that in 1957 the total number of prank calls on the police and sheriff's telephones was 10 percent lower on Halloween than on a normal Thursday night.

Out of the original Halloween Conference has evolved the Inter-High School Council made up of four student leaders from each high school. They meet once a month in executive session to act on any and all problems concerning high school youth in the community.

Inter-High Council works in five broad areas:
1. Law Enforcement
2. Traffic and Safety

300

3. Sportsmanship
4. Publicity
5. Leadership Training.

Community and school authorities are deeply convinced that the activities of Inter-High Council in Seattle have been a major force in precluding in Seattle the type of vicious gang delinquency prevalent in some other cities. School authorities are convinced that there is no finer way to teach responsible citizenship than to use the schools as a laboratory in the exercise in responsible citizenship. In a large way public agencies of the city such as the Police, Fire Department and Juvenile Court have come to use the Council as their means of reaching the students and to appreciate warmly the success of Inter-High School Council.

During 1957-58 the Inter-High School Council participated in the following projects.

1. The annual Halloween Conference on law enforcement involving students from all schools in the city.

2. Sportsmanship Conferences at the beginning of football season and again at the beginning of basketball season in which cheer leaders and song leaders met to discuss problems of crowd control at the stadium and the ethics of spectators at games.

3. A Sportsmanship Conference to which cheer leaders, student leaders, and song girls from all of the 16 participating high schools in the State High School Basketball Tournament were invited the evening before the opening of the Tournament to work on intersectional-loyalty problems involved when city schools play schools from other localities in the state.

4. A traffic and safety campaign in each school was sponsored in conjunction with the King County Safety Council and an all-day Teen-Age Driving Conference was held at a downtown hotel.

5. A series of eight half-hour television shows publicizing the activities and the policies of student government in the high schools was produced over educational station KCTS.

6. Members of the Inter-High Council took part in discussing "Contributions of Youth to Family Relationships" at a conference for social workers and other

adults in the community sponsored by the Family Life Education Department of Seattle Public Schools.

7. A Leadership Training Conference for officers of school governments at which the techniques of leadership including group dynamics were practiced.

Four years ago the Inter-High School Council began its most ambitious project, the sponsorship of a leadership conference at Seabeck, a resort on the Olympic Peninsula. At this meeting 160 student leaders from Seattle and neighboring high schools explore the techniques of leadership and work together for a week just before Labor Day. At the 1958 Conference four exchange students and two exchange leaders from Kobe, Japan, were in attendance. The idea of summertime leadership conferences has spread to neighboring areas, and now there is a demand for three times the enrollment that can be accommodated.

In each Seattle high school there is an activity coordinator with three hours release time from classroom work to direct the activities of the student government and the Inter-High School Council. The success of the Council's activities can be attributed to the nine activity coordinators who believe thoroughly in this means of promoting teen-age citizenship.

However, it is not always a school group that responds when a problem has been identified. For example, in two states nonschool organizations have instituted programs in research and special education as approaches to solving the delinquency problem. Both groups have published reports and educative materials based on their studies. When such materials, reports, and services are utilized by the school, their effectiveness is greatly increased.

THE STATE OF NORTH CAROLINA: The problem of delinquency has been a main concern of [the North Carolina Conference for Social Service] since its organization in 1912, and in recent years, the interest has centered more around juvenile delinquency. . . . During the past two years, the emphasis in our Committee on Adult and Juvenile Delinquency has been on special education as an instrument of preventing and treating juvenile delinquency, and action through treatment as an approach to juvenile delinquency. In both of these areas we have provided a number of programs.

302

Another recent project of our Adult and Juvenile Delinquency Committee has been the preparation of a folder on facilities for unwed mothers which has had a wide distribution. . . . We have had many requests for additional copies from . . . [high-school] principals. Unfortunately, many of the unwed mothers are of high-school age.

Another study by a nonschool organization dealt with detention facilities and probation services.

THE STATE OF NEW YORK: The State Committee on Children and Public Welfare [of the State Charities Aid Association] has been doing some surveys in the last two years in an effort to get information not available anywhere else on the 16-21 year age group. The survey we did last year was to find out the kinds of trouble those young people get into and what kind of treatment they received in the lower courts. This survey was conducted by volunteers in 14 counties throughout the state where we have local Committees on Children and Public Welfare. The material compiled was contained in a 14-county report. . . . In addition, reports of each local county were prepared for use by our citizens' committees in program planning to make needed changes and work toward meeting needs for youth services. As a result of that study, we became very much interested in the variety of treatment afforded young people both before and after trial, particularly in county jails. As a result, we have just completed another study which will give us some indication of the picture in some of our rural areas in regard to detention facilities and probation services. This has required getting information from county sheriffs, judges, commissioners of public welfare, probation officers, etc. The information will give us specific data on the number of young people detained in jail as well as a breakdown of the reasons for their detention and other pertinent information. In addition to this compilation, we have prepared a second part which is a compilation of an over-all report of programs on the state level which are designed to cope with the problem of youth crime and rehabilitation. As far as we know, this is the first time that such information on probation services, detention facilities, institutional care, psychiatric services, etc., has been brought together in one place. As a result of these two projects, we have prepared a list of

303

recommendations which quite logically have come out of our findings.

A major effort always calling for school-community cooperation is the recreation program. The school should not attempt to operate such programs alone but should always involve other community representatives in this activity. In Jamestown, North Dakota, the school works closely with those in charge of a teen-age canteen supported by the community through the United Fund. One program, formally organized by incorporation, is reported by Vale, Oregon.

VALE, OREGON: Our schools and community attempt to provide as many recreational and educational facilities for the young people as we possibly can. In Vale, we have an organization called Vale Sports, Inc., which, although operating on a very close budget, attempts to sponsor winter basketball for boys 8 to 13 years of age and summer recreational programs for boys between 8 and 17 years of age. Our recreational planning for girls is not very extensive in the summer. During the school months, the high school sponsors many activities for both boys and girls; namely, all types of sports programs, dances, yell squads, GAA, pep club, song-leader squads, drill team, Future Homemakers, Future Farmers of America, and others.

The problem of creating a recreation program for summertime and for nonschool hours during the regular school year is one that confronts almost every community, large or small. As is evident through this document, each community develops its own program with its own special features.

An idea of the variety of programs now in progress throughout the country may be obtained from the five reports which follow. Although their diversity is marked, these programs are alike in one significant respect: the school accepts responsibility for planning and cooperating in meeting community recreation needs. The first report is from New York City where the program employs a person to work within the elementary-school classroom from 11 a.m. to 3 p.m. and then to work with the same children in a recreational program from 3 to 5 p.m. The second report, from Pueblo, Colorado, emphasizes the cooperation of parents in interesting students in certain handicraft or sport activities. The third report, from San Francisco, relates how the adults themselves use the recreation program; the fourth, from Farmingdale, New York, is of interest to any suburban community which suddenly finds its population soaring; the fifth and final report in this section shows how Tacoma faces the problem of sharing responsibility in a community recreation program.

NEW YORK CITY: The All-Day Neighborhood Schools of the New York City Board of Education is a significant project that helps in the prevention of juvenile delinquency. These are elementary schools in which additional staff are provided to help children during the school day and in an after-school "club program" from 3 to 5 [p.m.]. The warm, personal relationship between teachers and children fuses home, school, and community into a sympathetic unit. Children of working parents who might otherwise be unsupervised in the empty after-school hours before the mother returns to the home, children needing help in learning processes, children with language and integration problems, children with emotional problems benefit from the program. Statistics show that there is a conspicuous lack of truancy and a minimum of vandalism in these schools and that the delinquency rate declines.

In an All-Day Neighborhood School, seven additional teachers and a psychiatric social worker from the Bureau of Child Guidance are assigned to the school in addition to the regular staff. These extra teachers, under the guidance of the Director of the program and the Principal of the school, assist classroom teachers in developing curriculum suited to the children. They also help in getting to know the needs of individual children and in exploring ways of meeting these needs.

Each of the six grades has an extra teacher, called a group teacher, whose duties from 11 a.m. to 3 p.m. include working with small groups of children from various classrooms. This is a structured program carefully planned at cooperative conferences by the classroom and group teachers. When two teachers plan together and each has the opportunity of working with a smaller group from the same class, children are reached individually and a meaningful educational program for all the children results.

From 3 . . . to 5 p.m. the group teacher provides an educationally sound recreation program for twenty-five selected children from the same grade. In charge of the six additional teachers is a seventh teacher called the Administrator. The continuity of guidance that is given to children through a program like this is of inestimable value. When the same person works with the child in the day school and in the after-school program, a fuller understanding of the child's personality results.

It is an interesting fact that the All-Day Neighborhood Schools were not started to prevent juvenile delinquency. The basic idea was that children could not be educated from 9 [a.m.] to 3 [p.m.] and recreated from 3 to 5 [p.m.] It was also our belief that children in low socio-economic areas, who often have limited cultural backgrounds and frequently come from broken homes, have emotional problems which make learning difficult. Many times the school is the only institution trying to meet the needs of such children.

The All-Day Neighborhood Schools work closely with parents and citizens to form a partnership of school and community working for the best interest of the children. It is our belief that schools must secure the cooperation of parents and citizens to assure a continuous educational pattern in home, school, and community. We also feel that they must work for the necessary financial support that will provide for the needed changes in the schools. . . .

One of the emphases of the All-Day Neighborhood School is pupil-participation in school living. As stated in Curriculum Bulletin No. 1, 1945-1946, Curriculum Development in the Elementary Schools: "Participating in the activities of the school means that gradually the children have opportunity to serve and to share experiences in a larger social group. Just as each member must do his share if the classroom community is to function properly, so should each class and each individual assume some responsibility for the effective functioning of the school community."

Beginning with the third grade, several classes in these schools engage in cooperative enterprises closely related to their work. These "service jobs," as they are called, become the class responsibility for an entire year. Much of the content of the daily studies of the pupils grows out of interests and needs which develop because of the job on hand. They have value to the children in proportion as they assume responsibility for the job and as the duties are so arranged that every child has his chance to do a definite part of the work. In general, it has proved valuable to rotate assignments so that each child has an opportunity at some time to work on each phase of the service job.

Each child must realize the responsibility for his own contribution toward the success of the service job as a class project, a job which is the responsibility of the class. It is not the special domain of the "good" child or the "gifted" child or a regard for individual accomplishment.

As the organization of the service job becomes routinized, the studying which grows out of the pupils' interest in the job is planned by them with the teacher. The areas of learning become specific: the child understands why he must learn how to make out a bill if he is handling the milk orders of the school; it is clear to him that he must learn how to add if he is responsible for collecting the money for school lunches; it becomes necessary to establish certain rules of behavior if he is to enter the classroom to carry on his business.

From these concrete necessities, it is logical for the child to find out how paper is made if his class is in charge of supplies for the school; or to go into an historical study of the growth of our country through the development of postal service if the class is in charge of the post office. Thus, the child has unified, dynamic learning experiences. Working in groups, some with the group teacher and some with the classroom teacher, brings greater efficiency and better results.

Many types of service jobs have been found valuable. Not all the jobs have been tried out in all the schools. The most successful ones have been those related to Milk, Post Office, Lunch, Library, Supplies, and Visual Aids.

Classes elect representatives to attend a weekly or biweekly meeting of a Student Council or Civic Club under the leadership of a teacher. Children are encouraged to discuss problems in which they can participate to improve the welfare of the school. Children have taken up problems related to the school and to the neighborhood. The matters discussed at the Council meeting are brought back for discussion in the classrooms. Usually representatives are selected from fourth, fifth, and sixth grades, but school-wide problems are brought to the attention of the younger children by having representatives from the upper classes talk to the younger children.

The children have participated in clean-up campaigns in the school and in the neighborhood. In one instance where a large number of children were living in a housing project, they reported the messy condition of halls and playground. Representatives of the Student Council went to neighboring schools to get their cooperation in a plan developed with the Housing Authority to set up additional waste receptacles and to generally improve the conditions. They are planning a continued campaign for next year.

In another school children wrote letters to other schools in the interest of getting a Branch Library. They saw the chief librarian in the Borough to solicit his interest in their behalf.

Children have undertaken jobs acting as hostesses in the lunchrooms to improve the atmosphere and to try and get the children to eat more balanced meals.

In two schools the children planned a more effective use of the playground during lunch hour, setting up areas for different types of games to avoid accidents and to attract children into the yard rather than running in the streets. A committee of children taught and supervised the games.

In another school the children became interested in seeing how they could secure a play street for this very crowded neighborhood. They have been interviewing the city officials and are getting the cooperation of the Parents' Association and other community groups.

New York City has been experimenting with putting musical instruments in Elementary Schools where a teacher adequate for teaching instrumental music is available. In the All-Day Neighborhood Schools a group teacher has been used or a teacher has been used in the afternoon center. Other schools have used classroom teachers. By giving the children an opportunity to learn a musical instrument, even though they cannot take private lessons, there has been a marked change in attitude in certain children.

The opportunity to achieve success and to be part of the school community has given many of these children a real incentive to participate in other school activities. Teachers have been amazed at the change in children by their participation in such activities. Parents are most enthusiastic as they, too, can see the change in attitude in many of the children. Certain children

308

with leadership ability and talent have been discovered, but the program is not limited to talented children only.

A year-round program which utilizes the services of parents to interest youngsters in handicrafts and sports is evaluated in the next report in this section on recreational activity.

PUEBLO, COLORADO: In June of 1958 the school district initiated a program of summer recreation approved and financed by the Pueblo School District 60 Board of Education.

This program took place in schools of the district and included many activities from the various games through the numerous handicraft-type activities. We are at present evaluating the effect of this program throughout the district. However, we have received numerous comments from parents and other citizens in the district. In every case they were highly laudatory and expressed appreciation and gratitude and a desire for the continuation of such a program. Our plans for this year include an extension of the program by approximately 50 percent and have been agreed to by a most cooperative and civic-minded board.

We have found that one of the greatest aids to our program has been the inclusion of various parent groups in our plans and in the supervision of our program. Their help was invaluable.

During the regular school year the . . . recreational phase is . . . important and receives much encouragement. Any suitable activity may be included when the students express an interest, and adequate supervision is available. This includes such activities as chess, checkers, table tennis, bingo, sewing, rug making, wood working, aluminum tooling, Spanish dancing, basket weaving, leather-craft, camera, cooking, etc. . . . these programs occur a minimum of three times per week after school and may also take place before school and at noon.

Another year-round program is operating on the West Coast. Here a particularly valuable feature of the program is that it offers the use of school facilities to both youth and adults.

SAN FRANCISCO, CALIFORNIA: This is the ninth year that the School District has conducted a recreation program on school facilities. . . .

The schoolyard playgrounds operate on a schedule of 3 p.m. to 6 p.m. on school days and 10 a.m. to 5 p.m. on Saturdays and school vacations. The program is planned for children of all ages but with special emphasis on the interests of the younger children who cannot travel any great distance to a recreation center or park. Activities include sports, games, competitive athletic leagues, arts and crafts, and during the summer—storytelling, talent shows, Day Camp, and weekly excursions to points of interest. During the summer vacation 37 of the 42 schoolyard playgrounds are open. Small attendance during the summer at the other 5 does not justify keeping them open.

Schoolyard playgrounds are located in those areas not served by a regular Recreation and Park playground, and a close working relationship is maintained between the two departments to assure city-wide coverage and to avoid duplication of services.

The evening gymnasiums are open on a year-round basis Monday through Friday, from 7 p.m. to 10 p.m., and provide recreational activities for adults as well as boys and girls. Gymnasiums are made available to churches, private agencies, military, and other organized groups. Recreation badminton and volleyball groups and competitive leagues and tournaments are organized and conducted for both men and women. The evening gymnasiums are closed part time during the summer to allow time for refinishing floors, new paint lines, and other work. . . .

In the after-school interscholastic program this past year there were 2500 boys participating in the junior high schools and 3000 in the senior high schools.[7]

The next reported recreation program functions within a community that is undergoing rapid population growth, supporting increased school-building activity, and providing expanded special services in its schools. The community's council uses school buildings as recreation centers. This report discusses the facilities in a school most adaptable to the needs of a recreation program as well as the financial responsibility for the supplies and equipment required in such a program.

FARMINGDALE, NEW YORK: The following is a brief description of Farmingdale which will help to orientate the reader. It is important to note that four new elementary buildings have been built within the last four years, leaving as the fifth the

310

original Farmingdale school built in the 1920's. The Junior and Senior High Schools share the same building on a split-session basis and both divisions are overcrowded.

Farmingdale is in a state of flux and its problems are dynamic. The number of pupils enrolled in school has jumped from 1,500 ten years ago to a registered enrollment of 7,540 as of April 2. 1958.

At this time, there are approximately 5,345 students in the elementary schools, 1,075 in the junior high school and 1,120 in the senior high school. During the year 1957-1958, 1,000 children were enrolled in our kindergarten program.

The problems of growth affected not only the building program and the need for increased facilities, but also the need for new staff members and the development of special services to deal with the many problems that were developing or being brought into the district. . . .

The Farmingdale Youth Council, a community-sponsored organization directed by a group of civic and recreation-minded volunteers, has scheduled the opening of all Farmingdale public schools as Recreation Centers.

Each Recreation Center best fulfills its function by servicing the differentiated needs of its own locale, hence operating procedures must vary with the needs of each Recreation Center. . . . [Below are listed the basic requirements.]

Space needs and maintenance
1. In general, the allocation of space should include:
    a. Gymnasium
    b. Toilets
    c. Lockers
    d. Necessary classrooms for arts and crafts and dancing
    e. Possible use of cafeteria and auditorium for special programs.
2. Control of facilities during Center's operation is most vital to the success of program. Rooms used should be centrally located and as close to the gymnasium as possible.
3. Recreation Center entrance should be door nearest to gymnasium. . . .

Equipment
1. Supervisor should have access to school telephone, typewriter, and mimeograph machine.

2. Supervisors are permitted to use their day-school physical education equipment (mats, volleyball standards, trampolines, etc.) for their program.
3. Equipment should be properly stored and treated.

Supplies
1. Basic Recreation Center supplies, such as basketballs, bats, softballs, etc., are to be drawn from the present-day school physical education supplies.
2. Special Recreation Center supplies, such as pool tables, nok-hockey, quiet games, etc., will be supplied by Youth Council.
3. A perpetual inventory of Youth Council equipment and supplies must be kept (this does not include school physical ed supplies). Equipment which becomes damaged beyond repair during the season should be held for final disposition at the close of the season.[8]

In Tacoma, the employment of a joint school-park recreational staff insures the sharing of financial responsibility and a coordinated and reciprocal program.

TACOMA, WASHINGTON: The superintendent of Public Recreation is jointly employed by the Tacoma School Board and the Metropolitan Park District Board of Park Commissioners. A supervisor of Evening Recreation Centers and playgrounds, a supervisor of Athletics, and a secretary are also jointly employed by the School and Park Districts. With this arrangement, all school and park facilities are available for leisure time activities.

School buildings are used for recreation programs after 6 p.m., Mondays through Fridays and on Saturdays. Some school playgrounds are used in the summer time. Five high school swim pools are used evenings, Saturdays, and summer vacations for instructional and recreational swimming, other than the regular day-school program.

Park ball fields, tennis courts are used by the school district for leagues and tournaments. Reciprocation of facilities is general. . . .

Today nine junior high schools are open on week-day nights for basketball leagues, boys' athletic centers on Tuesday evenings, and Teen Time Centers for junior high boys and girls on Friday nights. Senior high school gyms are used for basketball programs conducted by the Park school districts separate from varsity and day-school basketball programs. High school swim pools are used evenings, Saturdays, and during the summer vacation for swimming instruction and general recreational swimming.

Boys' athletic center programs consist of basketball, volleyball, wrestling, boxing, table tennis, and active [but simple] games. Boys in elementary and junior high may attend from 6:30 p.m. to 8 p.m. Boys in high school and out of school go to the school center from 8 p.m. to 9:30 p.m. This program is an opportunity for boys to work off their surplus energy. Any troublesome boy involved with the police because of the misuse of his spare time is referred to the school athletic center. Approximately 650 boys attend eight junior high-school boys' athletic centers once each week.

Teen Time programs in nine junior high schools attract approximately 1800 boys and girls each Friday night from October 15 through April 15.

Three hundred [basketball] teams . . . with 3500 participants enjoyed evenings in school buildings in park-school programs during their leisure time.

The school does not necessarily have to be the organizer or even an active co-worker in every worthwhile program for youth, but there are many ways in which the school can contribute. It may serve as a clearinghouse for information or as a channel for announcements. It may offer the use of its facilities for meetings and may play a supportive role for worthwhile community organizations by having their speakers appear before student or parent groups. Sometimes the school may serve as a referral agent to local groups or to such national organizations as the Police Athletic League and the Big Brother Association. The relations of the school to both organizations was briefly outlined by a discussion group at the NEA Juvenile Delinquency Project's National Invitational Conference.

NATIONAL INVITATIONAL CONFERENCE: The "PAL" Police Athletic League conducts a program for boys and girls and attempts to teach social teamwork and to provide wholesome leisure time activities. Referrals for Big Brothers and Big Sisters come to us from the schools. Conferences are often held in the schools with the youngster's family and Big Brother participating.

Our job placement and camping projects handle only referrals —mainly from schools.

Court referrals are handled by our PAL men (Juvenile Conference Committee) before—or rather than—a court appearance.

The schools (particularly school psychologists) have representatives on most committees of the Social Planning Committee of the Community Welfare Council. The police are also participants.

Our PAL follows through and has a visitation program for youths who are committed to correctional, treatment, diagnostic, and detention facilities.

The Big Brother program provides an excellent service to the school through its direct one-man and one-boy relationships with fatherless boys. This service relates both to the treatment of delinquents and to the prevention areas. The Big Brother meets the Little Brother once a week, for mutually enjoyable activities; as a result, after a long period the Little Brother may identify with the Big Brother. In essence, this is what we have to offer this boy who has had a poor relationship or no relationship at all with an adult male; it enables the boy to reach into this man's life and to take those things he wishes in his own life. He works out a better image of self; gain ideals and inspiration; and acquires better attitudes in respect to others, to property, to education.

The Big Brother also profits—he gets a valuable education in community service and in our schools and thus becomes a better and active citizen. Of course, the satisfaction and emotional values derived are limitless.

Other types of organizations, which are not school organized or sponsored but which could serve the school as a useful resource service, are exemplified by New York City's Boys Brotherhood Republic and the Centurions, one a regularly organized club and the other a "gang." Both of these have adult direction and sponsorship and have been extremely successful in giving youngsters a sense of direction and of belonging.

New York City: The Boys Brotherhood Republic of New York, Inc., is located in what is generally considered one of the prime breeding grounds for juvenile delinquency and adult crime. In the relatively small area of some 20 city blocks, there live close to 107,000 persons of many races and creeds, jammed into tenements and low-income housing developments. The juvenile population alone is estimated to number about 35,000—larger than the total population of most cities covering many times the area involved here. Almost without exception, these young people live in conditions of extreme poverty, or come from broken homes or homes in which both parents must work to subsist. Few of them receive the parental care, love and discipline necessary to the proper upbringing of youth. Most of them lack that feeling of "belonging" which every child and teen-ager needs. It is small wonder, then, that at the last count there were at least four named "gangs" of juvenile delinquents in the immediate area, with some 14 subgroups involving almost 400 youngsters. . . .

The government of the Republic is patterned after that of New York or any other large city. The citizens elect their own mayor, councilmen, business manager, city clerk, prosecuting attorney, and judges. There is also a chief of police, appointed by the mayor, and three police captains in charge of a "force" of 100 citizens, each of whom has one hour of duty per week. The citizens have their own penal code for various "crimes" and offenses, such as rough-housing and profanity; penalties usually consist of banishment from the premises for a stated length of time, depending upon the severity of the "crime." The accused is entitled to trial by jury and to defense counsel of his own choosing. The Republic has its own bar association, with procedures and requirements similar to those of the Bar Association of the City of New York. The councilmen enact laws and regulations by majority vote in public sessions, after lively and thorough debate in which each citizen may express his views. The citizens publish their own newspaper, *Boys' World*, and tax themselves 10 cents a month for eight months a year (supplemented, of course, by outside contributions).

Once a month there is a meeting of the Parent's Association of BBR. The purpose of this group is to seek ways and means to improve the community and to help raise funds to finance some of the projects and activities of the citizens. An important corollary benefit is that these meetings help overcome racial prejudices and tensions which are often stronger among adults than among youth. When the parents see their boys working, playing, and getting along with boys of different races and religions, and they then attend these multi-racial meetings of the Parents' Association, their prejudices tend to vanish, or at least diminish.[9]

One of New York's gangs, the Centurions, are known as New York's Christian Gang. They could just as well be a Jewish gang. The Centurions meet in a church, study the Bible, and never carry knives or zip-guns. They've never been challenged by another gang, because everyone knows they're the toughest young men in Manhattan's teen-age gangland. The adult leader of the Centurions tells his boys: "This is a *Christian* gang. If you join, you're going to act like a Christian whether you understand it or not. You don't steal, you don't carry a knife or gun, you don't use dope or push it, you don't fight except for sport with other Centurions. You'll study the Bible and learn to pray, and as we go along you'll get the idea why a Christian gang has to be different."

Some 40 percent of the 75 members of the Centurions have been on probation after conviction of a crime. The most common offense is theft, but the boys' "records" run the gamut from mugging to criminal attack. But no boy has ever been charged with an offense after becoming a Centurion.

The leader has found that as boys learn to fight scientifically, the urge to fight ebbs. When they know they're really tough, they don't have to fight to prove it. This toughness is brought about by a few weeks of judo, boxing, close-order drill, and war games. After this introduction, they come to a more modest estimate of their toughness. A few more weeks they begin to develop the genuine strength and skill that safeguard them against attack by the street-corner hoodlums that infest their neighborhood.

Another development in juvenile delinquency prevention and control has been the "roving group worker," who is assigned by a nonschool agency to establish contact with a street corner gang and try to channel gang interests into nondelinquent activities. Schools can aid such programs by making information and facilities available to the roving worker, whose efforts, when successful, directly benefit the school and its students.

SAINT PAUL, MINNESOTA: The Roving Group Work Units have worked closely with the schools attended by group members since September 1957.

316

A list of boys who are in Roving Groups was furnished the Marshall Junior High staff. Director of Roving Group Workers has participated in Pupil Problems conferences at Marshall and at Central High. After-school patrol in the Marshall area has enabled the Roving Group Work staff to intercede in several potential fights. . . .

Capitol Community Services held a series of meetings with the parents of six boys who were truanting from Central in early 1959. Probation officers cooperated in this venture, and this department worked closely with the assistant principal at Central in supporting the boys involved to stay in school.

A member of the Roving Group Work staff meets one afternoon a week for one hour with a group of boys from the club program at Marshall Junior High. These boys were not satisfied with their club choice at Marshall and are now learning skills in outdoor games.

Roving Group Workers have continually worked with group members to support their positive adjustment at school. Workers have talked to parents about supporting their boys at school and in one case an older brother who is a school drop-out is giving excellent support to a boy presently in school.

Several teachers have supported members of Roving Groups in finding jobs and have made contacts for some of the boys. The Principal at Mechanic Arts has had individual conferences with several group members and has helped them to make a much better adjustment in school. In some of the above instances, the contacts with teachers and administrators have been the first or one of very few positive contacts the boys have had with school personnel.

The cooperation which this department has received from the St. Paul Public Schools has been excellent. The interest taken in many of the marginal youth we know in our hard-to-reach groups has made a real difference to the boys. Several of the boys who could not function in school and dropped out have now been able to point out the help they received while in school and to urge their friends to stay in school.

The Roving Group Work Unit is giving service to eight groups at this time. Five groups are active Roving Groups, two groups have progressed to the point where they are receiving less service than the other groups and are classified as Post Roving Groups while the eighth group is a referral group from the Child Guid-

ance Clinic with one of its members active with the clinic. . . .
In addition to the 108 boys who were active in Roving Groups
during the last year, there are 27 boys who on occasion drift in
and out of group meetings. While these boys are not considered
members by the groups, they have an effect on group process,
and staff on many occasions has helped them to work out
problems such as school, job or probation contacts. . . .

The Roving Group Department sees itself as working at several
levels:

1. direct service to group members via group meetings and
    individual conferences
2. corollary services such as conferences with probation offi-
    cers, etc., including contacts with potential resources which
    can be used by or for all groups
3. contacts with interested persons and groups throughout
    the community to help improve existing services or create
    new services for the marginal youth—the work in the job
    area done by the Advisory Committee and supporting other
    settlements . . . fall in this third area, and
4. service on committees whose purpose is to improve services
    to youth on a community and state wide level. . . .

The job sub-committee has worked out the material on the
Youth Development Camp Program and the School-Work preparation program which have been the basis of bills in the State
Legislature which are being studied by special committees in
both Houses of the Legislature. . . .

[Weekend] camping . . . and cookouts are stressed during
the spring and summer. There was no winterized camp available during the past winter months.

Roving Groups have engaged in softball, touchfootball, basketball and hockey on an intra-club basis and played games . . . in
all the above sports except hockey. No schedule or league was
set up, as each game was planned individually. On several
occasions, members of two groups have shared the cost of outside officials. Only one knife pulling was noted in over 40
contests and the Worker stepped in before others noted what
had happened. Very favorable comments on team play and
sportsmanship have been registered by staff. . . . This represents
real progress for these individuals who in the past have lacked
the skill and determination to complete a ball game.

Bowling, fishing, cookouts, cooking, tobogganing and swim-

318

ming have been popular. Several evenings of "going to a drive-in" to eat and talk about various problems have been spent by the groups. One group is planning a series of programs on safe driving and may invite another group to join them. Another group has been interested in tumbling and several have made their high school team for the first time in any sport. Another group has had a personnel director from a local firm in to help them in learning how to fill out an application blank and have discussed how to look for a job.

One factor that creates problems in programming is the unique personality of each group. No two groups have the same problems or the same strengths. This fact limits programming on a department wide basis. Successful program . . . [activity] for one group is a sure-fire flop for another group. Individual plans and goals must be worked out for each group, for sub-groups within the group and for individual members.

The lack of skills, social, intellectual and physical, among group members is a major problem. What appears on the surface as apathy and disinterest is more often than not a cover up for fear and ignorance. We cannot hope to help these boys to behave up to the expectations of society until we can help them gain the skills society demands of its youth. Some of the skills needed for confidence can come through the group, other skills must be gained in school or on the job. How much time should the Agency staff give to staff of other Agencies to help them become more able to help the boys we and they serve?

The question of how far we should carry the Roving Groups has not been answered. Two groups have made enough progress . . . [to be] now classified as post roving and are receiving about one-third the service hours given to the Roving Groups. When do we drop them or should we drop them completely? Since we have no regular club program in which to move them, what is our responsibility? Do we continue to help them face emergencies in school, in the community and at home? Should we spend time in helping these boys in areas such as job or do we make a complete break?

What is our responsibility to non-group members who are delinquent or predelinquent who come to us to ask for help in seeking a job or help with a school problem? Do we refuse these youth our services or attempt to refer them to other agencies when we do not have staff time to follow up on a referral? [10]

An unusual program for working with the street corner gang is being developed in San Francisco. Here an attempt has been made to establish harmony among the gangs of the city and to create in the gang members an interest in service to others. The original move towards organization was opposed by some on the theory that once organization came, trouble would follow. Up to this time such is not the case. However, as in all the other programs reported in this book, it is evident that every new or experimental project will always carry some element of calculated risk.

SAN FRANCISCO, CALIFORNIA: [The American Friends Service Committee early in November of last year organized a Temporary Inter Club Council. This has developed into a Youth for Service Teenage Council.] The Council was formed to resolve the differences between teen-age clubs and to provide a sounding board for ideas put forth by these clubs working together. Gang fights had been prevalent in the area, and for the first time clubs confronted each other on a peaceful basis. It was a big step for many of them. "There are a lot of us here who shouldn't be meeting together," said one of the boys, "but since we're here, let's forget the past and go on from here."

It was hoped that through the projection of ideas from the group, more adults in the community could be involved in setting up programs, both volunteer and recreational. YFS was not set up to provide recreational activities for teen-agers in the commonly accepted sense. Some of the project alternatives suggested by the Council which were recreational in nature have now been sponsored by other groups, such as a boxing program sponsored by the Golden Gate Kiwanis Club. The basis for a club's involvement in the Council is still service to the community.

Outside groups that are now working with YFS on Council activities are the Junior League, Junior Chamber of Commerce, Unitarian Fellowship for Social Justice, the Dutton Club, and the First Presbyterian Church. Currently we are planning a large talent show, a conference with the attorney general in Sacramento, and sponsorship of one boy to the Youth March for Integrated Schools in Washington, D. C.

There are some 27 clubs [i.e., Aces, Road Runners, Lairds, Turbans, Frisco Apaches, Los Bandidos, El Royals] participating in the Council—car clubs, social and sports clubs, as well as

320

individuals not connected with clubs. There are no constitution or bylaws, . . . rules, membership cards, or other organizational structure, and membership is based completely on the principle of identification through interest. A significant factor, which it is hoped may be more than coincidence, is that from December 1958 to this writing, no gang fights have occurred in the areas served by the Council. Another important outgrowth of Council activities is the large number of speaking engagements filled by Teenage Council members and YFS staff. The boys have been well received by graduate and undergraduate groups at colleges and universities in the area, and no longer feel as intimidated by such contacts.

Other than these, Council accomplishments are difficult to pinpoint. The big factor, that of getting hostile clubs to work together, operates in far more subtle ways. Teen-age club members tend to identify with (the organization) in contacts with other teen-agers and adults, and feel a positive rapport with the total YFS program.[11]

The next section of this chapter will deal with a form of action commonly taken by most schools in organizing to help the norm violator in his community. The school may set up its own committee or join an existing group. These committees may take different forms and asume different functions and responsibilities. However, no school-sponsored committee can function independently of other agencies or groups in the community. The committee must at least consult with representatives of other agencies such as the court or clinic for information on their activities. In turn, these workers outside the school may become permanent members of the school-sponsored group.

The initial school delinquency committee may take many forms. It may be a committee representing a single school established because too many windows were broken in the school building over the week-end. A slightly more complicated design may be found in the regional-neighborhood school committee representing all the schools—elementary and junior high—supplying students to a certain high school. This group tends to work with one high school in a combined attack on the area's problems. Still another design is utilized by the school system that forms a committee composed of members drawn from all schools and special service divisions in the system, thus establishing a city, county, or state representative group. Running parallel to these three variants are the expanded community committees in which school membership is complemented by parents, police officials, welfare representatives, youth themselves, or, in short, the interdisciplinary community-wide committee representing all forces of the area.

These committees may come into being through two approaches. First, a group of teachers or principals may be talking together about school problems and decide to try to do something about a certain problem. They also determine to meet again at a certain time to continue the discussion. Soon this group selects a leader, a meeting time, and a specific plan of attack on a problem; thus, a committee has been formed and has begun its operations. Second, committees may form when an administrator discovers in his work that a certain problem needs rethinking and cooperative action. He decides to appoint an official committee. A group of volunteers is sought or members are appointed, and once again a functioning committee is the result.

In Redwood City, California, for example, the Youth Guidance Committee is formed along the regional-neighborhood plan and considers the problem of the norm violator as an individual and as a member of the group.

REDWOOD CITY, CALIFORNIA: In most of the high schools of our county we have what is known as a Youth Guidance Committee. This is centered around a high school and each feeder elementary school as well as representatives of police and sheriff's offices, welfare and probation departments, and other like departments, who participate as a coordinating committee once a month to determine what the best procedure may be in preventing pupils from straying too far from the norm. At these meetings, which sometimes become case conferences on an individual student, certain agencies may be given the responsibility to work the matter out and refer back to the central committee. In other cases, we discuss fundamental difficulties, such as gangs, hot rod clubs, recreation, and many other ideas on prevention. These have been very successful.

The city-wide committee is represented in this document by reports from Milwaukee, Saint Paul, and Detroit. These committees show three kinds of objectives. The Milwaukee committee functions as "a clearinghouse for all kinds of problems concerning youth in the schools." The emphasis is on the individual who has problems that go "beyond the resources of the school." The Saint Paul committee, however, has as its major concern the group characteristics of norm violators. This is a planning and "carrying-out" committee which has prepared a handbook and set up a training workshop for local youth workers. The third example, from Detroit, presents a committee with dual emphasis. Here a joint program is in operation, both specific and general in its attack; through a study of individual youngsters known to be vulnerable to norm-violating behavior, the committee members attempt to formulate new approaches to the general problem of delinquency.

MILWAUKEE, WISCONSIN: [The Community Referral Committee is composed] . . . of Representatives from the Department of Pupil Personnel, the junior and senior high-school principal, and selected members of his staff, and representatives from the Department of Municipal Recreation and selected members of his staff, and representatives from the Department of Municipal Recreation and Adult Education. . . . supplemented as the need arises with representatives from public agencies that are concerned with problem youth in the area served. This would include members from the Children's Court Probation Department, Police Department, Youth Aid Bureau, and Milwaukee Vocational School.

The general plan of action would be for the schools in the district to screen and refer cases of youth presenting serious problems which are beyond the resources of the school. Referrals would also come from other members of the permanent Committee where cases have come to their attention. In this way the Committee would serve as a clearinghouse for all kinds of problems concerning youth in school.[12]

SAINT PAUL, MINNESOTA: For the past two years a school

advisory committee on provisions for the maladjusted student has been at work discussing, planning, and carrying out such activities as seemed valuable and feasible within the limits of our own school organization. This planning has involved some 75 representatives from every department of the school system. They have met voluntarily and generally after school hours with only [one person's] services devoted full time to the implementation and coordination of their work. A handbook was developed for the Intra-School Pupil Problems Committees which are now functioning in every junior and senior high school. A workshop was conducted last spring as a result of committee planning.

DETROIT, MICHIGAN: [A project under the joint sponsorship of the Youth Commission and the Detroit Public Schools has the following objectives and procedures.]

To identify at an early age, those children who are more vulnerable to forces conducive toward delinquency.

To find ways of better using existing services of social work, recreational, educational agencies, and other community resources potentially effective in reducing the vulnerability.

To identify services which are needed, but not available.

1. Each school joining the project forms an action team. An action team consists of:
   a. An assistant principal—who acts as chairman—two or more classroom teachers, a visiting teacher, an attendance officer, and the school nurse
   b. Consultants—a psychiatrist, a nutritionist, a recreation worker, a social group worker, and other specialists to help with specific children.
2. Teachers survey all children in their classes.
3. They select some children as predelinquent on the basis of troublesome classroom behavior or adverse family conditions.
4. The action team checks this identification with test results from the Board of Education Psychological Clinic.
5. The action team holds case conferences on each child, tries to determine the unique needs of each child and how these needs can best be met.
6. The action team solicits aid from resources in the community to treat or diagnose a child's problems. This assistance includes a medical examination. Depending upon a child's need, the appropriate community resource.[18]

The County of Los Angeles, which is undergoing one of the highest rates of population increase in the United States, has been very active in juvenile delinquency prevention, and reports emanating from the county have been frequently quoted in this document. It is interesting to note that in each of the next three reports from this county, a particular type of committee and a distinctive function are delineated. The first is a committee seeking a policy and trying to identify conditions predisposing to delinquency. It is nonschool; that is, the school is represented on the committee but is not the controlling member.

Los Angeles County, California: The Case Conference Committee is a group process concerned with the discovery, examination, and referral of children exhibiting behavioral and personality difficulties. The Committee coordinates the referrals of children with behavior problems to the appropriate agencies. The Committee does no case-work, but considers the circumstances surrounding individual cases and suggests the appropriate resource for assistance. No child or adult concerned with the case is interviewed by the Committee.

The objectives are two-fold. One objective is the early discovery of behavior disorders. The Committee focuses its attention upon delinquent or predelinquent children. Children who have problems that require treatment are referred to case-work or group-work agencies as the circumstances warrant. Among common examples of a need for referral are the truant and the withdrawn or aggressive child.

The other important objective is the discovery of community conditions which predispose to delinquency. This involves the referral of these facts to the Community Council for either the expansion of existing youth services or the development of new facilities or programs which will counteract unwholesome environment. Occasionally there may be requests from countywide organizations, through the Federation Case Conference Committee, for information regarding local delinquency trends.

Due to the confidential nature of the work of the Committee, membership is limited to professionally trained people and people in official positions who are working with children and youth. Consequently, representatives of the schools, law enforcement agencies, probation and parole departments, and individual case work agencies are members. As the occasion demands other professionally trained persons such as psychiatrists, physicians, psychologists, group-work agency representatives, local ministers, public health nurses, recreation directors, and others may be called in to furnish information or to work with the Committee.[14]

A county-wide committee composed of representatives appointed by the superintendents of the larger school districts in Los Angeles County meets to formulate recommendations. It represents a committee formed by appointment and an example of its recommendations follows.

LOS ANGELES COUNTY, CALIFORNIA: That a model discipline code be cooperatively developed as a guide and that Boards of Education in individual school districts be encouraged to develop and adopt their own discipline code with specific policies and step-by-step regulations for handling their seriously disturbed pupils and those with behavior problems.

That the Commission on Credentials, California State Department of Education, be requested to include the subject of psychology as one of the teaching majors acceptable for the general secondary credential, in order that properly qualified teachers will be available in our junior and senior high schools for courses in personality development, marriage and the family, mental hygiene, boy-girl relationships, and other similar courses in psychology applied to adequate teen-age development.

That school administrators assume the responsibility for scheduling, on a regular basis, meetings involving school attendance supervisors, law enforcement workers, probation officers, health and welfare workers, and other youth case workers, who operate in the same geographic area, in order that constructive plans may be developed to help pupils.

That public-school administrators recognize and exercise their rights, under the Education Code, to request and transmit complete information concerning the seriously misbehaved pupils who transfer from one district to another.[15]

The third example from Los Angeles County is in the form of a request that a committee on delinquency prevention and control be established. As is obvious by the form of the report, a group is already in operation, brought together by a common interest and not by appointment. Here schools facing a common problem join in requesting that official steps be taken to bring a specific plan into action.

LOS ANGELES COUNTY, CALIFORNIA: Fourteen of the larger school districts . . . have asked the superintendent of schools to form a committee to investigate the possibilities for the prevention and control of juvenile delinquency, with particular reference to the role of the schools. It is suggested that each of the 14 school districts select . . . cases which are not now actually under the jurisdiction of the courts but which have the poorest prognosis for the future. Under the guidance of a committee representing the 14 districts, the fullest possible case history data will be gathered for each of the cases. The total sample (140 cases, if 10 are taken from each district) will be divided into matched pairs—one group being for intensive preventive treatment, the other group for control.

This intensive study and treatment is to be carried out by a team of paid professional workers employed for this purpose by and for the project, including at least the following: a psychiatrist, a psychologist, a neurologist, a psychiatric social worker, a clerical worker familiar with medical history and procedures.

The services of other law enforcement workers such as probation officers, juvenile court judges, and state legislators will also be needed, but their services may be arranged for and paid for as part of the activities of their regular full-time positions (not as paid personnel for this project). At the end of ___ months the performance of the treatment group vs. the matched controls will be compared to determine the effectiveness of the intensive preventive work.

Each of the school districts will consider assigning some portion of time and personnel to work with the paid project personnel in gathering data and implementing preventive procedures. Each district will also consider a budget appropriation to finance a part of the cost of the project. The balance of the cost of the project would come from research grant funds. . . .

The committee of school districts should hold monthly meetings to review policy, coordinate operations within school districts, etc. The probation officers, judges, and legislators who will cooperate with the project should be invited to the monthly meetings of the committee.

Whenever any committee identifies a factor which may contribute to delinquency, it is the committee's obligation to try to find a way to offset that factor by seeking the aid of any agency available, whether a service or welfare agency, a legal authority, or a neighboring university or college.

Los Angeles County, California: The Long Beach committee, in studying two youngsters who were becoming delinquent, found that their families were being disrupted by the inability of their mothers to handle ordinary housekeeping responsibilities. There was a need for assistance in such basic skills as managing family finances, organizing work time, and performing cleaning and cooking chores efficiently. The instability of the home was driving these children out in the community into delinquent behavior.

Through community contacts the committee learned that the Home Economics Department of Long Beach State College might be interested in making a student assignment to a situation of this kind. After consultation with the college, an agreement was reached and a referral was made. A graduate student was assigned to work with the mothers as a term project. It was her task to develop new skills in the mothers to help them cope with the situation.

At the year's end the project was regarded as having been of value to both groups, and a permanent agreement was reached between the college and the committee to make similar referrals possible in the future.[16]

The final section of this chapter will deal with a recent development—the state or municipal authority or youth commission designated by law to serve the public in the area of delinquency prevention and control. The enabling laws and the stated responsibilities for such authorities are usually broad and allow wide interpretation and leeway in programming. The activities are usually in one or more of the following three fields: originating and servicing programs of delinquency prevention and control, evaluating existing programs, or coordinating existing programs.

For example, both Illinois and Minnesota have state-appointed commissions and have designated the responsibilities

328

of originating and aiding local prevention and control programs. The Illinois Youth Commission has the additional responsibility of custodial care of juvenile offenders.

THE STATE OF ILLINOIS: The Illinois Youth Commission was created in 1953 by legislative enactment of the 68th General Assembly. In effect, the Youth Commission combines into a single organization all of the state services for the prevention of juvenile delinquency and the custodial care and treatment of juvenile offenders.

The Delinquency Prevention program of the State of Illinois is administered by the Division of Community Services, which is a unit in the Illinois Youth Commission.[17]

During the fiscal year ending June 30, 1958, the Division Staff gave service to community committees engaged in delinquency prevention in 187 different localities in the state. This is an increase of 16 committees over the previous year. The accomplishments of these volunteer organizations add up to an impressive total of increased youth services in the various committees. . . .

Some of the activities conducted by community committees are:

1. Equip and operate summer playgrounds and ballfields
2. Build and operate community centers
3. Provide social recreation, parties, dancing, or teen centers
4. Build and operate summer camps, or provide camping scholarships or memberships at gymnasium or pool
5. Help teen-agers find jobs
6. Conduct community social and/or fund raising events, such as picnics, summers, bazaars, to support the above mentioned activities
7. Cooperate with social agencies in extending services to the neighborhood for community drives
8. Serve as adult sponsors for probationers.[18]

In Minnesota, a similar state youth authority acts to originate and develop delinquency prevention programs.

THE STATE OF MINNESOTA: [The Youth Conservation Commission was given statutory responsibility for developing delinquency-prevention programs under the Youth Commission Act of 1947.] Being a separate state agency we have been able to work with all other state agencies. We have, in our total thinking, included the State Department of Education, the State PTA Congress, and each of the school structures throughout the total state. We have been involved in working with schools through community organization and [in] other plans attempting to assist local groups secure needed counseling and guidance teachers as well as other services within schools. In addition, we have been instrumental in working with all of the school officials from an adult and youth level in developing . . . [and] promoting what is known as the Minnesota Teen-age Code, a Traffic Safety Program, as well as a Physical Fitness Program.

With the application of the manual and consultant services from the Youth Conservation Commission, 38 councils have been formed in the state. By June 1956, these councils had completed or undertaken 352 specific projects. They completed youth accounting surveys, extended recreation programs, waged anti-indecent literature campaigns, fostered visiting nurse services, campaigned for annual physical examinations of children, fostered the development of remedial reading programs, promoted need for women police as well as adequate over-all law enforcement, assisted with police salary surveys, and in all ways demonstrated they cared for their youth.

With cooperation of the State Departments of Health, Welfare and Education, the Youth Conservation Commission performed 16 surveys of youth services for as many state communities. . . .

Requested by Governor Orville L. Freeman and his Advisory Council on Children and Youth, the mayors of 138 cities and communities called together all local officials and citizens to evaluate their youth programs and services, and to lay out plans to more completely serve youth. An Executive Secretary to the Governor's Advisory Council on Children and Youth, the Community Services Unit, prepared the guide booklet for each mayor and, through personal service . . . and communication, carried out the total program. These meetings were held in 66 of the state's 87 counties and more than one-third of the total state population were affected. . . .

These town meetings were successful, for in many communities it was the first time all forces in that community came together to mutually plan this extension of needed services. Forty-two of the towns have continued to meet and discuss youth problems. This further swelled the ranks of local communities accepting more completely their responsibility for their youth. . . .

An original Minnesota Teen-age Code draft was made, then mailed by the Council to the 370 Youth delegates who attended the Governor's Conference on Children and Youth. After discussion with other youths in their home community and with parents, these delegates forwarded their suggestions and approval to the Youth Council. A second draft was made and presented to the Advisory Council as a whole, which group of over three hundred adults changed only one word in approving the code. . . .

Today the Minnesota Teen-age Code is internationally known. Over 231 schools in the State have discussed social codes using the Minnesota Teen-age Code as a guide. Requests for copies have been received from 47 states, the territories, and five foreign countries.[19]

New York City provides an example of one youth commission with the function of evaluating the operations of various agencies and institutions in delinquency prevention and control.

NEW YORK CITY: [The Juvenile Delinquency Evaluation Project was set up by Mayor Wagner on January 1, 1956.] The staff consists of an assistant director, seven research associates, and two part-time experts who render special services. It is "interdisciplinary," representing the various areas of scholarship and practical experience—sociology and social work, municipal organization, social psychology, and law—requisite for the accomplishment of its task. It has enlisted also a group of voluntary consultants, specially qualified by their knowledge of the various areas under investigation, and it is aided by a Committee of Citizens, composed of persons distinguished for their public service and their informed interest in problems of social welfare. . . .

The Project is entirely independent, free to study any operations within its field and present any conclusions it reaches based on its findings. [The Juvenile Delinquency Evaluation Project has been examining or will examine the Police Department, the courts, detention of juveniles and adolescents, state and private institutions of "commitment," public-school system program for difficult children, mental health services under private auspices and the New York City Youth Board. The Juvenile Delinquency Evaluation Project is also making sample studies of city areas and special situations; i.e., the Lower East Side, the Puerto Rican situation.][20]

The third field designated for youth authority responsibility is the coordination of existing programs and services aimed to help the potential or active norm violator. Since many public and private agencies are presently engaged in this endeavor, a number of states and municipalities have assigned legal responsibility for coordination to offices manned by trained personnel. The first example is the Commissioners' Youth Council in Washington, D. C.

WASHINGTON, DISTRICT OF COLUMBIA: The Commissioners' Youth Council is charged with responsibility for the control, treatment and prevention of juvenile delinquency and, to this end, the coordination of all agencies and organizations in the District of Columbia which are concerned with the delinquency problem. . . .

The Youth Council consists of 18 members, five of whom are ex officio. The staff consists of a director, four professional persons to work with the Area Boards, and two clerks. The projects and programs of the Youth Council are effected through its various standing and special committees and through the Area Boards which are established throughout the entire city. The Area Boards have carried out many constructive projects which have helped to alleviate delinquency problems in their immediate neighborhoods. . . .

The Gangs Committee of the Council has continued active and has worked with the Gangs Committees of the various Area Boards. The Youth Aid Division has been alert to the movements of antisocial groups, and the two officers especially assigned to that work have kept the Youth Council informed. . . .

The Council staff has worked closely with the Roving Leaders who are assigned primarily to the areas where there is the greatest threat of gang activity. . . .

A study of the illegitimacy problem among adolescents has been conducted under the sponsorship of the Department Heads Committee of the Youth Council. . . .

A research and service project . . . is financed by the Eugene and Agnes E. Meyer Foundation. This is the third of a three-year grant to develop procedures for identifying the predelinquent and establishing preventive measures for him in the elementary schools. . . .

One of the problems now being studied by a Youth Council Committee is that of better distribution of *shoes and clothing* to needy school children. . . . The Committee is studying: more effective methods of collecting clothing; the possibility of establishing distribution points as needed throughout the city; Area Board responsibility for administering the over-all program; feasibility of purchasing surplus materials for repairs or construction by vocational schools or correctional institutions.

Another matter being considered is the establishing of a *Register* for multiproblem families in the District of Columbia. . . . The aim here is to determine ways in which the community can pool its experience with these families, and its information, in such a way that overlapping or duplication of service can be avoided, and the community can come up with a better rehabilitative plan for these families.[21]

The functions of a second coordinating authority, the Los Angeles County Youth Committee, are, in spite of some variations, quite similar to those of the District of Columbia Commission.

LOS ANGELES COUNTY, CALIFORNIA: In 1944, at the request of the Grand Jury, the County Youth Committee was appointed by the Board of Supervisors. It is an official committee which brings together a membership of county departments, Los Angeles City departments, and major organizations and agencies having an interest in children and youth. It has continued to provide a means of cooperative planning and coordination with reference to youth problems. During the quarterly meetings this year, major attention was focused upon the following:
1. Completing the report of recommended standards for a model teen-age dance ordinance

2. Reports of studies regarding 16-17 year old delinquents
3. Giving support to pending legislation pertaining to youth welfare
4. Report of the schools and the delinquency problems.

The Committee was also concerned with increasing its effectiveness and in relating more closely to the Federation of Community Coordinating Councils. A subcommittee was appointed to study these matters and make recommendations.

The Central Juvenile Index continued operation as a service to law enforcement agencies through the Fiscal year. However, the Central Juvenile Index Committee felt that the service would be more effective if it were available on a 24-hour basis and had access to teletype equipment. It was decided, therefore, that the service could be more economically performed by the sheriff's office. The Index was transferred to that office at the end of the fiscal year.[22]

A third such authority is the New York City Youth Board.

NEW YORK CITY: [In 1947, the City Board of Estimate created the Youth Board under the provisions of the State Youth Commission Act.] The Youth Commission is charged with the responsibility for giving guidance and state aid to localities to help them cope with their youth problems. It is empowered to reimburse local communities 50 percent of the cost of approved projects for the prevention and control of juvenile delinquency up to a ceiling which depends on the local youth population. . . .

Certain fundamental considerations, however, emerged early in the Youth Board's experience and continue to hold true today. Among these are the following:

The community's delinquency prevention effort, in order to have maximum impact, must be closely unified and carefully planned.

There is a vast untapped reservoir of leadership and energy for the prevention of delinquency in the city's many neighborhoods which must be stimulated, organized, and coordinated.

In order to have greatest effect, the Youth Board's program must be initially concentrated in areas of highest delinquency.

Methods must be developed for locating or detecting children and their families with incipient problems and getting them to needed services promptly.

334

The community's youth-serving agencies and facilities must be helped to work and plan more effectively to meet the problem of juvenile delinquency.

There is a need for planning and cooperation in the establishment of new services for youth and the demonstration of more effective techniques for preventing and treating juvenile delinquency.

The highest possible standards of professional practice must be maintained through the sharing of insights and experiences. The community must be informed as to the scope and causes of delinquency and the resources available to deal with it. . . .

At the neighborhood level, the Borough Community Coordinator works closely and actively with citizens groups, providing guidance, assistance and sometimes the initial impetus for their programs of delinquency prevention.

Neighborhood councils function best as independent, integrated groups representing the composition and thinking of their own communities. . . .

In 1950 the Youth Board initiated its central register, listing offenses by children and youth together with pertinent information about their background, including age, sex, home status, problems, etc. This index has been of great value in constructing a delinquency profile for New York City. . . .

Finding children and families with problems which may lead to delinquency and providing needed treatment for them has, from the start, been one of the Youth Board's most essential functions. There is a continuing need to seek out these individuals and families so that incipient difficulties can be dealt with before they have become sufficiently serious to involve them with the police and court.

Central to this vital facet of the Youth Board's functioning in each of the high-delinquency areas is the Referral Unit. These units, operated by the Board of Education, are located in each of the city's areas of highest delinquency and serve as "detection centers" to seek out children, young people, and their families with problems. Since the first of these units commenced operation in 1947 almost 30,000 children have come to their attention.

Referral Unit workers work closely with school personnel in identifying youngsters in need of help. Over the years they have developed an understanding in many teachers that the withdrawn, nonparticipating child as well as the overt, acting-out trouble-maker may often become delinquent. . . .

The city's areas of highest delinquency are also the neighborhoods where opportunities for healthy play have been fewest. In recognition of this fact, and of the positive preventive value of constructive, supervised recreation, the Youth Board, since its inception, has devoted a large part of its budget to expand recreational facilities in high delinquency areas. . . .

The Street Club Project's method consists fundamentally of sending skilled workers out into the places where the antisocial gangs congregate. They determine these locations through consultation with local law enforcement authorities, youth-serving agencies, school personnel, and residents. By watching for opportunities to inject themselves into the boys' conversations about sports, records, local happenings, etc., they gradually get to know the gang members and leaders. . . .

Always their influence is toward constructive alternatives to the gang's antisocial behavior. They make this shift possible by providing healthy outlets for the gang's energies. With the street club worker's help, athletic competition and dances replace vandalism and conflict as sources of status and excitement. Disputes with rival groups which would have led to violence are peacefully resolved around a conference table. Growth into adjusted, contributing citizenship becomes possible instead of the tragic waste of young lives.[23]

Summary

In Part 1 of this document an attempt has been made to present a cross section of the many different practices and adaptations that are visible in those schools of the nation which have concerned themselves directly or indirectly with delinquency prevention or control. The school's opportunity and responsibility have been illustrated in the early identification of the future or present norm violator, in the educational process within the regular classroom, through special services and curriculum adjustment via special schools and centers.

In Part 2 attention has been directed to the school's opportunity and responsibility in working with the parents, with law-enforcement and court personnel, and with all youth and family workers in the community.

Each chapter has offered a number of guidelines in the form of action-principles to enable local school personnel to check and evaluate their own approaches to helping the delinquent or predelinquent. These guidelines stemmed largely from the theoretical statement embodied in the first publication of the NEA Juvenile Delinquency Project, *Delinquent Behavior: Culture and Individual.*

Delinquent Behavior: Principles and Practices will not eliminate the need for fact-gathering and planning on the local level in order to meet the kinds of problems which will emerge in the community. However, it does offer the stimulation of theory-based actions which are supported through experience-validated programs. Many of these need further validation through controlled experimentation. It is hoped that this present report will serve as a resource for those who work in schools and are concerned with helping the norm-violating youngster, his family, and his teacher.

References

[1] United Nations. *First United Nations Congress on the Prevention of Crime and the Treatment of Offenders, Geneva, 22 August-3 September 1955.* A Report Prepared by the Secretariat for the United Nations, Department of Economic and Social Affairs. New York City: the United Nations, 1956. p. 46.

[2] Des Moines Public Schools, Central Committee on Special Education. "Report From the Committee on the Socially Maladjusted." Des Moines: the Committee, 1957. p. 9.

[3] New Jersey Youth Study Commission. *New Ways to Reach Unreached Youth: A Challenge to New Jersey.* Third Annual Report and Recommendations of the State of New Jersey Youth Study Commission. Trenton: the Commission, June 1958. p. 14.

[4] Von Christierson, Jean, "Schools Help Rebuild the Neighborhood." *The Nation's Schools* 59:50-55, June 1957.

[5] Massachusetts Secondary School Principals Association, Committee on Citizenship. "Responsibility—Price of Freedom." Boston: the Committee, 1955. p. 1.

[6] Los Angeles County Public Schools, Department of Community Services. *Annual Report 1956-1957.* Los Angeles: the Department, 1957. p. 13.

[7] San Francisco Board of Education. "Spear's Comments on Youth Problems to Board of Supervisors of San Francisco." Report to Board of Supervisors on Youth Problems, Part III. *San Francisco Public Schools Bulletin* 30; 3-4; February 23, 1959.

[8] Board of Education of Farmingdale, Youth Council. "Farmingdale Youth Council Recreation Handbook." Farmingdale, New York: the Council, 1958. p. 10.

[9] Boys Brotherhood Republic of New York, Inc. "The Boys Brotherhood Republic of New York, Inc.: A Unique Pilot Project in Juvenile Democracy." New York City: the Boys Brotherhood Republic, 1958. p. 2-4.

[10] Capitol Community Services, Roving Group Work Unit. "Roving Group Work Unit Report: Board-Staff Workshop, March 12, 1959." Saint Paul: the Unit, 1959. p. 1-4 *passim.*

[11] American Friends Service Committee. "Progress Report, April 6, 1959, Youth for Service." San Francisco: the Committee, 1959. p. 2.

[12] Milwaukee Public Schools, Department of Pupil Personnel. "Community Referral Committee." Milwaukee: the Department, 1958. p. 1.

[13] Detroit Board of Education and the Detroit Commission on Children and Youth. "The School-Community Project for Reducing Delinquent Behavior." Detroit: the Board and the Commission, 1958.

[14] Los Angeles County Department of Community Services and the Federation of Community Coordinating Councils, Case Conference Committee. "Manual for Case Conference Committees." Los Angeles: the Committee, 1958. p. 1.

[15] Los Angeles County Public Schools, Committee of Five. "Problems of Delinquent Behavior." Los Angeles: the Committee, 1957. p. 1-3.

[16] Los Angeles County Public Schools, Department of Community Services, *op. cit.,* p. 12.

[17] Illinois Youth Commission, Division of Community Services. *Handbook: Delinquency Prevention Through Community Organization.* Springfield: the Division, 1956. p. 4.

[18] Illinois Youth Commission, the Division of Community Services. "Summary of Activities of Community Organizations Cooperating with Delinquency Prevention Program of Division of Community Services." Springfield: the Division, 1958. p. 2-3.

[19] Saint Paul Youth Conservation Commission, Community Service Unit. "A State Program in the Prevention of Delinquency." Saint Paul: the Unit, 1958. p. 9-12.

[20] City of New York Juvenile Delinquency Evaluation Project. "A Progress Report." New York: the Project, 1958. p. 1-4 *passim.*

[21] The District of Columbia Commissioners' Youth Council. "Annual Report—Fiscal 1958." Washington: the Council, 1958. p. 1-3 *passim.*

[22] Los Angeles County Public Schools, Department of Community Services, *op. cit.,* p. 9.

[23] New York City Youth Board. *New Directions in Delinquency Prevention, 1947-1957.* New York City: the Board, 1958. p. 7-28 *passim.*

ANNOTATED BIBLIOGRAPHIES

Books and Pamphlets

Barron, Milton I. *The Juvenile in Delinquent Society.* New York City: Alfred A. Knopf, Inc., 1954. 350 p.

Views the problem of juvenile delinquency in a comprehensive, societal frame of reference and calls for orderly modification of the American social structure and of some of the values and functions of American society.

Beck, Bertram M. *Five States: A Study of the Youth Authority Program as Promulgated by the American Law Institute.* Philadelphia: American Law Institute, 1951. 146 p.

Presents a critical appraisal of the state programs under way in the pattern of the Youth Authority Act as first established in California and presents an orientation for future developments.

Beck, Bertram M. "Delinquents in the Classroom." *NEA Journal* 45:485-87; November 1956.

Discusses and illustrates various types of delinquents: social, asocial, neurotic, organic, and accidental.

Bloch, Herbert A., and Flynn, Frank T. *Delinquency: The Juvenile Offender in America Today.* New York City: Random House, Inc., 1956. 612 p.

A comprehensive and critical review of significant research related to causation, diagnosis, and treatment of delinquency.

Cohen, Albert K. *Delinquent Boys: The Culture of the Gang.* Glencoe, Illinois: Free Press, 1955. 202 p.

Considers the social origin of juvenile behavior and shows how juveniles who share similar problems draw together by forming a delinquent subculture for social reinforcement.

Cohen, Frank J. *Youth and Crime.* New York City: International Universities Press, Inc., 1957. 274 p.

A report of the proceedings of the Law Enforcement Institute on Youth and Crime held at New York University in July 1955. Covers topics relating to concepts and methods for reducing juvenile delinquency.

Ellingston, John R. *Protecting Our Children from Criminal Careers.* New York City: Prentice-Hall, Inc., 1948. 374 p.

Traces the theory and origin of the California Youth Authority in relation to all aspects of the delinquency problem.

Glueck, Sheldon, editor. *Problems of Delinquency.* Boston: Houghton Mifflin Co., 1959.

A compendium of writings concerning definition, causes, and treatment of juvenile delinquency.

Glueck, Sheldon, and Glueck, Eleanor. *Unraveling Juvenile Delinquency.* New York City: The Commonwealth Fund, 1950. 400 p.

Presents data gathered over a 10-year period on 500 delinquent boys and an equal number of matched controls. Concludes that a boy's relations with his parents; his physical, personality temperament, and character type; and how he gets along with people constitute three prime factors in the complex of delinquency causation. Attempt is made to work out "prediction tables" for use at an early age.

Kvaraceus, William C. *Juvenile Delinquency and the School.* Yonkers-on-Hudson, New York: World Book Co., 1945. 338 p.

Describes an urban-community program under which the school system assumes chief administrative responsibility for the scientific study and treatment of active and potential delinquents.

Kvaraceus, William C. *The Community and the Delinquent.* Yonkers-on-Hudson, New York: World Book Co., 1954. 566 p.

Outlines a community-wide program for study and control of juvenile delinquency. Indicates what various agencies can do to identify the delinquent and predelinquent at an early date, to study and diagnose his needs, and to administer treatment, using all community resources.

Lander, Bernard. *Towards an Understanding of Juvenile Delinquency: A Study of 8464 Cases of Juvenile Delinquency in Baltimore.* New York City: Columbia University Press, 1954. 144 p.

An extensive analysis of a variety of data available on a census tract as related to the study of differential juvenile delinquency rates.

Mackie, Romaine P.; Kvaraceus, William C.; and others. *Teachers of Children Who Are Socially and Emotionally Maladjusted.* U.S. Department of Health, Education, and Welfare, Office of Education, Bulletin 1957, No. 11. Washington, D. C.: Superintendent of Documents, Government Printing Office, 1957. 92 p.

Reports findings based on deliberations of a committee of experts and the questionnaire returns of experienced teachers.

Merrill, Maud A. *Problems of Child Delinquency.* Boston: Houghton Mifflin Co., 1947. 404 p.

Presents a report of a comparative study of 300 technically delinquent and a like number of nondelinquent children. Results indicate certain traits and pressures which appear to be associated with delinquency.

National Congress of Parents and Teachers. *What PTA Members Should Know About Juvenile Delinquency: A Guide to Action.* Chicago: the Congress, 1957. 96 p.

National Society for the Study of Education. *Juvenile Delinquency and the Schools.* Forty-Seventh Yearbook, Part I. Chicago: University of Chicago Press, 1948. 280 p.

Various experts discuss the meaning, causes, and approaches to the delinquency problem.

New York State Youth Commission. *Reducing Juvenile Delinquency.* Albany: the Commission, 1952. 34 p.

Considers promising techniques for noting vulnerable children. Reports data concerning actual adjudicated delinquency in the region of Albany and efforts of treatment of delinquent children.

Nye, F. Ivan. *Family Relationships and Delinquent Behavior.* New York City: John Wiley & Sons, Inc., 1958. 168 p.

Tests the significance of relations between family attitudes and behavior and delinquent behavior.

Powers, Edwin, and Witmer, Helen. *An Experiment in the Prevention of Delinquency. The Cambridge-Somerville Youth Study.* New York City: Columbia University Press, 1951. 650 p.

Reports and evaluates results of an eight-year study of two matched groups of 325 boys each. The "treated" group received all the aid that

344

a resourceful counselor could give. Very few significant differences are reported between the control and the experimental boys. The co-author, who was not connected with the original project, presents a separate and objective evaluation of the experimental methods and results.

Roucek, Joseph S. *Juvenile Delinquency.* New York City: Philosophical Library, 1958. 370 p.

Fourteen papers prepared by specialists on a variety of topics including definitions, search for causes, evaluation of attempted solutions, and international trends.

U.S. Department of Health, Education, and Welfare, Social Security Administration, Children's Bureau. *Recommended Standards for Services for Delinquent Children.* Washington, D. C.: Superintendent of Documents, Government Printing Office, 1953. 21 p.

An evaluative guide intended for professional workers interested in appraising certain agencies and institutions which deal with delinquent children. The standards of organization and practice are culled from the publications of various national professional organizations.

U.S. Department of Health, Education, and Welfare, Social Security Administration, Children's Bureau. *Helping Delinquent Children.* Children's Bureau Publication No. 341. Washington, D. C.: Superintendent of Documents, Government Printing Office, 1953. 48 p.

A simple and concrete statement of the types of services that must be provided for delinquent children in an effective program of prevention and treatment.

Vedder, Clyde B. *Juvenile Offender: Perspective and Readings.* Garden City, New York: Doubleday & Company, Inc., 1954. 510 p.

A compilation of readings culled from the periodical literature on many aspects of the delinquency problem.

Reviews the meaning and implications of delinquency and provides practical suggestions for community action.

Witmer, Helen L., editor. "Prevention of Juvenile Delinquency." *The Annals of the American Academy of Political and Social Science* 322:1-213; March 1959.

Presents a series of reports, experimental and demonstration in nature, aimed to reduce norm-violating behavior. Some attempts are made to evaluate outcomes.

Witmer, Helen L., and Kotinsky, Ruth, editors. *New Perspectives for Research on Juvenile Delinquency.* U.S. Department of Health, Education, and Welfare, Social Security Administration, Children's Bureau. Washington, D. C.: Superintendent of Documents, Government Printing Office, 1956. 92 p.

The report of a conference on the interrelation and relevance for delinquency of certain concepts from sociology and psychiatry.

Publications Available from NEA

Hill, Arthur S.; Miller, Leonard M.; and Gabbard, Hazel F. "Schools Face the Delinquency Problem." *Bulletin of the National Association of Secondary-School Principals* 37:181-221; December 1953.

Discusses types of services schools might render the delinquent and predelinquent. Gives specific illustrations of school programs in action.

Kvaraceus, William C. *Juvenile Delinquency.* What Research Says to the Teacher, No. 15. Prepared by the American Educational Research Association in cooperation with the Department of Classroom Teachers. Washington, D. C.: National Education Association, August 1958. 32 p.

Presents implications for classroom teachers based upon research and theory.

Moore, Bernice Milburn. *Juvenile Delinquency: Research, Theory, and Comment.* Washington, D. C.: Association for Supervision and Curriculum Development, a department of the National Education Association, 1958. 64 p.

Analyzes social problems related to delinquent behavior and examines the school's role in alleviating delinquency.

National Education Association, Research Division. "Schools Help Prevent Delinquency." *Research Bulletin* 31:99-132; December 1953.

An over-all look at the problem of delinquent behavior, with specific reference to what schools can do and are doing to prevent and control undesirable behavior.

National Education Association, Research Division. "Teacher Opinion on Pupil Behavior, 1955-56." *Research Bulletin* 34:57-107; April 1956.

Presents the opinions and judgments of 4270 classroom teachers concerning the nature and trend of current misbehavior among children.

Motion Pictures on Juvenile Delinquency*

Primary Sources of Motion Pictures Listed Below

Athena—Athena Films, Inc., 165 West 46th Street, New York 36.

Brandon—Brandon Films, Inc., 200 West 57th Street, New York 19.

Christophers—The Christophers, Inc., 18 East 48th Street, New York 7.

E. B. F.—Encyclopaedia Britannica Films, Inc., 1150 Wilmette Avenue, Wilmette, Illinois.

I. F. B.—International Film Bureau, Inc., 57 East Jackson Blvd., Chicago 4.

McGraw-Hill—McGraw-Hill Book Company, Text-Film Department, 330 West 42nd Street, New York 36.

M. H. F. B.—Mental Health Film Board, Inc., Film Service Department, 267 West 25th Street, New York 1. This organization was terminated in July 1959. Films are now being distributed by I. F. B.

M. H. M. C.—Mental Health Materials Center, 1790 Broadway, New York 19. Films now being distributed by I. F. B.

M. T. P.—Modern Talking Pictures Service, Inc., 3 East 54th Street, New York 22.

NEA—National Education Association, Press & Radio Division, 1201 16th Street, N.W., Washington 6, D. C.

NET—NET Film Service, Indiana University, Audio-Visual Center, Bloomington, Indiana.

N. A. A. J. S.—National Academy for Adult Jewish Studies of the United Synagogue of America, 11095 Fifth Avenue, New York 28.

United World—United World Films, Inc., 1445 Park Avenue, New York 29.

U. S. C.—University of Southern California, Audio-Visual Services, Dept. of Cinema, University Park, Los Angeles 7, California.

Age of Turmoil. 20 min., b & w. 1953. McGraw-Hill.
Six adolescents, ages 13-15, representing different personality types, are used to illustrate the behavior that reflects the emotional turmoil of an early teen-ager.

Angry Boy. 33 min., b & w. 1951. I. F. B.
The story of emotional disturbances engendered by family tensions and how a psychiatric team traces these disturbances in a preadolescent boy to their basic causes.

Borderline. 27 min., b & w. 1955. McGraw-Hill.
A teen-age girl on the "borderline" between useful citizenship and delinquency is hindered by a lack of guidance from her parents.

Boy With A Knife. 19 min., b & w. 1957. I. F. B.
Dramatizes a group of adolescent boys on the verge of crime and shows a skilled social worker helping one boy and his father.

Discipline During Adolescence. 16 min., b & w. 1958. McGraw-Hill.
Results of both too little and too much parental control are dramatized in a typical family setting.

Emotional Maturity. 20 min., b & w. 1958. McGraw-Hill.
Shows the important role played by adults in helping adolescents develop emotional maturity.

Farewell to Childhood. 23 min., b & w. 1952. I. F. B.
The story of a normal teen-age girl and the bewilderment of her parents

---

* This bibliography was compiled and edited by Anna L. Hyer, director, and Robert C. Snider, assistant director, Division of Audio-Visual Instructional Services, National Education Association.

as they try to understand the swift emotions and uncertainties of adolescence.

First Lessons. 22 min., b & w. 1952. I. F. B.
Deals with the adjustment problem of a new, aggressive pupil in a class of second-graders and how a normal balance is regained through the skill of an understanding teacher.

Glass Houses. 25 min., b & w. 1954. Brandon.
A community is awakened to its responsibilities when a teen-age boy is caught stealing and is brought before a prosecutor who indicts the agencies of society that helped shape the boy's character.

H—The Story of a Teen-Age Drug Addict. 22 min., b & w. 1951. McGraw-Hill.
Documentary story of a teen-age drug addict designed to alert community groups to the dangers of drug addiction among adolescents.

Hard Brought Up. 40 min., b & w. 1955. I. F. B.
When two 10-year-old boys are brought before a juvenile court, a child welfare worker attempts to get to the bottom of the case. In so doing, the parents and the community see the real problem of juvenile delinquency and bring about a solution.

Head of the House. 37 min., b & w. 1953. United World.
Shows how a social worker, a policeman, and a minister can join forces to help a young boy and his parents through the serious troubles of adolescence.

Howard. 27 min., b & w. 1957. I. F. B.
A teen-age boy is confronted with a serious conflict of opinion between his wishes and those of his parents.

Kid Brother. 27 min. b & w. 1957. I. F. B.
Depicts the vain efforts of a 16-year-old, through overindulgence in alcohol, to express his anger and frustration.

Meaning of Adolescence. 16 min., b & w. 1953. McGraw-Hill.
Reviews problems facing adolescents such as physical change, social acceptance, getting along with the opposite sex, and learning to make moral decisions.

Meeting the Needs of Adolescents. 19 min., b & w. 1953. McGraw-Hill.
Needs of adolescents are presented in this story of a 14-year-old boy and his 17-year-old sister that shows what parents can do to help.

Mike Makes His Mark. 29 min., color, b & w. 1955. N. E. A.
Shows the positive effects of a well-staffed school in helping a confused teen-age boy to overcome his frustrations and resentment.

Mirror in the Mountains. 19 min., color, b & w. 1956. M. T. P.
The story of a hostile, bitter youth from a sordid family background who is slowly transformed into a happy, healthy, useful citizen by his experiences at Berkshire Industrial Farm.

Old Man Stone. 30 min., b & w. 1956. N.A.A.J.S.
Produced by NBC Television. The film presents the true story of Louis Stone, immigrant druggist in a Detroit slum, who fought juvenile delinquency by having faith in individual boys and girls.

Physical Aspects of Puberty. 19 min., b & w. 1953. McGraw-Hill.
An animated description of the development of the primary and secondary sex characteristics in boys and girls during adolescence. Shows how normal variations in development can have social repercussions.

348

The Protest. 25 min., b & w. 1959. U. S. C.
Presents the case of a 13-year-old boy in trouble with the law and shows how over-worked juvenile officers attempt to help by working with his parents who do not understand the needs of their son.

The Quiet One. 67 min., b & w. 1948. Athena.
A mentally disturbed Negro boy receives the training and emotional comfort that help him rehabilitate his personality.

Roots of Happiness. 25 min., b & w. 1953. I. F. B.
Stresses the role of the father in building and maintaining a happy family environment. Dramatizes contrast between a family where father loves and respects his wife and children, and a family where discord and hostility prevail.

The Search: Wayne University (Juvenile Delinquency). 27 min., b & w. 1955. McGraw-Hill.
Produced by CBS Television. This film tells the story of the joint attack being made on juvenile delinquency by Wayne University and the city of Detroit.

Searchlights On Delinquency (13 films). 29 min. each, b & w. 1956. NET.

Addiction Among Teenagers. Outlines some of the causes of teen-age addiction and considers the possibilities of treatment.

The Broken Home. Shows boys from homes with various forms of impaired relationships and explains how these lead to seeking satisfactions outside the home that result in delinquent behavior.

The Culture of Delinquency. Develops thesis that delinquents are products of a delinquent culture. Describes conflicts within our culture.

Delinquency Areas. Describes areas which produce the majority of delinquents and pictures life of young people in these areas.

The Delinquent Self. Outlines the ways in which an individual develops a concept of himself as a delinquent or criminal.

Emotionally Disturbed. Graphically presents the high incidents of emotional disturbance among delinquents and explains causes.

The Gang. Describes delinquents as a group phenomenon and contrasts the boys' gang and the boys' club.

IQ and Delinquency. Discusses and refutes some often heard ideas about the relationships between mental ability and crime.

Narcotics Traffic. Featuring an interview with an addict, this film explains how drugs are distributed and used and outlines factors contributing to the narcotics traffic.

Parole and Probation. Explains the role of parole and probation in combating delinquency and in preventing crime.

Poor Little Rich Boy. Discusses the effects of overindulgence on children and youth and indicates that even an economically secure home may be a disorganized one.

Who are the Delinquents? Reviews kinds and causes of delinquency, refutes popular myths about delinquents, and reviews the basic hostilities of the delinquent personality.

Social Acceptability. 20 min., b & w. 1958. McGraw-Hill.
Illustrates the correlation between social acceptability and the successful adjustment and happiness of the average adolescent.

349

Social Class in America. 16 min., b & w. 1957. McGraw-Hill.
Significant contrasts are shown in the lives of three boys who come from different social classes and whose graduation from a public high school marks the start of increasingly different lives.

Social-Sex Attitudes in Adolescence. 22 min., b & w. 1953. McGraw-Hill.
Depicts the importance of personal experiences and the influence of parents and friends in the struggle of a teen-age boy and girl to achieve mature social-sex adjustment.

Step By Step. 20 min., b & w. 1954. I. F. B.
Revolves around playground situations and shows situations which breed delinquency and gangs.

The Teens. 26 min. color, b & w. 1957. McGraw-Hill.
Shows the normal behavior of three teen-agers in the everyday life of an urban middle-class family and the active interest and sympathy required of parents to help teen-agers become adults in their behavior and personalities.

Three Steps To Start. 25 min., b & w. 1955. McGraw-Hill.
Illustrates how a parent group works with various community agencies to develop a unified program to cope with problem of juvenile delinquency in all parts of a city.

What About Juvenile Delinquency. 12 min., b & w. 1955. McGraw-Hill.
A teen-age gang on a reckless driving spree crash into a man's car and assault him. A group of students go to city council, which is seeking measures to curb delinquency. Film ends as council asks for suggestions.

Why Vandalism. 16 min., b & w. 1955. E. B. F.
Three boys from unhappy home situations destroy school property. Film ends as a judge summarizes the factors which led boys into vandalism and how it might have been avoided.

World Starts With Jimmy. 28 min., b & w. 1955. Christophers.
Presents Bing Crosby, Dorothy Malone, and William Campbell in this dramatization of a positive approach toward correcting and forestalling the problems of young people.